Transfo ... 5
in the Twe ... ury

Graham Black argues that museums must transform themselves if they are to remain relevant to twenty-first century audiences – and this root and branch change would be necessary whether or not museums faced a funding crisis. It is the result of the impact of new technologies and the rapid societal developments that we are all a part of, and applies not just to museums but to all arts bodies and to other agents of mass communication.

Through comment, practical examples and truly inspirational case studies, this book allows the reader to build a picture of the transformed twenty-first century museum in practice. Such a museum is focused on developing its audiences as regular users. It is committed to participation and collaboration. It brings together on-site, online and mobile provision and, through social media, builds meaningful relationships with its users. It is not restricted by its walls or opening hours, but reaches outwards in partnership with its communities and with other agencies, including schools. It is a haven for families learning together. And at its heart lies prolonged user engagement with collections, and the conversations and dialogues that these inspire.

The book is filled to the brim with practical examples. It features:

- an introduction that focuses on the challenges that face museums in the twenty-first century
- an analysis of population trends and their likely impact on museums
- boxes showing ideas, models and planning suggestions to guide development
- examples and case studies illustrating practice in both large and small museums
- an up-to-date bibliography of landmark research, including numerous websites.

Building upon and complementing Graham Black's previous book, *The Engaging Museum*, we now have a clear vision of a museum of the future that engages, stimulates and inspires the publics it serves, and plays an active role in promoting tolerance and understanding within and between communities.

Graham Black is Reader in Public History and Heritage Management, at Nottingham Trent University. He is also a consultant Heritage Interpreter, and exhibitions on which he has acted as Interpretive Consultant have won the first UK £100,000 Museum Prize (2003) and been on the final 2007 shortlist, as well as winning its predecessor the Gulbenkian Prize, a Museum of the Year Award, the Special Judges Prize at the Interpret Britain Awards and the English Tourist Board's 'England for Excellence' Tourist Attraction of the Year Award. He is a Fellow of the Association for Heritage Interpretation (UK). He is the author of *The Engaging Museum* (Routledge, 2005).

Transforming Museums in the Twenty-first Century

Graham Black

Routledge
Taylor & Francis Group

LONDON AND NEW YORK

First published 2012
by Routledge
2 Park Square, Milton Park, Abingdon, Oxon OX14 4RN

Simultaneously published in the USA and Canada
by Routledge
711 Third Avenue, New York, NY 10017

Routledge is an imprint of the Taylor & Francis Group, an informa business

British Library Cataloguing in Publication Data
A catalogue record for this book is available from the British Library

Library of Congress Cataloging in Publication Data
Black, Graham.
Transforming museums in the 21st century / Graham Black.
    p.   cm.
"Simultaneously published in the USA and Canada"—T.p. verso.
Includes bibliographical references and index.
1. Museums—Social aspects. 2. Museum attendance. 3. Museum visitors. 4. Museums—Technological innovations. 5. Social change. 6. Community life. I. Title.
AM7.B57 2011
069—dc23
2011026784

ISBN: 978-0-415-61572-3 (hbk)
ISBN: 978-0-415-61573-0 (pbk)
ISBN: 978-0-203-15006-1 (ebk)

Typeset in Myriad Pro and Arno Pro by The Running Head Limited, www.therunninghead.com

MIX
Paper from responsible sources
FSC® C004839

Printed and bound in Great Britain by
TJ International Ltd, Padstow, Cornwall

For Sam and Edward

Contents

List of figures

Acknowledgements

I must begin by expressing my absolute gratitude to Anne Lidén, Lecturer, Art and Museum Education, Stockholm University, who commented on the original proposal and then waded her way through the bulk of the text.

Andrew Ashmore, actor (ashmoreacts@yahoo.co.uk), kindly gave permission to use his image from *The Accursed Thing*.

Mette Boritz, of the National Museum of Denmark, helped me develop my ideas both by providing information on her work and through email conversations.

Yael Borovich, Director and Curator of Education, Tel Aviv Museum of Art, kindly commented on part of the text, helped me with the description of the museum's gallery shows and permitted me to use a number of her wonderful photographs.

Steve Burt, Museum Director (Operations), Royal Armouries, read and made insightful comments on Chapters 3 and 5.

Matthew Gibbons and Amy Davis-Poynter of Routledge gently steered me through the various crises of authorship.

Natalie Heidaripour, Curator of the Herbert Art Gallery and Museum's Peace and Reconciliation Gallery, gave essential support in the case study of her gallery.

Tony Jackson, Centre for Applied Theatre Research, University of Manchester, was a fount of knowledge on museum theatre, making possible my brief case study in Chapter 6.

Bob Janes, editor of *Museum Management and Curatorship*, read and commented on Chapter 8, generously allowing me to benefit from his great depth of understanding in this field.

Benedict Johnson, photographer, generously permitted me to use his image from the British Museum Samsung Discovery Centre.

Lynda Kelly, Director of the Australian Museum Audience Research Centre, commented on the original proposal and kindly read and commented on Chapter 4, as well as ensuring I did not lose sight of the importance of the internet and social media.

Lyndsey Mackay, Curator of St Mungo Museum of Religious Life and Art in Glasgow, and previously of the Open Museum in Glasgow, gave me welcome assistance in developing the Open Museum case study.

Shelley Mannion, Digital Learning Programmes Manager, Samsung Discovery Centre, British Museum, was instrumental in enabling me to complete my case study of the Centre and in obtaining an image I could include.

Katja Meith, Director of Museum Affairs of the Free State of Saxony, Germany, supported and inspired me through the early gestation of the book and gave invaluable help with the case studies on the GDR classroom in Leipzig and the New Green Vault in Dresden.

Susan Pacitti, Managing Editor, Glasgow Museums, gave essential help on locating images on the Blind Faith project and Open Museum.

Kym S. Rice, Director of the Museum Studies Programme, George Washington University, commented on the original proposal and kindly met with me in Washington to discuss early drafts.

Lucy Roe, Research and Interpretation Co-ordinator for Natural Sciences at Otago Museum, helped me develop the case study on family engagement at the museum.

Anthony Schrag, artist, generously permitted me to use his powerful *Rebelland* work created for Glasgow Museums.

Liz Weston, Curator, and Jodie Henshaw, Museum Development Officer, thrilled me with their work at Mansfield Museum.

David Williams of The Running Head Limited led me sensitively and enthusiastically through the process of converting my text into a book.

Maren Zeise invited me to give a keynote paper at Schloss Genshagen, near Berlin, in September 2010 – without this, I doubt that the book would have really taken off.

My colleagues Stuart Burch, Deborah Skinner and Neville Stankley enjoyed laughing when I complained but supported me throughout.

My students generously acted as guinea pigs and kept my feet firmly on the ground.

Finally, and most importantly, I must thank my wife Carolyn who has had to put up with a lot!

Introduction: change or die

We are witnessing a complete renovation of our cultural infrastructure. Those 'bricks and mortar' culture houses, citadels of experience, towers of inspiration, that for so long have stood steadfast as symbols of cultural continuity and comfort, while the streets around them have whizzed and clattered to multiple disruptive transformations, are being **turned inside out** . . . this wholesale renovation is born out of an urgent requirement to change or die, and it is just beginning.

Fleming (2009: 1), his emphasis

Few museums, outside the nationals and any other rock stars of the tourist world, can continue to exist in their present form. This Introduction sets the future of museums in the context of the rapid societal developments that we are all part of. There must be equally rapid changes in the definition and public practice of museums if they are to remain relevant to twenty-first century audiences and, therefore, to survive. The challenges facing museums belong to two inter-related fields: those that are the result of wider societal change, and those that directly challenge the traditional roles of museums. The future is now, and change is long overdue. The future for museums must focus around two forms of sustained engagement:

- the externalisation of purpose of the museum, driven by engagement with its publics and ultimately with the communities it serves (Pitman and Hirzy 2011: vi); and
- the self-initiated, self-directed, self-sustaining, collaborative engagement between the museum and its users.

CHALLENGES FROM SOCIETAL CHANGE

The impact of new technology

We are living through a period of profound change in Western society, underpinned by the rise of new media and by a resultant fundamental shift in Western economies to a globally interconnected information economy. Both have had a profound impact on the skills individuals require to succeed in work and life. The debate around what are being called twenty-first century skills – including information and communications literacy, problem solving, creativity and critical thinking, cross-disciplinary collaborative working, adaptability and multi-tasking – has grown in the last decade and is beginning to influence formal education. It is also breaking down the barriers between formal and informal education, with a general recognition that learning is a lifetime pursuit.

Figure 0.1 **Is this the future for museums?**

The impact of new media has gone beyond the economic to transform how we live our daily lives. This was dramatically brought home to us all by Barack Obama's campaign for the US Presidency in 2007–8 – 'a societal shift ... played out before our eyes' (Brown 2009: 24). Building on his background as a community organiser Obama used social networking to conjure 13 million email sign-ups and over $500 million of campaign funding. During the campaign, around 2 billion email messages were sent and over 5 million bloggers took part (Mintz 2011), illustrating that new media had 'transformed participation from something limited and infrequent to something possible anytime, for anyone, anywhere' (Simon 2010: 3). And much of that networking and participation is mobile: 'When he accepted the Democratic nomination in Mile High Stadium, tens of thousands held up their glowing mobile phones like candles at a rock concert' (Brown 2009: 24).

Obama's campaign also revealed how powerful social networking can be in creating an online community of interest. If anyone thought that this was a one-off, or only possible in the USA, the abortive Green Revolution in Iran after the disputed election in 2009 and the Arab revolutions of 2011 have shown the extent to which informal online networks on Facebook and Twitter have emerged as potent tools for democratic engagement, producing 'a heady atmosphere seeded by new freedoms of expression and information' (*The Times* 2011: 2).

Social networking is having a profound effect on the nature and behaviour of Western society. We communicate in different ways. We learn differently. The pull of place has lost its power as we create other ways to 'meet'. We require new skills to play an active role in contemporary life. And it has given birth to both a new creativity, for example, in Facebook and YouTube, and to new levels of collaboration, as in Wikipedia. Meanwhile the mobility of this new technology, combined with the attitudinal change it supports, means people today increasingly refuse to be passive recipients of whatever governments, companies or cultural institutions such as museums offer; instead they seek to be active members of what Scott McNealy (2005), chairman of Sun Microsystems, has declared to be 'the age of participation'.

Demographic and generational change

Yet new technology, and its impact on the economy and society more generally, represents only one aspect of the changes we are living through. We are also witnessing global movements of peoples on an unprecedented scale. There are an estimated 214 million migrants worldwide, potentially rising to 405 million by 2050 (IOM 2010: xix). The populations of Western cities in particular, where so many museums are located, are in the midst of rapid demographic change, with immigration and a rise in birth rates radically altering the ethnic and racial make-up. One third of current London residents were born outside the UK, and more than 55 per cent of births were to mothers born overseas (Ford 2011: 7). 'Diversity is becoming more and more diverse' (Wallace Foundation 2009: 15), while previously marginalised communities are less and less willing to remain silent or let others speak for them. In this environment, issues around identity, sense of belonging and community cohesion are high on the agenda for individuals, communities and political leaders.

We are also on the cusp of a generational shift. Of course, as life expectancy increases, the Baby Boom generation will be around for a long time to come. But the tastes, interests and behaviour of those born since the 1960s – Generations X, Y and M – are beginning to dominate cultural activity. These generations are not only more diverse but also have much more choice in what they engage with; they are more demanding, and can be much harder to reach by cultural institutions. And the young represent the fastest-growing group of mixed race people, leading to complex identities and new, hybrid forms of cultural expression that break down racial and ethnic categories. Many see these categories as not fitting contemporary realities.

DIRECT CHALLENGES

Financial uncertainty

In 1995, Stephen Weil warned museums that they must inevitably face a funding crisis, and must prepare themselves for it:

> When (not if, but only when) the anticipated crunch in public and private funding materializes, worthiness alone may not justify the continued support of every

museum or similar institution. The questions that each museum may have to answer are just these hardball ones: Are you really worth what you cost or just merely worthwhile? . . . Are you truly able to accomplish anything that makes a difference, or are you simply an old habit?

Weil, quoted in Nolan (2010: 118)

And so, with the banking collapse in 2007–8, a 20-year expansion in funding for the arts came to a painful end. By 2010, national surveys in the USA revealed that 53 per cent of museums lacked the staffing to deliver their programmes and services (Johns Hopkins University 2010: 7), while 67 per cent reported financial stress (Katz 2010). In the UK, publicly financed museums were faced with cuts of at least between 20 and 40 per cent in their budgets. An August 2010 survey of regional museums in England by the UK Museums Association (Heywood 2010) suggested cuts would lead to many reductions in outreach, events, activities and temporary exhibitions; less staffing; shorter opening hours; and site closures, with a risk of 'dragging museums back into the dark ages' – and this is what seems to be happening. In Germany, 10 per cent of museums and cultural institutions face closure by 2020 due to funding cuts (DW-World.de 2010). Meanwhile newspapers have been filled with stories of the impact of funding cuts on museums in France, Italy, Greece and elsewhere.

Public funding to museums can only continue to decline across indebted Western nations. Weil's 'hardball' questions will come back to haunt museum leaders as they seek to fill the gap in their business plans by joining the competition for cash from the limited available pots of grant aid and private funding – is my museum worth it? Do we make a difference? Such a continuing funding crisis reflects 'a business model which is fundamentally flawed' (Antrobus 2010: 1). Museums and galleries generate less of their own income than any of the other art forms. What is more, increasing engagement – which the public wants – costs much more, but without any corresponding increase in income. It is no surprise, if profoundly depressing, that the chief response by museums to public funding cuts has been to decimate the teams who engage directly with the public. Can museums and galleries instead turn increased engagement into a funding stream, and how would this match up to the commitment to reach out to the lower socio-economic groups who are under-represented in museum attendance? Alternatively, will reduced engagement not just bring the death of the museum that much closer?

Loss of certainty about what museums are for

There is nothing new about museum conflict over purpose, with a range of current functions listed in Box 0.1. Museums have always had to select where to focus and then build a clear mission around that. But today many museums seem torn in all directions and unable to define for themselves why they are here, let alone broadcast this to their potential audiences. Lack of certainty of purpose can only bode ill for future survival.

Box 0.1 What are museums for?

- a cultural treasure house
- a leisure and tourism attraction
- a source of local pride
- a resource for informal and structured learning
- an income generator
- an agent for physical, economic, cultural and social regeneration
- a memory store for all in the local community, relevant to and representative of the whole of society
- accessible to all – intellectually, physically, socially, culturally, economically
- a celebrant of cultural diversity and promoter of social inclusion, with a core purpose of improving people's lives
- a place of dialogue and toleration, and a community meeting place, committed to promoting civil engagement
- proactive in developing, working with and managing pan-agency projects
- an exemplar of quality service provision and value for money
- all of the above?

This lack of certainty, linked to public funding cuts, is a reflection of a much deeper malaise. Primarily, museums (alongside other public institutions) face a collapse in the general concept of the 'public good' in Western society. This is reflected directly in the willingness of public bodies to cut funding for being 'merely worthwhile', as Weil put it, and the increasing need to justify the funding that is received in terms of demonstrable outcomes. Public funding, while falling, is therefore coming with more and more strings attached in the form of what seem like constantly changing and certainly ill-defined public agendas. As a result, museums must find new ways to demonstrate what they are for, in terms of being 'for the benefit of the public'.

They are also being challenged by the public at large in their core function as repositories of material culture. Why do you need a museum when you can have virtual access to millions of cultural artefacts online? Why visit a museum at all when there is so much competition in the marketplace for leisure and cultural activities – and museums must compete for public attention while faced with frequently out of date, negative perceptions of their offer. One consequence of these issues is that many museum professionals themselves seem to have lost certainty about what museums are for.

A decline in attendance by traditional audiences and continuing failure to engage new audiences

Museum audiences in the Western world remain overwhelmingly white, are substantially from the well-educated and affluent professional classes, are aging, and are in decline at many – particularly smaller – museums. Their leisure time is increasingly fragmented largely due to the work commitments of dual-income households, while they have more options on how to spend their time. Survey after survey shows a decline in their attendance at cultural sites and events, except when on holiday. Meanwhile, audience research across Western museums continues to reveal a growing failure to attract the under-35s or to replace the declining traditional audiences, particularly with the new communities living in our cities. The impending crisis in attendances is hidden by a continuing boom in cultural tourism, by the short term boost to visitor numbers following major capital schemes and by the continuing popularity of blockbuster exhibitions (Bradburne 2004).

The challenge of the World Wide Web

The web could be seen as the pre-eminent challenge to the role of museums in contemporary society. Its existence is a direct threat to the position museums hold as gatekeepers to and interpreters of the cultural memory of humankind. Rather than having to visit a museum, internet users now have access to millions of cultural objects online, and to information about them. The web also offers an alternative to the authority of museums. Its growth questions what expertise actually means in contemporary culture. With the web has come a new collaborative approach to knowledge generation and sharing, a recognition of multiple perspectives, and an expectation by users that they will be able to contribute and adapt/manipulate content to meet their own needs.

> A curator's authority pales in comparison to the audience's vast collective stores of knowledge and passion. How can gatekeepers redefine their role in ways that harness the power of the audience without losing the sense of subjectivity and personal risk that lie behind [their] decisions?
>
> Connor (2009: 9–10)

In a broader context, the web is also gradually changing what people want from a cultural experience. Leadbeater (2009) suggests users at arts and cultural venues have always sought an overlapping 'mix of three different experiences', – Enjoy, Talk, Do – outlined in Box 0.2.

In the past, he believes the overwhelming demand was for Enjoy experiences. But with the rise of the web, Talk and Do are overtaking Enjoy. Potential museum users

---

Box 0.2 Enjoy, Talk, Do: three forms of cultural engagement

- **Enjoy**: to enjoy being entertained and served; to watch, listen, read. These are passive only in the sense that people do not do much. But inside their heads, such Enjoy experiences can be intensely engaging.
- **Talk**: experiences in which the content provides a focal point for socialising and interacting. The value lies in part in the Talk that the content sets off.
- **Do**: some people also want experiences that allow them to be creative, to get involved, to contribute.

based on Leadbeater (2009: 11)

are becoming not only more diverse but also 'more critical, promiscuous, challenging and even subversive. On the flip side ... more open, willing, adventurous, engaging and collaborative. Put short, *demand is more demanding*' (Fleming 2009: 3). This has overwhelming implications for the development of museum content, for the roles of the curator and others who are involved in the development of this content, and for the very structure of arts and cultural organisations – with a new focus on openness, equality and pluralism (Antrobus 2010: 2).

In my view, these are *positive* challenges that will drive museums on to higher standards. The reality is that, to be successful, museums must now operate across three spheres – physical, internet, mobile – and these are increasingly coming together (Kelly 2011). Together, they provide us with opportunities undreamt of by our predecessors to share our collections, enthusiasms and expertise with the world, and to work with our publics for the benefit of all.

Inertia

Museums must either grasp the opportunities offered by our changing society or lose relevance within a generation. They must redefine their roles and discover ways, through engaging with their users, not only to reposition their offer but also to open up new funding streams. A few are actively engaged in this process but, for many others, the response to date has been one of inertia.

Inertia is linked to weak leadership, uncertainty of purpose, a staff structure geared to another age, lack of funding and responsibility for the expensive maintenance of historic buildings that often do not meet modern requirements. It is very easy to bury one's head in the sand and hope it all goes away. But this will not happen. There has been a transformational shift in public attitudes, expectations and behaviour. Museums have still to understand or respond properly to this, but try asking the other old mass communication media like television, newspapers, the pop music industry or even bookshops about the impact of the web on their activities as audiences move online:

> Here's a hypothesis: the old giants of the mass media age were slow to recognise that the world was changing. They adapted late to the changed conditions brought by the Web and attempt to do so now only out of grim necessity. Their resistance to change offered an opportunity for disruptive innovations from upstarts and outsiders [like YouTube and political bloggers].
>
> Connor (2009: 2)

If museums do not change to respond flexibly and rapidly to changing public demand, that public will go elsewhere.

WHAT DOES THIS MEAN FOR MUSEUMS?

In a November 2007 survey, the American Association of Museums asked its members 'What do you think is the single most significant challenge facing the museum profession over the next several years?' (AAM 2007). Alongside funding, technology and leadership, they identified maintaining the public relevance of museums. So, there is the underpinning issue for this book – what do we need to do *now* to ensure our museums are still relevant in, say, 2030? This date was not chosen at random but reflects projections by the Smithsonian Institution and the American Association of Museums' Center for the Future of Museums. It also relates to the usual lifespan of the expensive new permanent exhibitions many museums have installed in recent years, not to mention the many new museum buildings we have seen constructed. The decisions we are making *today* will be there to haunt us in 2030. In these terms, the future is already with us.

In hard times it is very difficult to take the long view, but that is what I want to try to do here. In 2004–5, when writing *The Engaging Museum*, I could speak of the pressure for change in museums coming from a growing legislative framework, political agendas and lobbying from both excluded groups and committed museum staff. Now I can add both necessity and urgency. Society is changing much faster than we are. We must accept the need for rapid change in museum ethos and practice, even in times of financial hardship, in order to respond to twenty-first century demands – a big challenge for a profession that is notoriously resistant to change. For the necessary change to happen, we must all be futurists now.

Most urgently, we require a shared vision centred on the 'Why' of what we do – what is our 'mission' for in the twenty-first century and why is it so important? What difference will it make to future generations that we are still here? And this vision must be strong enough to:

1   persuade the public at large, as well as funders, of the essential value of museums to society as a whole
2   convince individuals, families, social groups, schools and communities of the unique benefits they will gain through the experience of engaging with what museums have to offer, whether on-site or online, and
3   persuade local communities to work in partnership with museums.

In my view, this mission *cannot* involve a 'safety first' return to a twentieth century focus on museums that were little more than collection warehouses, with exhibitions targeted at elite audiences. Equally, while many are benefiting from the ongoing boom in cultural tourism, museums – as the cultural memory of humankind and as major social and civil spaces within their communities – must strive to be much more than tourist attractions and providers of leisure activities (although I am happy for them to perform those functions as well).

The key lies in the word I would place at the heart of the vision: *engagement*. This refers to two tasks: museums must support the active, prolonged and meaningful engagement of their users, and they must look outwards to reach out and engage directly both with their communities and with contemporary issues.

Borrowing from the Dallas Museum of Art strapline, we must *ignite* the power of museum collections (Pitman and Hirzy 2011) in four ways.

1 We must enable our users to engage with the cultural memory of humankind

Culture, and its representation and inclusion within the collective, is an essential element in the construction of both individual and community identity. It reflects a sense of belonging over time and space, of a place in the human story. Through cultural forms we can explore and gain an understanding of differing beliefs, attitudes and opinions, and such understanding must form the bedrock of a cohesive, culturally diverse society and a globalised world. A twenty-first century museum, aware of the increasing diversity of society, will be a place where ideas and cultures can collide positively, learn off one another, ask new questions and stimulate new thoughts and dialogue (Lavanga 2006).

2 We must stimulate creativity and imagination

The cultural heritage is not there simply to be preserved in aspic, but to be constantly re-examined and recontextualised for contemporary society. And creativity is central to expressive life and the creation of meaning. It enables people to lead productive and fulfilled lives. It is worth spending a moment here to examine the most famous work of psychologist Abraham Maslow: his 'hierarchy of needs', in the form of a pyramid, developed in the 1950s (2nd edn 1970). His pyramid gave absolute precedence to physical survival and security. He makes room for higher needs – social belonging, self-esteem and self-actualisation – but only once the more basic needs have been met. However, this contrasts dramatically with research on what motivates people at work. Here, basic factors give rise to *dissatisfaction* if not adequate. However, *satisfaction* depends entirely on the things Maslow regarded as higher needs – advancement, responsibility, the work itself, recognition, a sense of achievement. Zohar and Marshall (2004: 16–17) argue that in the developed Western world, basic needs are met as a birthright and that Maslow's higher needs bring more than satisfaction and happiness. In their view, Maslow's pyramid should be inverted: 'We need a sense of meaning and driving purpose in our lives. Without it we become ill or we die.' This viewpoint is surely reinforced in societies that are increasingly reliant on industries of the mind.

3 We must benefit society as a whole through the impact of cultural engagement

In the USA, the Greater Philadelphia Cultural Alliance has shown conclusively that higher civic engagement is directly correlated with higher cultural engagement – investments in culture are also investments in civic engagement and quality of life (Greater Philadelphia Cultural Alliance 2009). Museums, through the opportunities for creative encounters that their collections offer, are essential to modern society – but only through the dynamic manner in which they support active use of those collections. Their continuing relevance depends on their ability to meet this challenge.

4 We must help strengthen communities and encourage them to engage with the great issues of today

The potential role of museums in promoting and supporting civil engagement introduces a further issue concerning their capacity to remain relevant in the twenty-first century: the ability of museums to tackle contemporary issues. Doug Worts speaks of the 'winds of change' (http://douglasworts.org) in wider society and the responsibility of museums to engage their users in the great issues of the day. Beyond that lies the wider capacity of museums to support previously marginalised individuals and communities to develop the skills and confidence to engage fully within civil society.

WHAT DOES THIS MEAN IN PRACTICE?

Twenty-first century museums will seek to engage and involve their users, on-site and online, on a number of levels:

1   still providing enjoyable, exciting and stimulating experiences for families and groups of friends to participate in together, whether on a one-off visit or as regular users
2   focusing on developing their audiences as long term, regular users rather than one-off visitors (although still welcoming the one-off visitor)
3   engaging with users as active participants, contributors and collaborators on a learning journey together, rather than as passive recipients of museum wisdom
4   reaching out to build relationships and partner their communities
5   continuing to change and take on new meanings and roles as society continues to transform itself, and
6   through building ever-closer relationships with their users, creating new funding streams (not a subject for this book, but one that needs urgent attention).

Engagement

The word *engagement* highlights the dynamic role of museums as user-focused institutions. Focusing on meaningful engagement as the core outcome changes museums from being inward-looking institutions centred on their collections to outward-looking organisations confident in the important role they can play in the lives of individuals and the positive contribution they can make to wider society. Museums have the ability to make a difference to people's lives through their capacity to inspire, excite, empower, give confidence, help people grow as individuals and communities, and assist them to explore and interact with the world in new and stimulating ways. However, making this positive difference requires sustained interaction with museum content – what the Exploratorium in San Francisco has called 'active prolonged engagement' (Humphrey and Gutwill 2005) – which in turn leads to personal and social meaning-making. Engagement is, preferably, for the long term – relevant to one-off visitors but most effective for regular users.

With

Engagement, in turn, cannot be separated from the expectation by modern audiences that they will be able to participate actively, which has the potential to transform the nature of cultural exchange. Charles Leadbeater, in his essay *The Art of With*, speaks of an industrialised world in which goods and services are delivered *to* and *for* people. This world applies not only to the commercial sector but also to much of the educational and cultural environment: 'Often in the name of doing things *for* people traditional, hierarchical organisations end up doing things *to* people' (Leadbeater 2009: 2). A classic example is the transfer of knowledge from the expert to the passive receiver that forms the basis of our formal educational system. It also applies to much of the public side of museum provision where the curator and/or educator provides content for and delivers it to the audience. As Leadbeater almost puts it, the curator bases this on his/

her assessment of the audience's needs, rather than reflecting the latter's capabilities and potential.

For a museum to truly engage its users, it must cease acting as a controlling gatekeeper to its collections and expertise. Rather, the museum must work with its users and communities to unlock the stories its collections hold (Lynch 2001), responding to the choices its users make. As such, it must give up its traditional authoritarian voice so that users are free to question, debate, collaborate and speculate – seeking out those issues that most concern them – and are given the support and inspiration required to do so. *With* is at the heart of the engaging museum. It can be seen, for example, in the way staff at the USS *Constitution* Museum in Boston work with families to develop new exhibits. It underpins the concept of participation promoted by Nina Simon in her book *The Participatory Museum* (2010). The principle of *with* also changes the way knowledge in the museum is developed to a process that is co-created, reflective of many sources and shared. Such collaborative learning is already a mainstay of how many people use museums, reflecting the social nature of most museum visiting. It can be expanded exponentially if museums grasp the opportunity to reach outwards that new technology offers. Web 2.0, and the principle of *with* it embodies, represents a chance to share authority and collaborate for the benefit of all. By collaborating with contributors worldwide, the expertise of museum staff will increase.

Crucially, *with* is central to the development of a long term relationship between the museum and its users, symbolising the shift in mind-set and behaviour from the one-off visit to an ongoing association, online as well as on-site, over time. It ensures that the user's voice is at the heart of the museum experience.

Finally, *with* is also about partnerships. Museum relevance in the long term will depend on an ability to forge partnerships – with communities, with schools and others working in the field of complementary education, with other cultural institutions, with other relevant agencies, and with their users:

> Partnerships allow museums to extend the boundaries of what is possible: to share risks, acquire resources, reach new audiences, obtain complementary skills, improve the quality of service, achieve projects that would otherwise have been impossible, acquire validation from an external source, and win community and political support.
>
> Anderson (1997: 69)

Social responsibility

> In the museum context, being truly relevant demands identification of external challenges to which the museum's expertise can be directed and make a positive difference. It is not simply a matter of trying to engage the community in what the museum wants to do (Carbonne 2003). Rather it needs to be about a wholehearted externalisation of purpose.
>
> Koster and Baumann (2005: 86)

The engaging museum of the twenty-first century must work to place itself at the heart of the communities it serves. As such, it is incumbent on the museum to seek to attract as diverse an audience as possible, to reflect the complexity of a changing society and to represent all its communities through collections, content and programming. It must strive to enhance tolerance, build community capacity and promote civil engagement. It should actively encourage and incorporate user contributions, represent multiple perspectives, and willingly share authority. It must not flinch from tackling contentious issues but must instead focus on promoting dialogue and understanding.

Driving change

A museum cannot transform itself overnight. It is like any long-established institution which had in the past a clear sense of purpose and direction, and developed its staff structure, business plan, activities, etc. accordingly. The seismic change involved in transforming a traditional museum into an engaging and campaigning museum will not happen by accident. If there is to be more than a piecemeal response to the need for change, it must be driven by a committed governing body and leadership, a focused staff structure and a shared purpose.

From the leadership must come a clear vision, an explicitly stated mission, a commitment to work actively to achieve their goals and an effective strategy for doing so. But leaders cannot operate in a vacuum, as noted by Jack Lohman, Director of the Museum of London:

> A leader has got to give the message that this has got to be embedded, that it's the responsibility of all of us. Leaders have to grow a critical mass of support for this agenda because that in turn supports their leadership. They can't carry the burden and the responsibility and actually the pleasure of leading in this agenda ... It's got to be shared, you know: dispersed leadership, empowering people, embedding this so that it's sustained.
>
> Lohman (2010)

Sustained change will take time and will require a shared responsibility by all who work in – and use – museums. As part of this, the knowledge and expertise of museum staff will be needed more than ever, but in a different way that extends their role to develop new technical and interpersonal skills, from using social media to working in partnership with their communities. This transformation has already begun. We see it in family-focused museums across the world. It shines through in the work of curators who mediate between community memories and work with communities to draw out relevancies from existing collections (for example Denniston 2003, Bott et al. 2005 and the Collective Conversations project at Manchester Museum). We also see museums, particularly in the USA, committing themselves to supporting civil engagement.

WHAT FOLLOWS

In the following chapters I attempt to represent the ethos and practice of a museum in the twenty-first century that has committed itself to remaining relevant to its communities of users. The book is divided into two unequal parts. The first, shorter section focuses on the key underpinning issues of knowing our audiences, reaching out to build relationships and supporting their engagement through the creation of a user-friendly environment. Chapter 1 begins with a short overview of visitor surveys before focusing on profiling by motivation and key issues around longer term visitor trends, finishing with an analysis of the impact of cultural tourism. Chapter 2 explores the key role marketing can play in winning hearts and minds, stimulating visits, building relationships and helping to convert people from visitors into users. Chapter 3 concentrates on the visitor experience, looking at issues around visitor services, creating a user-friendly environment and enabling users to customise their visits.

Section 2 – which forms the bulk of the book – then examines what I believe is meant by a twenty-first century museum in practice. Beginning with the changing landscapes of informal (Chapter 4) and formal (Chapter 5) learning, it then places conversation at the heart of user engagement and learning for adult (Chapter 6) and family (Chapter 7) visits. By contrast, the key word in Chapter 8 is *dialogue* as the book looks in breadth and depth at the museum's engagement with its communities. It uses case studies and exemplar activity throughout to project the concept of the engaging museum. The book concludes with a short endpiece examining what all this means for the stalwart of the museum, the permanent exhibition.

Section 1
From visitor to user

The value of museums begins and ends with the relationship with our visitors. It's a contract that is renewed each and every time they engage with us, and if we don't live up to it, we will be usurped.

Falk (2010)

The ambition for the twenty-first century museum should be to change the mind-set of museum audiences, converting them from one-off visitors into regular users who see themselves as active partners in the work of the museum. For this to happen, we must begin by learning much more about current and potential users and responding to what this reveals. But museums must also transform themselves in both attitude and practice. This cannot wait. Apart from the continuing growth in cultural tourism, museums are currently haemorrhaging traditional audiences while not replacing them with new ones.

In the last 20 years, the argument within the museum profession that the twenty-first century museum should be people-centred has largely been won. Yet over the same timespan the audiences for museums, and for cultural institutions more generally, have remained largely white, have been in decline and are getting older, while the nature of many of the local communities within which museums are located has changed dramatically. If we want our museums not only to survive but flourish during the demographic transformation that will continue to take place over the *next* 20 years, it is imperative that we develop a much fuller understanding of existing visitors and of the current and future communities we want to serve, and work to transform our relationship with them.

This section of the book examines the basic issues of knowing our users better, stimulating visits and both caring for and supporting users on-site. The first step on the road to transforming visitors into users is to increase our understanding of actual, potential and future audiences, their demographics, the dynamics of new generations, their changing motivations and the choices they all have in the use of their leisure time. The second is to begin the process of building relationships for the long term – winning hearts and minds, stimulating visits both on-site and online, converting visitors into users. Much will depend on the images museums project and how successfully they create an atmosphere of belonging.

1   Getting to know our users better

All our traditional arts organisations were developed in very different times, for audiences very different from those we address now. If we are to adapt at the speed set by the fast-changing world around us, then audience insight is the catalyst we need to help us match that pace of change.

Morris and McIntyre (undated: 2)

INTRODUCTION: FROM VISITOR TO USER

This book is not primarily about visitor studies, but about visitor engagement. However, as the Introduction discussed, the changing nature and demands of museum users and potential users are a primary reason why museums must transform themselves or die. Unless museum change can keep pace with the needs and expectations of their publics, they are lost. And the issue is made more complex by the fact that users are now engaging with museums across three spheres – physical, online and mobile (Kelly 2011).

The starting point is a much greater understanding of users and non-users. Morris and McIntyre define the two tools that will enable us to achieve this challenge:

- *Intelligence*: an awareness of the changing world around us that looks way beyond our own database, and
- *Insight*: an understanding of the needs, attitudes and motivations of our existing and potential audiences.

Morris and McIntyre (undated: 2)

This chapter seeks to provide a brief overview, beginning with basic visitor surveys, before focusing on profiling by motivation and key issues around longer term visitor trends. It is completed by an examination of that continuing success story for museums, the growth of cultural tourism. The bulk of the chapter examines on-site users. While there is a growing understanding of those who are engaging with museums online and via social media, the situation is changing so rapidly that it is difficult to give definitive information. I will return to this theme later in the chapter.

Beyond the continuing success of major tourist draws, on-site museum audiences are in a state of flux. Traditional visitors are coming less often. Emerging new generations have different demands. Museums, on the whole, have failed to engage adequately with new communities. Until recent years, visitor research in museums, if it occurred at all, was driven by marketing departments and focused on market segments.

Such research tells us, for example, that:

- the 'traditional' on-site visitor to a Western museum is white, professional class and well educated
- for most of our users, a visit to a museum represents an occasional leisure-led event
- the family group is frequently the largest audience, characteristically making up from 40 per cent to 55 per cent of total visitor numbers
- slightly more adult females than males visit, except to military and industrial museums
- ethnic and racial minority groups, young people and families with children under 5 years old are under-represented among museum visitors, and
- there are clear peaks and troughs in visitation through the week and year, with different segments also coming at different times.

This sort of data is easily quantifiable and provides a core understanding of existing visitors and an essential underpinning for business plans. However, it tells us little about the motivations behind museum visits or the strategies that audiences use during their visit. Today it is increasingly supported by more focused research into why people come (or do not come), their expectations of the experience the museum will provide and the impact this has on the way they seek to personalise their visits.

For longer term planning, museums must also look at future population and leisure trends. Our users in the future will make different demands on museums. Given that many of the long term exhibitions that museums are developing now will still be in place in 10 to 20 years' time, we must immerse ourselves in these trends to ensure we plan for the future, not to continue to meet the needs of past audiences.

Audience segmentation

No introduction to visitor studies can begin without an understanding of market segmentation. Segmentation is a market research method for breaking down audiences into groups that behave in similar ways or have similar needs. Most visitor surveys provide basic quantitative data on audiences, using established market segmentation techniques to provide audience breakdowns. Classic market segmentation breaks down 'traditional' heritage audiences in terms of:

1. Demographics:
   - age
   - gender
   - educational level attained

   Family status is heavily used in segmentation, as it can be such a major predictor of behaviour (dependant; pre-family; family at different stages; late life-cycle, including empty nesters). In the past, ethnic or racial origin has been a rare factor in visitor surveys, but this has changed as museums seek to respond to the needs of changing local communities and broaden their audience base. There is substantial evidence that the higher the educational level attained, the more often people will visit museums.

2   Geography:
    - resident/local
    - day tripper
    - tourist: – VFR (visitor staying with friends or relatives)
                 – national
                 – international

3   Class/occupation:
    There is ongoing controversy over the concept of social class and its relationship to income, education and occupation but here is not the place to discuss it. Social class and occupation, however, continue to be used as key market segments. Although the British government introduced a new National Statistics Socio-Economic Classification in 2000, the Social Class based on Occupation classification is still the most commonly used by heritage sites and museums in the UK because it enables comparisons to be made with previous surveys:

    A = higher managerial, administrative or professional
    B = middle managerial, administrative or professional
    C1 = supervisory, clerical or managerial
    C2 = skilled manual workers
    D = semi- and unskilled manual workers
    E = pensioners, the unemployed, casual or lowest grade workers.

    All the available evidence suggests people on higher incomes are more likely to visit museums and galleries. Among higher income groups in the USA, art museum attendance rates varied from 34 per cent of adults in households making $100,000 to $150,000 to 52 per cent of adults in households earning more than $150,000 (NEA 2009). In the UK, those with a household income of £30,000 or more are twice as likely to have visited a museum as those who earn less than £17,500 (MLA 2004: 5).

4   Structured educational use:
    primary/elementary (to age c. 11/12)
    secondary/high (aged c. 11–16/18)
    student (college/university).

5   Special interest:
    subject specialist
    self-directed learning
    booked group, e.g. a local history group.
    This can also be referred to as a part of behaviouristic segmentation, linking groups of people according to interest in or relationship with particular subjects/products.

6   Psychographic:
    Segmentation relating to lifestyles, opinions, attitudes, etc. is still infrequently used, although it is becoming more common to hear reference to these terms as museums increasingly take leisure trends and visitor profiling into account.

VISITOR SURVEYS

As already noted, museum visitor surveys began largely as the tool of the marketing office. As such, the *quantitative* information they contain can give us key insights into visitor trends – who the visitors are (in terms of market segmentation analysis), where they are coming from, who they are coming with, how they are getting to the site, maybe how often they are coming, and how current attendance compares with that in the past. This, in turn, can enable museums to define who is missing or underrepresented, and thus also forms the basis for a systematic approach to the development of new audiences. For historic data, Hood (1993, 1996) provides an effective summary of USA surveys while Davies (1994) is a classic quantitative 'survey of surveys' for museums in the UK.

Today, however, surveys are also widely used to provide broad *qualitative* insights into visitor motivations, expectations and needs, as well as exploring visit satisfaction, learning and other potential elements that can be measured to reflect museum or government policies. Motivations, expectations and needs are discussed below, and the evaluation of visitor learning in Chapter 5.

National surveys of participation

Public participation in the arts has become a matter of concern for governments internationally, and it has gradually become the norm to carry out regular surveys involving nationally representative samples of the adult population. In the USA, the National Endowment for the Arts (NEA) has been carrying out its *Survey of Public Participation in the Arts* (SPPA) since 1982, most recently in 2008 (NEA 2009). Unfortunately NEA data tracks only art museums and gallery attendance, not cultural, historical or science museums. For these, one must rely on the proxy of visits to historic sites. In England, government agencies have been commissioning national surveys of museum visiting since 1999, initially carried out by MORI (1999). Since 2005, the work has been incorporated within a wider rolling survey commissioned by the Department for Culture, Media and Sport: *Taking Part: England's Survey of Leisure, Culture and Sport* (DCMS 2007 and ongoing), which measures not only participation and non-participation but also satisfaction, enjoyment, volunteering and barriers to participation. It is providing consistent year-on-year data. In Canada, Hill Strategies Research Inc. (2007) has profiled the cultural and heritage activities of Canadians since 1992, drawing on data from Statistics Canada's General Social Surveys. The Australian Bureau of Statistics has been collecting data on both adult and child participation in leisure and cultural activities every three years since 2000. These surveys now provide an underpinning for our understanding of museum visitors and, increasingly, allow us to make comparisons over time.

What the surveys reveal: the 'traditional' museum audience

The CASE programme (Culture and Sport Evidence) is a three year joint research programme in the UK involving the Arts Council, English Heritage, the Museums, Libraries and Archives Council and Sport England to inform UK policy on culture and sport. It is closely linked to the *Taking Part Survey* referred to above. One aspect of the research is on the 'drivers, impact and value of engagement' in culture and sport. This strand was reported in 2010 (CASE 2010), including a summary of general trends influencing the likelihood of engagement. These are outlined in Box 1.1.

Box 1.1 CASE summary of general trends in cultural engagement

- Increasing age predicts increasing cultural engagement but diminishing engagement in sport.
- Self-reported childhood experience of engaging in all types of culture is positively associated with engaging in culture as an adult.
- Those with higher levels of education are more likely to engage in culture.
- Those of higher socio-economic status are more likely to attend arts events, visit a heritage site, or visit a museum.
- Media consumption is positively associated with engagement in culture and sport.
- Men are much more likely than women to participate in sport, but less likely to attend arts events, visit a museum, or visit a library.
- The probability of ethnic minorities engaging in culture varies with age. For young people, ethnic status has no effect … while among older people, those from a BME group are less likely to engage in culture.
- Families are more likely than non-families to visit heritage and museums.

CASE (2010: 6)

This summary supports research on museum visitation across the Western world. The NEA data suggests that 75 per cent of visitors to museums in the USA are aged under 55, with most age ranges represented almost equally, but a slight majority in the 45–54 category. Davies (1994) reveals comparable attendance in UK museum audiences, but with smaller percentages at 16–24 and over 55 years old. The more recent surveys of UK visitors suggest increasing problems in attracting the adult audience under 35. Rubenstein and Loten (1996) place most adult museum visitors in Canada within the 35–44 age range. At the Australian Museum, Sydney, 28 per cent of visitors are within the 35–49 age range, 25 per cent are over 50 and 22 per cent are aged 25–34 (AMARC 2003). People tend to visit in groups or families, as a social outing, rather than on their own, although more people go on their own to art galleries. At the Australian Museum, Sydney, 45–55 per cent of visitors come in family groups, 15 per cent come with their partner, 15 per cent come alone and c. 15 per cent come in organised school parties.

Potentially, up to 33 per cent of museum visitors are under 16, making it highly likely that 60+ per cent of visitors include children in the group – either as families or on organised school trips. Some 41 per cent of Australian children visited a museum or art gallery in the 12 months up to April 2009 (Australian Bureau of Statistics 2009). Rubenstein and Loten state that, for Canadian museums, family groups are the key audience. Percentages will, however, vary from site to site and exhibition to exhibition, depending on the approach taken to the presentation, marketing and operation of the site, and specific exhibitions and programmes.

The two genders are relatively equally represented at museums, although this is dependent on the nature of the site – in Canada, for example, art gallery audiences are

60 per cent female and 40 per cent male (Rubenstein and Loten 1996), while in the USA they are 55 per cent female and 45 per cent male (NEA 2009). Less information is available on the racial or ethnic origin of visitors, although this situation is changing. What there is suggests strongly that all groups other than whites are under-represented. The 2001 MORI survey suggested just under 30 per cent of white and Asian people in the UK visited museums and galleries in the 12 months up to November 1999, but only 10 per cent of black residents. About 26 per cent of non-Hispanic whites, 15 per cent of Hispanics, 12 per cent of African-Americans, and 23 per cent of adults in other racial/ethnic categories (largely Asian Americans and Native Americans) visited an art museum or gallery in the USA in 2008 (NEA 2009).

For Canada, Rubenstein and Loten suggest most visitors are either local residents or tourists. In the UK, the research suggests day-trippers and local resident populations make up the core market for most heritage sites and museums, except for those in major tourist destinations, including London.

> The lifeblood of the South-East [UK] is the day visitor drawn dominantly from socio-economic groups ABC1, and aged between 40 and 60, of whom 60% are female. More than 70% are from the region and visit the sites for leisure rather than for educational reasons.
>
> Berry and Shephard (2001: 166)

Most museum visitors in the UK, except in central London, go by car and prefer to travel no more than one hour to a museum, which is crucial in defining catchment areas. This can vary depending on the scale and popularity of the site and whether it is on a greenfield location with easy access and free parking, or in a traffic-packed city centre, but travel time is rarely more than 1.5 hours. A market survey of museums in the East Midlands, carried out in 1994–5 (still one of the largest of its type carried out in the UK) showed that 83 per cent of visitors travelled less than one hour, with 60 per cent travelling less than half an hour (East Midlands Museums Service 1996). From the limited research available, local people represent the bulk of repeat visitors, reflecting an unwillingness to travel far to revisit a site. Some day trips can require pre-planning and booking but the majority do not, which means they can be a spontaneous decision. The weather can, not surprisingly, be a real influence on choice. For sites outside the major tourist destinations, by far the most substantial tourist audience at UK sites is the VFR (visitors staying with friends or relatives). This audience is discussed in more detail below.

However, the most striking evidence from visitor surveys, revealed by any analysis of adult museum visitors, is that the largest group and the most over-represented in comparison to their percentage within the general population, consists of the better-educated, more affluent, white professional classes (even more extreme for art galleries than for museums), with education the most important factor. Hood summarised the traditional USA audience as:

> in the upper education, upper occupation and upper income groups ... This social class factor applies across the spectrum of museums – from zoos, science-technology centres and children's museums to historical sites, botanical gardens and art museums.
>
> Hood (1993: 17)

In the USA, among adults who visit an art gallery or art museum at least once in 12 months, 80 per cent have some college education, with 52 per cent of those with graduate degrees visiting (NEA 2009). In the UK, 65 per cent of people with a university degree or above visited museums, while only 19 per cent of people with no qualifications did (MLA 2004). The average educational profile among visitors at the Canadian Museum of Civilisation shows 48 per cent with some university education or higher, 22 per cent with pre-university college, 22 per cent with high school and only 8 per cent with elementary school (Rabinovitch 2003). Rubenstein and Loten (1996) reinforce this for Canada as a whole, stating that most adult visitors are professionals with post-secondary education. Visitor studies at the Australian Museum, Sydney, suggest 50 per cent of their audience have a university education or above (AMARC 2003). Those with higher educational levels are also significantly more likely to attend *regularly* than those with other or no qualifications (Bunting et al. 2007: 25).

A word of caution here, however. Not all highly educated people visit museums, and the available research does not explain why. Equally, many less well-educated people visit museums regularly. So other factors must play a key role, not least exposure to museums as a child. This is explored further below.

Lack of access to private transport is often given as a key reason for lack of use by lower socio-economic groups, particularly as many heritage sites are in rural locations. But visitor surveys show that, on the whole, there is no significant difference in the social class profile between rural and urban sites, where public transport is more readily available (Light and Prentice 1994: 92). High admission charges are also given as a key cause, but work by Prentice (1989) and others seems to show that manual workers were not being deterred at the gates of heritage sites by high admission charges – instead they were not arriving at the sites in the first instance. As Been et al. suggest, increasing the admission fee will only have a limited effect, more so for museums that are major tourist destinations rather than dependent on local visitors:

> A main reason for the limited price elasticity of visiting museums is the small share of entrance fees in the total costs of a visit: about 17 percent. The other 83 percent consist of travelling expenses, food, drinks and in some cases even accommodation costs. The weight of these costs increases along with the distance to the museum. Therefore foreign tourists are hardly influenced by the level of the entrance fee.
>
> Been et al. (2002: 3)

Davies (2007), in his research on UK museum visitors since 1991, goes even further, suggesting that there is actually evidence of a substantial shift in the proportion of higher occupational class visitors (ABC1) compared to those from lower occupational classes, shown in Table 1.1 (overleaf).

Davies discusses potential reasons for this apparent failure in what has been a major museum and government agenda in the UK over the last 15 years to broaden the audience base for museums. He points out that the population as a whole has become more middle class but also that this table charts *proportions*, not actual numbers. He suggests that there is a possibility more C2DEs are visiting but *even more* ABC1s.

This explanation is supported to some degree by research following the reintroduction of free admission to UK national museums in December 2001. By the early

Table 1.1 **Shifting proportions of socio-economic classes visiting UK museums (%)**

	ABC1	C2DE
1991	55	45
1994	56	44
1999	66	34
2003	75	25
2005/6	72	28

Davies (2007a: 366)

summer of 2002, the Department of Culture, Media and Sport was able to announce a 62 per cent increase in visitor numbers to these museums in the seven months since entry charges were scrapped. Free entry was designed to encourage those who normally did not visit museums. Research by MORI in their omnibus survey of August 2002 showed a substantial increase in museums and gallery visiting when compared with 1999, outlined in Table 1.2, while comparable activities like cinema or concert going remained comparatively stable. Free admission could therefore be seen as a major cause of this rise.

Table 1.2 **Proportion of the UK public who have visited a museum or gallery (%)**

	1999	2002
Total	35	45
15–34	33	43
35–54	42	48
55+	24	43
AB	56	62
C1	39	53
C2	29	39
DE	23	25

MORI (2003: 4)

However, what the survey showed is that, while the percentage of more difficult to reach audiences did increase, so too did that of the traditional audiences and the overall profile of the audiences remained stable.

What the surveys reveal: why people do not use museums

Arts organisations now tend to break down people who are traditionally underrepresented in attendance at museums and galleries and other arts events and activities into three broad categories, outlined in Box 1.2.

Box 1.2 **Under-represented audiences at UK museums and galleries**

- *disabled people*: i.e. people defined by themselves as having any longstanding illness, disability or infirmity that limits their activities in any way
- *black and minority ethnic groups*: i.e. defined by themselves as Asian or British Asian (Indian, Pakistani and Bangladeshi, other Asian background); black or British black (black Caribbean, black African, other black background); mixed ethnicity; Chinese; and other ethnic groups. For reasons of space, black and minority ethnic is sometimes shortened to 'BME' in charts and tables
- *lower socio-economic groups*: using the National Statistics socio-economic classification (C2, D and E), i.e. those in supervisory and technical roles, semi-routine or routine occupations, and who have never worked.

based on Bunting et al. (2007: 12–13)

But these categories, by focusing on marginalised groups, fail to incorporate those other gaping holes in museum attendance, namely families with young children and – central to the future of museums – increasingly, the under-35s.

The UK *Taking Part Survey 2005/6* (Aust and Vine 2007), in revealing that about 60 per cent of the UK population did not visit a museum, suggested three central reasons:

1 They do not know the museum exists

Ignorance of the museum's existence, contents, programmes and their relevance to individuals and communities is *the* major barrier for many who might be potential visitors. For example, in 2002, 40 per cent of the UK population did not know admission charges to national museums had been scrapped (MORI 2003: 6).

2 They know it exists but do not see any relevance to their lives

When we turn to those who are aware of a museum's presence but are non-visitors, responses to the survey, illustrated in Table 1.3 overleaf, provided two main reasons:

- They say they are not interested.
- They say that they do not have enough time – which in my mind means they are not interested enough to make time.

3 Poor health

was also a significant issue.

Table 1.3 **Reasons given for not visiting a museum (%)**

1	Not really interested	35.5
2	It's difficult to find the time	29.2
3	Lack of transport/I can't easily get to it	10.4
4	Never occurred to me	9.8
5	Health isn't good enough	9.5
6	No need to go	8.1
7	I wouldn't enjoy it	4.5
8	It costs too much	4.4
9	Not enough information on what is available	3.3
10	Have been in past/no need to go again	2.0
11	Not child friendly/children too young	1.2
12	I have no one to go with	1.1
13	Other reasons	5.0

Aust and Vine (2007)

Bunting et al. (2007: 49), however, suggest that the picture looks quite different when higher and lower socio-economic groups are examined separately. Lack of interest is the real barrier for lower socio-economic groups, but for higher socio-economic groups lack of time is more of a problem. It is impossible to avoid the conclusion that it is a reflection of a class divide, which in turn creates a 'participation divide' that affects social and civil engagement across the board, not just in the arts (Bunting et al. 2007: 62). But how does this apply to the young professionals who are not visiting – is it lack of time for them, or is it lifestyle choice based on lack of perceived relevance to their lives? And will this change if and when they have children? This is discussed below when exploring future trends.

It is essential to try to look beyond this. Here we can turn to the work of Hood and others in defining criteria by which people judge their leisure experiences, including museum visits. The core attributes Hood listed as underlying their choices were, in alphabetical order:

- Being with people, or social interaction
- Doing something worthwhile
- Feeling comfortable and at ease in one's surroundings
- Having a challenge of new experiences
- Having an opportunity to learn
- Participating actively

Hood (1983: 51)

Hood's research defined the characteristics museum non-visitors valued most highly as being with people, participating actively, and feeling comfortable and at ease, and that these three leisure attributes – the ones they value most highly – are frequently not present at all in museums:

They perceive museums to be formal, formidable places, inaccessible to them because they usually have had little preparation to read the 'museum code' – places that invoke restrictions on group social behaviour and on active participation. Sports, picnicking, browsing in shopping malls better meet their criteria of desirable leisure activities.

Hood (1983: 54)

Such a negative image can last long after the reality has changed. Although museums have transformed themselves over the last thirty years, they are still thought of by many non-users as dry, dusty places, with cobwebs on the displays, and staffed by surly, unwelcoming or even rude museum attendants who are clearly out to ensure you do not enjoy your visit. This is substantially what marketers would refer to as an 'organic' stereotype, one that is the result of half-remembered, distant experiences, conversations, television programmes, etc. An attitudes survey of non-visitors to London museums (Trevelyan 1991) discovered that a significant proportion of adult non-visitors had received a negative experience of museums as children and, unaware of modern developments, had not been stimulated to try visiting a museum again. Hood (1983) reinforces this in making the key point that, generally, non-participant adults were not socialised into museum going when they were children. This is discussed further below.

Underpinning lack of interest and time, and expressions of boredom, are core issues relating to inclusion, representation, relevance and equality of participation. The study of these issues has focused on black and minority ethnic groups. When researchers for the Yorkshire Museums Council explored usage of museums by the local black and Asian community they examined barriers preventing visits, and saw the attitudes and assumptions of non-users to be a key element:

- "They don't do activities that interest me"
- "Not enough black culture"
- "Doesn't relate to me"
- "Don't feel included"

Woroncow (2001: 2)

However, museum focus on segmentation as a means of defining under-represented groups has seriously over-simplified the situation by emphasising individuals' socio-demographics rather than their motivations and attitudes (McCarthy and Jinnett 2001: ix). Many groups, particularly with younger members, resist being addressed through or constituted by racial or ethnic categories, and see these as not fitting contemporary realities. For example,

Younger generations of African Americans, he suggested, in many ways have more in common with young people of other races than with older individuals within their own ethnic group. For instance, hip-hop is a defining cultural influence for young people across ethnic groups, but has little appeal for older generations of African Americans—thus, the "rap gap."

Omar Wasow, quoted in OP&A (2004: 5)

Despite any or all of this, the evidence 'suggests that the greatest inequity in arts engagement is along socio-economic lines – that the least affluent in society benefit least from the wide range of arts opportunities available' (Bunting et al. 2007: 65). What new ways can museums find to connect better with those who are disengaged? What more can we do to overcome the 'lack of interest', or whatever that phrase masks? It is time to look more closely at motivations.

VISITOR MOTIVATIONS

Visitor surveys explore mass demand arising within defined segments of the market; from this they attempt to generalise the nature of users and their expectations. The problem is that when you take a close look at museum audiences, the picture is much more complex, right down to the level of the individual. Central to this is motivation – why the choice is made to visit a museum, and the extent to which this is due to its ability, for example, to provide a focus for a social outing or for an essentially unshareable, individual, personal or social group/family interest. From this it follows that visiting individuals, families or social groups are audience segments in their own right; their personal needs motivate their choice of site to visit and, once there, of which aspects to engage with. Museums must develop a much more sophisticated understanding of the varying motivations of individuals, families and social groups and must then find ways to support visitors who seek a more personalised experience based on their motivations and interests.

People have many reasons for choosing one leisure activity over another and will of course, over time, involve themselves in a wide range of different activities. Since individuals differ, the criteria applied in deciding what activity to engage in will differ. A central issue for museum attendance, therefore, is whether the make-up of the traditional museum audience is limited not by constraints but rather by choice. To what extent do the professional and/or highly educated classes see goal-oriented activities as an important use of an element of their leisure time, and does this go some way to explaining their disproportionate use of museums and heritage sites? As Hood put it,

> they are attracted to the kinds of experiences museums offer and they find those offerings and activities satisfying ... These folk emphasise three factors in their leisure life: opportunities to learn, the challenge of new experiences, and doing something worthwhile for themselves.
>
> Hood (1993: 17)

Professional class museum visiting may also be motivated by past experiences. As Light and Prentice (1994: 98) suggested, those activities which an individual has previously experienced as rewarding are more likely to be repeated, and so behavioural consistency is maintained. Important influences on this process will include the activities with which an individual has been socialised – and here the family is a key agent. Is professional class heritage visiting self-perpetuating, passed on from one generation to the next? There is growing research evidence on the importance of 'arts socialisation' during one's early years. Childhood and adolescent exposure to museum visiting, and the arts in general, is a major factor in adult leisure choices (CASE 2010; McCarthy and Jinnett 2001; OP&A 2007b; Orend 1989).

I discussed above the six attributes Hood (1983, 1993, 1996) listed as the criteria by which people judged their leisure activities. Alongside these, research at the Australian Museum, Sydney, between 1999 and 2001 (Kelly 2001: 9) highlighted five main motivations for museum visiting as: experiencing something new; entertainment; learning; the interests of children/family; and doing something worthwhile in leisure. McManus (1996), based on survey work at the Science Museum in London, sought comments from visitors on the motivation for that specific visit, and the associated expectations:

Motivation to visit:	Family visit with children	20%
	Recreation	20%
	Reputation of the museum	18%
	Interest in science	17%
	Revisiting the venue/an exhibit	17%
	Museuming	8%
Expectations of visit:	Finding out/learning	26%
	Fun	22%
	General interest	21%
	Specific aspect of museum	18%
	No structured plans	7%
	None defined	6%

Her general conclusion was that 'we can say that visitors are highly motivated to attend to exhibit communications within a social recreational context. Their interest is general and not focused in a studious, academic style' (McManus 1996: 59–60).

As with Hood and Kelly, her study emphasises the combination of an opportunity for learning and the 'social recreational context' of the visit. So, most of our users seek to develop their skills, and enhance their understanding through active involvement with museum content and programming in the context of a casual, social visit where they want to enjoy themselves rather than feel they are being made to work hard. Attitude of mind matters as much as motivation. We are speaking here of what Ham (outlined in Box 1.3 overleaf) calls 'non-captive' audiences rather than the 'captive' users on structured educational visits.

Box 1.3 Captive and non-captive audiences

Captive audiences	Non-captive audiences
Involuntary audience	Voluntary audience
Time commitment is fixed	Have no time commitment
External rewards important	External rewards not important
Must pay attention	Do not have to pay attention
Will accept a formal academic approach	Expect an informal atmosphere and a non-academic approach
Will make an effort to pay attention even if bored	Will switch attention if bored

Examples of motivations:
- grades
- diplomas
- certificates
- licence
- jobs/employment
- money
- advancement
- success

Examples of motivations:
- interest
- fun
- entertainment
- self-enrichment
- self-improvement
- a better life
- passing time (nothing better to do)

Ham (1992: 7)

And attitudes and levels of engagement will vary between audience segments and at different times of the year:

> A number of years ago I visited the Gateway Arch Museum in St. Louis, Missouri. I remember talking to one of the park rangers assigned to interpretation about differences in visitors as a function of the time of year. He explained that the fall visitors, many of them empty nesters and retired persons, were a much more rewarding audience for interpreters. These visitors would pay careful attention to his interpretation and ask meaningful questions. In contrast, the summer audience was large, somewhat hectic in nature, and motivated more by wanting to ride the tram over the Arch. They paid less attention and asked fewer questions.
>
> Loomis (1996)

Other factors that influence motivation will include, for example, the types of participation involved – through media (television, online), through attendance or through a desire for active involvement (which can be on-site and/or online). Equally, 'the participation behaviour of frequent, occasional, and rare participants may be motivated by different factors' (McCarthy and Jinnett 2001: 12).

The bulk of those interviewed by McManus are clearly occasional or rare participants and their motivations and expectations reflect this. But this is the norm for museums. One aspect of motivation all surveys reveal is that, for the vast majority of the audience, a museum is something one visits as a special occasion rather than being something used regularly. For example, in the UK, the first report on the *Taking Part Survey* reflecting data collected in England in 2005/6 notes that only 8 per cent of the c. 40 per cent of the population who visited museums did so more than four times a year (Aust and Vine 2007: Figure 4.2.1).

Learning as a motivator

Thomas noted that professional and managerial workers were more likely to visit historic monuments to be informed, whereas manual workers were more likely to visit for relaxation and entertainment, and that an important motive for visiting museums is a prior interest in museum or gallery content (Thomas 1989: 86, 90).

Museum-led literature relating to the motivations behind museum visits overwhelmingly emphasises the importance of learning (see, for example, Falk et al. 1998; Hood 1983, 1996; Kelly 2001; Prentice 1998; Prentice et al. 1997). Ostrower suggests 65 per cent of Americans who visit museums say they are strongly motivated by a desire to gain knowledge or learn something new (Ostrower 2005: 4). Clearly this often relates to a specific interest in the subject matter. Ostrower's survey revealed that 'African-American and Hispanic respondents were far more likely than white respondents to express a desire to learn about or celebrate their cultural heritage as a major motivation for attendance: 50 percent of African-Americans and 43 percent of Hispanics, but only 15 percent of whites gave this response' (Ostrower 2005: 4).

In recent years, this focus on learning has resulted in the segmentation of museum and heritage visitors in new ways. As an independent researcher, John Falk has developed visitor profiles based on individual needs and the internal processes that he believes drive visitors to museums and strongly reflect personal identity. These are outlined in Box 1.4.

Box 1.4 John Falk profiles

Explorer: the need to satisfy personal curiosity and interest in an intellectually challenging environment.

Facilitator: the wish to engage in a meaningful social experience with someone whom you care about in an educationally supportive environment.

Experience seeker: the aspiration to be exposed to the things and ideas that exemplify what is best and intellectually most important within a culture or community.

Professional/hobbyist: the desire to further specific intellectual needs in a setting with a specific subject matter focus.

Recharger: the yearning to physically, emotionally and intellectually recharge in a beautiful and refreshing environment.

Falk (2009: 63–4)

Most museum and heritage organisations have sought to define motivational segments rather than personal profiles. In the UK, for example, Arts Council England (2008) has established 13 segments, including non-visitors, while the National Trust has broken its audiences down into seven segments, outlined in Box 1.5, and used these to influence the way the Trust develops new interpretation for its sites.

Box 1.5 National Trust visitor profiling

Out and About: Spontaneous people who prefer chance encounters to making firm plans and love to share their experiences with friends.

Young Experience Seekers: People who are open to challenge, in a physical or horizon-broadening sense; they make and take opportunities in their journey of personal discovery.

Curious Minds: Active thinkers, always questioning and making connections between the things they learn. They have a wide range of interests and take positive steps to create a continual flow of intellectual stimuli in their lives.

Live Life to the Full: Self-driven intellectuals, confident of their own preferences and opinions and highly independent in their planning and decision making; these people are always on the go.

Explorer Families: Families that actively learn together, the adults will get as much out of their experience as the children. To fit in the interests of all family members planning, sharing and negotiation are essential.

Kids First Families: Families who put the needs of the children first and look for a fun environment where children are stimulated and adults can relax; they're looking for a guaranteed good time.

Home and Family: Broad groups of friends and family who gather together for special occasions. They seek passive enjoyment of an experience to suit all tastes and ages.

National Trust (2004)

We can be more specific for those who go beyond informal museum visits to take part in adult museum programmes. Sachatello-Sawyer et al. (2002) used the results of a three year research study to profile participants based on their motivations, illustrated in Box 1.6.

But it is essential to look back to the research of Hood, Kelly and others and recognise that learning is rarely the sole motivator behind a museum visit. In particular social interaction is an essential element of almost all visits. Museums are one of a range of leisure-learning-related experiences that our visitors use for the pleasure of learning and for personal development. This is most obviously the case for families, discussed in Chapter 7. What is clear from both anecdotal evidence and the research available is that the demands and expectations of informal visitors are rising, and there is continuing pressure to improve the product.

Box 1.6 Categories based on primary motivation for attending museum programmes

Knowledge seekers	demonstrate a strong desire to learn new things. They seek challenging content, a broad array of learning activities and additional resources that allow them to follow up their interests.
Socialisers	attend expressly for social interaction. Often family members, friends or neighbours attend together – participants also share the experience after the programme is over.
Skill builders	like to learn by doing. Their goal is to improve specific skills and gain new ones.

based on Sachatello-Sawyer et al. (2002: 8–10)

Today's reality: the 'traditional' audience is in decline

> After topping 26 percent in 1992 and 2002, art museum attendance slipped to 23 percent in 2008 . . . For the first time in the SPPA [*Survey of Public Participation in the Arts*], women reduced their rate of attendance . . . The proportion of US adults touring parks or historical buildings (25 percent) has diminished by one third since 1982.
>
> NEA (2009: 2)

It is vital for museums to understand that they cannot take their existing audiences for granted – in fact, museums are at risk of losing many of them while not replacing them with new audiences. Museum audiences across the Western world are currently at best on a plateau, at worst falling steadily. They are aging and they are not particularly diverse – and they are often not very welcoming of the changes museums need to introduce to reach younger generations. The museum audience does not exist in isolation, but must be seen in the context of wider leisure trends, with an explosion in leisure opportunities and the impact of new technology and media transforming demand and expectations.

The fragmentation of leisure time

There is an assumption in Western society that everyone is leading busier lives, with less time for leisure than ever before. If we accept a definition of leisure time as that not spent on work, biological necessities like sleeping or eating, or basic household tasks, but instead used for fun, relaxation or personal enrichment (OP&A 2007b), the reality is more complex. While we have seen an ongoing increase in dual income households, with the movement of married women into the workplace and more time therefore committed to a rigid work schedule, the time spent on basic household tasks has declined dramatically with, for example, the rise of ready meals, the use of new technology and paying for tasks such as cleaning or gardening to be done.

In the USA, studies have concluded that there has actually been an *increase* in adult leisure time, but that this leisure time has become more fragmented – it is increasingly difficult, because of fixed work commitments, to coordinate leisure activities with friends and partners, and this is having a significant impact on leisure time choices, with blocks of joint time often too short to do other than relax at home (OP&A 2007b). In this report, evaluation of available quantitative market research data suggested that:

- Americans are becoming more home bound, passive and vicarious in their leisure activities, and
- flexibility in scheduling leisure activities is becoming ever more important.

One effect has been a growing demand for personalised on-demand experiences that are easy to access and share, and which can be found increasingly at home. When linked to the rise of new media, these have resulted in a major shift in how people are using their leisure time. Since 2003 television viewing in the USA has increased by 9 per cent on all days of the week, while the time spent playing video games and using computers has increased by 32 per cent. By contrast, time spent attending or hosting social events or attending out-of-home cultural, entertainment, sporting or recreational events have all seen significant decreases of anywhere from 20 per cent to 50 per cent (White 2010). Museum visits have declined less than many other activities, perhaps because they are more time flexible – available eight hours a day, most days of the year.

More means less

Whether people choose to stay at home or go out, there are more options for how they spend their time. At home there is home cinema, a multitude of television and radio channels and a plethora of electronic equipment (with the social networking opportunities this provides), as well as conversation, books, etc. If they go out, they will find more choice for eating, drinking, film-going, and so forth – whatever their area of interest, there are more options – 'a greater choice of leisure options and a greater number of choices within each option' (Scott 2000b: 39). And all these are, of course, alternatives to visiting a museum. Even with museums, there are now many more to choose from. The end result is that a smaller percentage of the available market will select each of the individual options.

Shopping

The major competition for museums lies in alternative uses of leisure time. One thinks of in-home entertainment, the rise of the garden centre and health club, eating out and, most important of all, shopping. Shopping is now the second biggest leisure activity in Western society, after watching television. In the UK, shopping centres such as Bluewater Park in Kent, or Trafford Park in Manchester, attract 30–35 million visitors a year, more than the attendances at all the national museums put together. The introduction of Sunday trading in the 1990s has had a disastrous impact on what used to be the busiest day of the week for museums in the UK. While there has been a substantial increase in both day trip and tourist visits, particularly to historic towns and cities, much of the drive behind this has been about doing 'normal' things in a new environment – most importantly this has meant shopping. What we are seeing here is the rise of historic towns as 'consumption centres', with more and more consumption activities being added to those already available. While the historic built fabric remains a core element of heritage tourism – and a 'critical mass' of relevant attractions, mainly museums and galleries, is seen as an essential support – shopping and dining out are frequently the key factors:

> Visitors can experience heritage first hand in a way that cannot be achieved at a purpose built facility such as a heritage centre. They can engage with history while undertaking activities that could be carried out elsewhere, e.g. shopping ... combined shopping and tourism trips are now just as important a reason for visiting an historic town as its heritage.
>
> English Tourism Council et al. (1999: 11 and 13)

Museums and galleries urgently need to sharpen up their external image and appearance to match the standards demanded by the modern consumer, and make themselves at least as attractive to the potential visitor as shopping and afternoon coffee.

Changing demographics, the changing demands of the under-35 market and the impact of new technology

These three issues are inter-related and are key to any analysis of current or future demand. As discussed in the Introduction, the populations of our cities, where so many museums are located, are in the midst of demographic change, with immigration and the rise in the birth rate radically altering the ethnic and racial make-up. For many museums, their traditional audience is simply no longer there in the same numbers. There is also evidence that the under-35 audience of young white professionals is not being attracted to museums. One reason for this has been the tectonic shift in the way Western society operates, represented by the rise of new media.

These issues are explored below in looking to future visitor needs and at the ability of museums to develop new audiences.

ANTICIPATING FUTURE VISITOR MOTIVATIONS, EXPECTATIONS AND NEEDS

> This is what this YouTube-Facebook-instant messaging generation does. Witness. Record. Share.
>
> Vargas (2007), quoted in OP&A (2007a: 2)

In the Introduction, I spoke of the focus of the Smithsonian Institution and the AAM's Center for the Future of Museums on the early 2030s in exploring the demands users are likely to place on museums in the future. What will our audiences want from museums in 2030? Because each generation can be associated with different sets of interests, lifestyles and values, a core approach has been to look at generational distinctions and their potential impact, as outlined in Table 1.4. This must, however, also recognise that each new generation is partly shaped by the previous generation – the adults and society they live and grow with.

Table 1.4 **Generational characteristics of USA audiences**

Generation	Characteristics
Silent/Mature Generation	Born between 1927 and 1945. Raised in the era of the Depression. Came of age during the Second World War. Broad assumptions of this generation include that government is a catalyst for growth, sacrifice is a virtue and that leisure time and retirement are rewards for years of hard work.
Baby Boomers	Born between 1946 and 1964: an increase in the birth rate of 30 per cent over the Silent/Mature generation. Helped fuel the enormous growth of suburbia. Witnessed the explosion of mass media, as television in particular united the nation. As teens and young adults they were shaped by the social upheaval of the 1960s and early 1970s and by the introduction of the birth control pill. As children and young adults (especially those born pre-1954) they also witnessed unprecedented economic expansion, leading to a dramatic increase in their income and wealth.
Generation X	Born between 1965 and 1978. Markedly smaller numbers than the Baby Boomers who preceded them – annual birth rates dropped c. 15 per cent after mainstreaming of 'the pill'. Shaped by growing up amidst a rapidly changing family structure – twice as likely to see their parents divorce. They are the 'latchkey kids'. Generation X women became 70 per cent more likely to go on to higher education than women from the start of the Baby Boom – major impact on how families operate today. The rise of dual income families. Have higher debt burdens than previous generations, largely owing to housing costs, and are about one third less likely to have pensions – have less disposable income than the Baby Boomers had.
Generation Y	Starts roughly 1979 when annual birth rate in USA increased c. 10 per cent. Had mostly Baby Boomer parents who put off having children longer than previous generations. Extraordinary diversity – ethnic minority youth population 50 per cent greater than that of their parents. Thanks to the internet and especially social networking sites, they have a different way to filter the world around them than the traditional mass media. Continuing increase in the percentage of women going on to higher education.

Generation M   Difficult to define starting point – probably mid-1990s
(Millennials)   Growing up as the 'wired' generation – they are immersed in a world of media and gadgets. They expect to be able to gather and share information in multiple devices, in multiple places. Their technology is mobile. The internet plays a special role in their world.

based on Wilkening and Chung (2009: 8–10) and Rainie (2006), quoted in OP&A (2007a: 9–10)

The Center for the Future of Museums and the Smithsonian Institute have pinpointed trends reflecting these and other issues, outlined in Box 1.7.

Box 1.7   Key trends for future museum visitors

- People will live longer. Physical access will become an increasingly important issue for all public provision. There will be growing numbers of older people who want opportunities to volunteer, with educational institutions like museums high on their agendas. There is likely to be increasing demand for programming and website provision that supports brain exercise.
- People will be more highly educated than their predecessors and less likely to accept a passive role in their museum visiting – if museums do not respond to their expectations, people will look elsewhere.
- Generation X will seek increasing opportunities for social interaction and civil engagement, reflecting their growing interest in community involvement.
- The population will continue to become more diverse but also increasingly fragmented. By 2050 the USA will have a population where no single group will constitute more than half the population.
- People will become more tolerant on social issues such as immigration, race and homosexuality.
- Women will continue to have their children later. Their economic importance will also continue to grow.
- With increased sharing of family responsibilities, there will be growing demands for family-focused programming.
- There will be a continuing advance in the nature and use of technology, especially among the young. But older audiences and those with disabilities also increasingly use the internet for access.
- The Internet will become less about knowledge transmission and more about social networking
- The social experience of museum visiting will be increasingly important. People will also be looking for the experiential, participative experiences shaped by their lifelong exposure to the internet.
- There will continue to be vastly more options for how people, especially younger people, gather and spend their leisure time.

based on Center for the Future of Museums (2008) and OP&A (2007a)

The key conclusion the Smithsonian reached from its analysis of these trends is that 'our constituencies are changing faster than we are':

> Responding to audiences that increasingly, look, think, behave, and process information differently requires museums to not only get to know these audiences better, but to be willing to make bold changes in marketing, programming, and infrastructure to meet future visitor needs.
>
> OP&A (2007a: 15)

By 2030 the Baby Boomers will all be over 70 and likely to be still seeking new experiences, while Generation X will be contemplating retirement. Generation Y will be entering their 50s and the Millennial Generation will be parents, we hope bringing their children to our museums. Will the number of children being born continue to increase as it has since Generation Y? Will we see the same or greater diversity? What types of experiences will they want?

Generations Y and M – the current under-35s – appear to be more demanding, seek more-active experiences, have higher expectations from what is on offer and are less willing to accept poor quality. They are also leading increasingly frenetic lives. Research suggests many do not like traditional museums. They do not want to 'learn' but seek a more sensual/emotional experience. They are seeking a leisure environment that can provide all their requirements in one location – museum galleries, shopping, an animated public space in which to meet, eating, activities, events and changing exhibitions – and extended opening hours to match. Sites seeking to attract this audience must be able to reflect the under-35 lifestyle – in these terms it is perhaps no surprise that Tate Modern in London was such an immediate success.

Yet, under-35s are also closely associated with the shift in consumer demand towards greater freedom of choice, customisation, personal involvement and individual service. The research by Kelly et al. (2002), on *Indigenous Youth and Museums* in Australia, highlighted themes relevant to all young people (defined there as aged 12–24 but in my view applicable to all those seeking a more active engagement). This audience wants:

- [To see] themselves reflected in content, programmes and staffing;
- Active learning experiences that cater for their individual and collective interests and learning styles in a comfortable and supportive atmosphere
- Involvement in programme development and delivery
- Contemporary modes of information exchange . . .
- Examination of contemporary youth issues . . .

> Kelly et al. (2002: 4)

The under-35s are also those most at home with modern technology and most likely to organise their social lives through social networking sites:

> The median age of a Twitter user is 31, which has remained stable over the past year. The median age for MySpace is now 26, down from 27 in May 2008, and the median age for LinkedIn is now 39, down from 40. Facebook, however, is graying a bit: the median age for this social network site is now 33, up from 26 in May 2008.
>
> Pew Internet (2009)

If museums can rise to the challenge, modern technology is an important way to grow both audiences and levels of engagement. It also offers a shining opportunity to develop new relationships with users.

What does this all mean for the museum audience?

Unless we see major change by museums, the core audience will continue to consist of the well-educated professional classes, but they will attend less often and expect more from their visit. A higher percentage of the audience will be white than in the wider population, and much of it may also be getting older. Basic issues of physical access will become more important. Amidst this potential gloom, the family audience will continue to grow, provided its needs are met.

All the research available suggests that future audiences will be increasingly demanding in terms of service quality, no matter the type of museum or heritage product they seek. Sites will require strong individual identities and will have to increase visitor choice and add novelty to their approaches. The pressure towards greater visitor participation will increase, as will the demand for a subtler, more personalised interpretation – the demand will be for individual, family and social group *experiences*, with the concept of the 'experience economy' rising to the fore. Museums must also recognise that for the majority of visitors they will continue to represent only one choice of leisure activity among many. In this context, they must balance their own commitment to learning with their visitors' usually more leisure-led, recreational frame of mind.

The demand for participation will include a desire for changing content and more active programming, as well as opportunities to see behind the scenes, to meet staff and to be involved in product development. However, most of all, visitors will be looking for opportunities to engage with collections and with each other. Retail and catering services will also have to be transformed to meet contemporary standards – quality, and the ability to match consumer lifestyles, will be key to long term success. The quality of the social experience of the museum visit will become increasingly important.

In the UK a number of newly developed contemporary art galleries – beginning with Tate Modern but now including Nottingham Contemporary, the Turner Contemporary in Margate and Hepworth Wakefield – have already responded to these changing demands by becoming 'social hubs', combining the gallery and shop with a good restaurant, a space for screenings and a place for performance, readings and other activities. Alongside their more traditional role they have become for a regular audience a focus for evening activity. This approach is also developed to a much greater extent in places like Brooklyn Museum and Dallas Art Gallery, which will be discussed in Chapter 2.

The use of new, particularly mobile, technologies will transform the relationship between museums and their users, taking the museum beyond its walls and its physical community. Technology will make both content and participation more accessible, extending opportunities for user contributions and the representation of multiple perspectives. It will push the issue of the museum sharing authority for content.

This is the context in which museums now operate. Museums must grow and change with their audiences. They must demonstrate their relevance to people's lives in the twenty-first century, and they must enable both social interaction and participative engagement with collections. It is essential to keep up with research. Indispensable websites include the Center for the Future of Museums (www.futureofmuseums.org), Museum Audience Insight (http://reachadvisors.typepad.com/) and, for new technology, the Museum Next blog (www.museumnext.org/2010/blog) and Pew Internet (www.pewinternet.org).

A case study on the practical application of futurist predictions at the Valentine Richmond History Center can be found on the Center for the Future of Museums website at: http://futureofmuseums.blogspot.com/2011/06/practical-futurism-case-study.html

THE GROWING IMPORTANCE OF CULTURAL TOURISM

There will continue to be a symbiotic relationship between museums, heritage sites and the leisure and tourism industry. Many museums worldwide depend on tourism, both domestic and international, to generate visitor numbers and income. A survey of cultural tourists in Australia, illustrated in Table 1.5, reveals the extent to which cultural visits form part of their holiday.

Table 1.5 **Australia: share of cultural and heritage visitors by activity (2008)**

Cultural and heritage tourism activity (%)	International visitors	Domestic overnight visitors	Domestic day visitors
Attend theatre, concerts or other performing arts	24	23	22
Visit museums or art galleries	57	44	35
Visit art and craft workshops or studios	18	7	8
Attend festivals and fairs or cultural events	21	17	19
Experience Indigenous art and craft and cultural displays	22	3	1
Visit an Indigenous site or community	11	2	n/a
Visit historical or heritage building sites or monuments	61	30	24

Tourism Research Australia (2008)

Not surprisingly, for the tourism industry the cultural and heritage tourist is now regarded as a key figure – growing in numbers, and likely to both stay in an area longer and to spend more money. Compared to other travellers, cultural and heritage tourists:

- Spend more: $623 vs. $457
- Are more likely to use a hotel, motel or B&B: 62 percent vs. 55 percent
- Are more likely to spend $1,000+/–: 19 percent vs. 12 percent

- Travel longer: 5.2 nights vs. 3.4 nights
- Historic/cultural travel volume is up 13 percent from 1996, increasing from 192.4 million person-trips to 216.8 million person-trips in 2002.
- The demographic profile of the cultural heritage travel segment today is younger, wealthier, more educated and more technologically savvy when compared to those surveyed in 1996.
- 35.3 million adults say that a specific arts, cultural or heritage event or activity influenced their choice of destination.

Travel Industry Association of America (TIA) and Smithsonian Magazine, *The Historic/Cultural Traveller, 2003 Edition*, quoted in US Department of Commerce (2005: 5)

Not surprisingly, there is a remarkable similarity between the analyses of the cultural and heritage tourist and of the traditional museum visitor, as they are the same people. A major motivating factor behind cultural heritage tourists lies in their desire to gain a deeper understanding of the culture and heritage of a destination. Although the TIA research quoted above suggests the demographic profile of the cultural tourist is getting younger, it is still the case that households headed by Baby Boomers are more likely to engage in cultural activities, and the average age of the cultural and heritage tourist is older (49 vs 47). Richards (2001a), reflecting on a major survey carried out in 1997 of cultural heritage tourists in western Europe, pointed out that the proportion of cultural and heritage tourists with a higher education qualification was almost double the European Union average, while more than 40 per cent of heritage visitors were aged 50 or over. Almost 60 per cent had managerial or professional jobs; this, together with their older age profile, meant their average incomes were significantly higher than the European average.

One of the key findings of the *State of the American Traveller Survey 2009* was that 68.8 per cent of those surveyed said their trip included a visit to friends or relatives, while 47.5 per cent stayed in a friend's or relative's home (Destination Analysts 2009). In the UK, for sites outside the major tourist destinations, by far the most substantial tourist audience for museums and heritage sites is the VFR (visitors staying with friends or relatives). The accompaniment of VFRs also accounts for a substantial proportion of repeat visits by local residents: people want to, or feel obliged to, take visitors out, and preferably to places they have been to and liked. The VFR market is notoriously difficult to measure as most is domestic, comes in its own transport and does not stay in commercial accommodation – so there is very little data. The general view, however, is that it is increasing as families and friends are separated by work and other reasons and more people have cars and housing that can accommodate visitors comfortably. One perhaps surprising factor seems to be the importance of students to this market, as they study away from home, make new friends and visit each other, and are visited by family and friends.

The *State of the American Traveller Survey 2009* broke down the activities of cultural tourists as illustrated in Table 1.6 (overleaf). But they were also engaging in a wide range of other activities. In Richards' study (Richards 2001b) only 18 per cent classified their holidays as being cultural – rather, a heritage visit was just part of their holiday. The *State of the American Traveller Survey* records the full range of activities (additional to Table 1.6) travellers participated in while on leisure trips of over 50 miles (Table 1.7).

Table 1.6 **Participation in cultural heritage tourism activities: USA domestic tourists (% participating at least once in past 12 months while on a leisure trip)**

Visit an historical attraction	42.0
Visit a state or local park	29.8
Drive a designated scenic byway	24.8
Visit an art gallery or museum	24.8
Visit a national park	24.7
Attend a concert, play or musical	20.4
Visit a national forest	14.0
Visit an ethnic heritage site	11.6
Visit an ecological site	6.6

Destination Analysts (July 2009)

Table 1.7 **Other core tourism activities USA (%)**

Dine in restaurants	78.7
Visit friends or relatives	68.8
Shopping	66.2
Going to a beach or lake	56.3
Sightseeing in cities	49.3
Visit small towns/villages	41.7
Sightseeing in rural areas	38.2
Casinos/Gambling	34.8
Visit a theme/amusement park	34.4
Attend a family re-union	21.7

Destination Analysts (July 2009)

The tables show that research within the leisure and tourism field contrasts with museum-produced literature in seeing beyond the museum visit to the bigger picture of the day out or holiday.

Either [museums and heritage sites] serve the purpose of occasionally offering a more specific destination in the context of a general day-trip, or they provide an alternative, and usually subsidiary, recreational activity to those on holiday in their vicinity. In either event, the role of such activities is of secondary recreational significance, but nevertheless appears to constitute an important element of leisure-based behaviour.

Thomas (1989: 67–8)

Given the clear importance of the cultural and heritage tourist market to museums, it would be useful to know if this audience is growing or falling. Both the Travel Industry of America and the *State of the American Traveller Survey* would suggest that it is growing, with 81 per cent of leisure travellers now defined as cultural and heritage tourists, a considerable growth from the 61 per cent recorded in 1998 and the 65 per cent of 2001. According to *Visitor Attractions Trends in England 2008*, there has been an annual increase in visits to museums and galleries in the UK since declines in 2001/2 following 9/11 and a foot and mouth disease outbreak, with a rise of 8 per cent in 2008 alone (BDRC 2009). The tourism economy in the UK is projected to grow by 2.6 per cent a year between 2009 and 2018 (Heritage Lottery Fund 2010: 8), and heritage is the mainstay of UK tourism. Between 2000 and 2008 cultural and heritage tourism for international visitors to Australia had an average annual growth of 3 per cent, increasing to 2.7 million visitors (Tourism Research Australia 2008). Figures for 2009, the year of the 'staycation', show 57.4 per cent of museums in the USA reported an increase in total attendance (Katz 2010), while in the UK, annual visitor numbers at National Trust properties grew by almost 20 per cent (Heritage Lottery Fund 2010: 1).

But these positives are not necessarily all they seem. The 8 per cent growth in visitation to UK museums in 2008 was based on increased attendance at 57 per cent of the sites surveyed, but a decrease at 35 per cent (BDRC 2009: 16), reflecting a continuing trend for visitation to migrate to larger sites (BDRC 2009: 20). It is also based on a self-selecting return by only 29 per cent of those museums surveyed. Overall, there does seem to have been an increase in the proportion of the population visiting UK museums, but any increase in the number of visits does not match the growth in tourist trips and day outings. Anecdotal evidence suggests that small local museums are the ones suffering the largest falls in visitor numbers.

In the USA, the increase in visits represented by tourism research seems to contradict the evidence from the NEA's survey of participation in the arts (NEA 2009). The suggestion must be that while people are visiting museums and heritage sites while on a leisure trip, they are reducing the amount they do so while at home, supporting the research noted above (OP&A 2007b) that Americans are becoming more homebound, passive and vicarious in their leisure activities. Again it seems to be the small local history museums where audiences are in decline – while history museums comprise more than 48 per cent of the total number of museums in the USA, median attendance is now only 10,000 visitors a year (Merritt and Katz 2009: 43).

Yet overall, the tourism picture seems more positive for museums than it did when I was writing *The Engaging Museum* in 2004–5. This is good news not just for museums in tourist areas. Growing numbers benefit all those that can reach out to visitors who stay locally with friends and relatives. These VFRs not only visit museums but bring their local friends and relatives with them This both boosts visitor numbers and gives museums an opportunity to turn those locals from one-off visitors into regular users.

2 Stimulating visits, building relationships

INTRODUCTION

Museum funding from public subsidy and grant aid has declined dramatically since the global financial crisis of 2007–8. As a result, the *economic imperative* of generating income has become ever more important. Museums and heritage sites are under immense pressure to increase their visitor numbers and grow income from them while expanding corporate usage and developing their role as tourist destinations. And most are expected to achieve these tasks while also further developing educational usage, broadening their audience base by attracting currently under-represented groups, and maintaining their traditional roles in collecting, conserving, displaying and protecting key heritage resources for the long term benefit of society. As late as 1999, only 29 per cent of UK museums admitted to having a PR and marketing policy (Runyard and French 1999: 1). It would be a rare museum that did not have a policy today.

This chapter does not seek to outline how museums can develop a strategic marketing plan – the best starting point for this is Kotler et al. (2008). (Box 2.1 is a useful matrix can that help too.) Rather, its function is to look beyond the immediate economic

---

Box 2.1 The beginnings of a strategic marketing plan

Where are you now?	**Where do you want to get to?**
Losing traditional audiences	Win hearts and minds
Not attracting new communities	Stimulate visits
Failing to engage new generations	Build relationships
Strapped for cash	Turn visitors into users

How are you going to get there? | **What resources will you need?**

How will you know if/when you have got there?

---

issues. In difficult times, it is all too easy to focus the marketing effort purely on income generation and lose sight of the major contribution it could make to promoting the core mission of museums: the *cultural imperative* to collect, care for and interpret what is the material memory of humankind and, through these collections, to encourage and support visitor engagement in cultural learning. Furthermore there is the *social imperative* to develop sustained access by as broad an audience as possible. This chapter explores the role that marketing and visitor services, underpinned by audience research, can play in supporting these latter two imperatives. To this end it has three primary objectives:

- *winning hearts and minds*: to transform the 'museum' brand, the perceptions that the public at large have of museums, into one that more effectively projects the value of museums to society as a whole alongside a positive image of museum visiting as an enjoyable and life-enhancing experience
- *stimulating visits*: to highlight the importance individual museums must place on researching and reaching out to potential audiences, stimulating visits and motivating people to engage with displays and activities when they arrive
- *building relationships*: to explore the need to persuade audiences that visiting a museum should be a regular occurrence rather than an occasional one-off event – in effect, to transform visitors into users.

WINNING HEARTS AND MINDS

Brand is the promise that exists in the public's mind about who you are and what you do.
Gardella (2002)

Museums are here for the long term. They have responsibilities that go beyond their public face and that most members of the public do not fully understand. Yet, as discussed in the Introduction, to remain relevant to twenty-first century audiences, we must persuade the public at large of the continuing value of museums to society as a whole. We must convince individuals, families, social groups and communities of the benefits gained through the experience of engaging with what museums have to offer. This will involve changing the images and perceptions that public bodies and many individuals and communities have of museums. All too often, the images and perceptions held are negative: formed through lack of awareness, through entrenched negative attitudes or through the 'wrong' positive attitudes. It is only by changing these attitudes – effectively changing the museum brand – that we can hope to win hearts and minds in the twenty-first century.

Value to society as a whole

The term *brand* first appeared in the 1980s and is now seen as an essential part of a company's identity and marketing. In one sense, the brand is projected by a company to its target market as a combination of the company or product name and the unique qualities that the product and company's services supposedly contain. Most importantly, however, it is the public's perception of the company and its product – marketing brands is about attempting to construct the perception that the company wants in the minds of the public. However, the *brand identity* that a company seeks to project is not necessarily the same as the *brand image* perceived by the public.

Companies with strong identities in the minds of the public, like Coca-Cola or Cadbury's, effectively had a brand image before the term was invented, whether they sought it or not. The same applies to museums – the concept of the museum is a brand in its own right. To the museums profession, it is a *values brand* based on authenticity, trust, cultural provision and learning opportunities. As such it 'creates a long-term bond with those sectors of the population sharing the same values' (Scott 2000a: 35). Research among both users and non-users of museums provides clarity in terms of what those values are:

> The public finds that museums stimulate the creativity and innovation which are fundamental to the new 'ideas' economies. Museums provide opportunities for individual learning and skill building. They build community capacity and contribute to social cohesion. Moreover, museums create public value through providing equitable access to collections and through being the 'honest information brokers' in a world where other sources of information are becoming increasingly suspect. Importantly museums are valued by more of the population than those who make visits. Irrespective of direct engagement, the existence, option and bequests value of museums is prized.
>
> Scott (2007: 8–9)

Scott also comments that museums are prized for their role in preserving, providing access to and interpreting history, not least that of local communities, and that this plays an important role in engendering a sense of identity and belonging. Her conclusions, based on audience research at the Australian War Memorial Museum in Canberra and the Powerhouse Museum in Sydney, reflect similar research in the USA, the UK and Canada. Research in the UK (MLA 2004: 6) showed that the majority of people think it is important for their local town or city to have its own museum, even including most of those (76 per cent) who have not visited one in the last 12 months. A survey of almost 24,000 Canadians seeking their views about the country's museums, published in 2003, found:

- 68% of respondents see museums as offering an educational as well as an entertainment/recreational experience;
- 92% believe it is important for children to be exposed to museums;
- 96% believe museums contribute to quality of life;
- 94% believe museums play a valuable role in showcasing and explaining artistic achievements;
- 97% believe museums play a valuable role in explaining the natural heritage;
- 96% believe museums play a valuable role in showcasing and explaining achievements in science and technology;
- 93% believe museums play a valuable role in explaining other regions and cultures; and

- 97% believe museums play a critical role in preserving objects and knowledge of Canada's history.

Canadian Museums Association (2003: executive summary)

So – museums matter to people. They are a crucial part of the wider cultural provision that underpins society. As a profession, we need to stand united to make this case much more strongly. We also need to join forces with other cultural bodies to project the importance of cultural engagement more widely within society.

Selling the benefits to individuals of engagement with museums

A widely held recognition of the public value of museums is essential to the positioning of museums within contemporary society, but it can also be to the detriment of individual museums trying to increase the size of their audience and broaden its scope. Among those we would see as the 'traditional' audience for museums most people have what museum professionals would consider highly positive attitudes towards museums. A brand audit carried out by the Powerhouse Museum, Sydney, in 1998 saw museums described as 'educational, places of discovery, intellectual experiences, challenging, thought-provoking, absorbing, fascinating, innovative and places where one can touch the past' (Boomerang 1998, quoted in Scott 2000a: 37).

These responses must be balanced against the attributes respondents defined for the ideal leisure experience – one which was 'a relaxed atmosphere, entertaining, a good place to take family and friends, friendly, fun, an exciting place to be, great value for money, plenty of room to move' (Boomerang 1998, quoted in Scott 2000a: 37). This is reflected to some degree in the external activities respondents to the Boomerang survey participated in most frequently:

- going to restaurants and cafes   66%
- exercising and playing sport   64%
- shopping for pleasure   59%
- visiting pubs and clubs   52%
- visiting parks and gardens   46%
- going to the theatre/movies   41%
- going to the beach   35%
- attending sporting events   34%

Boomerang (1998), quoted in Scott (2000a: 37)

Visits to art galleries and museums were frequent events (by which the survey meant monthly) for only 5 per cent and 3 per cent of respondents respectively.

Museums need to take care here. We know that we can provide enjoyable, exciting and stimulating experiences for families and groups of friends to participate in together, while remaining 'absorbing' and 'thought-provoking'. Yet we have to prevent the perception of museums and galleries as intellectually challenging actually becoming a barrier to visiting. If people perceive that a museum visit always requires serious mental engagement and hard work, they will go elsewhere:

> Museums are *fun,* they are *exciting,* they are *good places to take the family* and they offer *great value for money.* However, it appears that museums are failing to capitalise on and claim these attributes to demonstrate the valid synergy between want and what museums have to offer. The opportunity exists for museums to include in their branding not only the attributes that they meaningfully own, but also the attributes associated with an ideal leisure experience.
>
> Scott (2000a: 37)

Rather than presenting an image of museums (and other forms of heritage sites) as educationally 'worthy', we need to present an image as quality leisure destinations, but then build on this by emphasising that museums 'add value' to an outing through the very positive attributes noted above – a unique, authentic engagement with the 'real thing' that differentiates us from all other forms of leisure outing. This is not an easy task. Core characteristics of what the marketing industry might call the 'museum product', particularly its intangibility, make it difficult to sell.

Overcoming entrenched negative attitudes

Reasons why people do not visit museums are discussed in Chapter 1. At their heart lie negative, often age-old, attitudes to museums as dry, dusty, elitist, unwelcoming, formal and boring, alongside more challenging concerns about content that excludes and fails to represent the life experiences of many communities.

Changing attitudes and persuading people to visit will take more than a re-branding exercise. What is really required is behavioural change: 'people must unlearn old habits, learn new habits, and freeze the new pattern of behaviour' (Kotler and Andreasen 1996: 393). There is a medical model for this: Prochaska's Stages of Change model (Prochaska et al. 1994). However, McCarthy and Jinnett simplify this to four key stages:

> The *background stage* consists of the individual's general attitudes toward the arts; *stage 1* is the individual's formation of a predisposition to participate in the arts; *stage 2* is his or her evaluation of specific participation opportunities; and *stage 3* is the individual's actual participation experience and subsequent assessment of his or her inclination to participate.
>
> McCarthy and Jinnett (2001: xii)

If museums are to include everyone, present multiple perspectives and actively seek user contributions, they will need to make a sustained commitment to work in partnership with their local communities. This kind of transformation is discussed in depth in Chapter 8.

STIMULATING VISITS

Alongside the need for a collective campaign to transform people's attitudes to museums in general must sit site-specific image projection. These two elements are inseparable. It is only through new audiences coming to, and being inspired by, individual sites that widespread negative attitudes will be broken down. Yet image alone is not enough. It must be linked to visitor research and to the development of relevant content that will attract people to your museum in particular. The image you want will be hard-won and equally difficult to sustain, but your museum's future probably depends on it. On the one hand, the challenge is to make more people aware of the museum and what it has to offer (cognition), achieve a responding positive reaction (emotion), and then motivate/put people in an active frame of mind to visit (behaviour). On the other hand, the challenge is to know much more about what potential audiences want and accept that you will need to change your marketing, content and associated programming radically in response.

Raising awareness

There is a tendency, if you work in a museum, to assume that everybody knows it is there. In fact, ignorance of your existence is a major barrier for many who might be potential visitors. For example, street studies of black and minority ethnic groups in

Figure 2.1 **Weather forecast, pirate style**
The regional weather forecast is broadcast from Mansfield Museum on 'National Talk like a Pirate Day' – a fun and free way to reach out to the family audience. Courtesy of Mansfield Museum.

London (Tissier and Nahoo 2004) found that 74 per cent had not heard of any local museum in their areas, although awareness of national museums in London was much higher. Common sense tells us that people are bombarded with information daily, and much of that attempts to persuade them into courses of action. According to a 1997–2000 study by Yankelovich and Partners, the number of advertising messages hitting people each day in major US markets now exceeds 3,000 (Gardella 2002). To survive this bombardment requires people to have an ability to be selectively attentive, and to be able to do this rapidly and subconsciously. We seem to have a built-in skill in screening out all those messages that do not relate to our own beliefs and interests.

If museums want to reach the broad range of audiences who currently do not visit, their initial challenge is to break through that screen and persuade people to pay attention to their existence.

Countering intangibility

If you are buying a car, you can test-drive it. In contrast, you cannot experience a museum visit before deciding to 'buy' it. How do we get potential visitors to buy the museum product – a service/experience rather than a manufactured good? If the ultimate museum experience itself is intangible, we must take every opportunity to present 'signs' of quality to back up the experiential nature of the visit – to give the visitor the sense of being engaged in something welcoming yet special and of the highest quality. Marketers refer to this as 'making the intangible tangible'. This incorporates every aspect of the external presentation of the site: the point of arrival, the quality of staff, their cleanliness and the way they are dressed. All are used as evidence by which a visitor views the quality of their museum experience (Box 2.2).

Box 2.2 'Making the intangible tangible'

Think of:

- the messages about the site you are putting across in the media
- the quality of your advertising material and promotional literature – what does it promise the potential visitor? How does it influence expectations?
- the look and branding of your website
- the effectiveness of the signage that leads first-time visitors to your site
- the first impression of the site – for both visitors and passers-by. How does this impression compare to the expectations raised in the media and in your literature?
- the appearance/motivating appeal of the entrance
- how you actually deal with visitors on arrival – from orientation to ticketing arrangements etc.
- all the members of staff, or volunteers, who may have any contact with your audiences – from telephone to in-person
- how you handle enquiries, complaints, etc.

Positioning the museum

> All characteristics of a museum – both as an institution and as a physical space – condition its public image . . . The image projected by a museum should not result merely from chance, but should be consciously determined, consistent with the museum's role and directions.
>
> Royal Ontario Museum (1976: 7)

I made reference in the Introduction to the uncertainty that many museum professionals feel about the role of museums in the twenty-first century. If the survival of your museum depends on the perception potential audiences have of you, then clarity is essential. As a values brand, we can appeal to the underlying allegiance of much of the potential audience, but each individual museum must also project an external image that will ensure it has a strong, positive individual identity in the public mind, and particularly in the minds of target audiences. You need to consider the key characteristics that will attract targeted audiences to the museum, and distinguish your museum both from every other one and from other types of competitors. This will begin with an internal analysis of your current position and a *brand audit* to discover what your museum stands for in your potential audience's eyes.

The internal analysis will concentrate on defining what you might consider to be your key positive attributes (remarkable building, welcoming atmosphere, unique collections, participative displays, friendly staff, etc.), and highlighting those you consider of greatest appeal to the audiences you want to visit. It should also highlight negative attributes to overcome, including changes needed to your basic product. The external analysis will concentrate on the attitudes of existing visitors and non-visitors. The starting point here is baseline research on how you are currently perceived in your own right and *then* in comparison with your competitors.

Scott (2000a) discusses the brand audit carried out for the Powerhouse Museum in Sydney, a museum of applied arts and sciences established in 1879 that had moved to the site of a historic power station in 1988. Despite receiving 600,000 visitors a year, a decision was taken in 1998 to 'take stock' and examine the need to respond to growing competition, from museums and other leisure activities. The results of the audit revealed what people believed made the Powerhouse different. They also showed the wider awareness of the importance of museums in general as a values brand combined with the leisure preferences of the Sydney public:

> It is *not a traditional museum*, it is *a place of discovery* offering *exciting, hands-on* experiences. Visitors have the opportunity to become *engaged*. . . . [I]n a leisure environment where passive consumption is readily available, a leisure experience with the added dimension of *engagement* can be promoted as an attractive alternative.
>
> Scott (2000a: 38), her emphases

BUILDING RELATIONSHIPS: TURNING VISITORS INTO USERS

As discussed in Chapter 1, in the UK, the first report on the *Taking Part Survey* (2005/6) noted that only 8 per cent of the c. 40 per cent of the population who visited museums did so more than four times a year (Aust and Vine 2007: Figure 4.2.1). Earlier in this chapter, I referred to research carried out for the Powerhouse Museum in Sydney which showed that visiting art galleries and museums in Sydney was a frequent event (by which the survey meant monthly) for only 5 per cent and 3 per cent of respondents respectively (Boomerang 1998, quoted in Scott 2000a: 37). This is the norm for museum visitation. The bulk of museum audiences do not attend structured educational sessions, projects or special events. Their engagement with the museum and its collections comes through visiting exhibitions and any associated activities, or through online access. Most who attend physically see this as a one-off event, not a regular occurrence. Museum professionals share that mind-set, calling them visitors rather than users.

We need to work actively to transform this situation. Museums more than ever require the sustained allegiance of regular users. More importantly, as will be discussed in Chapter 4, it is through regular engagement with museum content that meaningful cultural learning takes place, not through intermittent visits. If we believe in the power of museums as learning institutions and the ability of cultural learning to change lives, a primary focus must be on transforming the visitor experience for all so that it is something that people want to come back to time and again. Of course, this regular engagement can be virtual as well as physical.

We must look to shared values as an underpinning for the development of a closer relationship. We must then build from this core to develop new content, activities and programming, both real and virtual, that meets specific needs and supports regular engagement.

Using profiling to turn visitors into users at Dallas Museum of Art

To turn visitors into users, museums must begin by developing a much more sophisticated understanding of their needs and motivations. Building a profile of your users and personalising contact with them through *relationship marketing* is a common feature in the commercial world, and is being adopted by many in the museum and heritage field. The most obvious example is Amazon – if you have bought books from them, you will have received the email: 'Hello Mr. Black, we notice you bought *xxxx* and as a result we thought you might be interested in *yyyy*.' In the UK, the National Trust has 3.5 million members and a target of 5 million by 2020. Improving the member offer is seen as central to this being achieved. Their membership card now has a barcode on the back, so they are beginning to track what members do. I have no doubt that within ten years the Trust will have a clear idea of what its individual members enjoy and will be working hard to deepen and personalise member relationships through online contact based on individual preferences.

Not all visitors seek the same experience from museums. In fact, the opposite is the case – museum users increasingly seek to customise their visits to meet their own specific needs. To date, perhaps the most specific example of visitor profiling to examine the differing needs of frequent, occasional and rare participants and in turn lead to a transformation of the museum offer comes from the Dallas Museum of Art, where a study from 2003 to 2009 of visitor preferences and behaviours led to the identification of four related 'visitor clusters' (Box 2.3). Resulting fundamental change to all aspects of the museum's public practice – from exhibition and programming development to new marketing strategies and interpretation tools – led to a 100 per cent increase in attendance and motivated more than 50 per cent of the museum's visitors to participate in its educational and public programmes.

Box 2.3 Dallas Art Museum 'visitor clusters'

Observers
26 per cent of on-site visitors

Observers are somewhat tentative about looking at art and being in art museums. Among the clusters they are the least comfortable analyzing or talking about their experience of art, though almost half have some educational background in art and art history, and the majority stay informed on exhibitions and related events. Some Observers may be new to looking at art and visiting museums ... Among the clusters, Observers include the highest proportion of males ... They are the least likely to visit museums or attend lectures and symposiums.

Participants
24 per cent of on-site visitors

They enjoy learning and the social aspects of their experiences. They have a strong knowledge of and interest in art, and they like to connect with works of art through music, dance, dramatic performances, readings and a variety of other ways. Participants easily provide thoughtful descriptions of what a meaningful experience in an art museum is, value 'real' works of art, and actively use interpretive resources and programmes.

Independents
20 per cent of on-site visitors

Independents like to view art on their own and develop their own explanations and interpretation. Their interactions with works of art are intense. They are confident about their art knowledge, have a strong educational background in art, and are comfortable with art terminology. They talk easily with others about art and have passionate responses to art. They feel the Museum needs to create a setting that encourages and allows visitors to slow down and look at works of art.

Enthusiasts
30 per cent of on-site visitors

Individuals who are confident, knowledgeable and enjoy looking at all types of art. They connect with works of art emotionally, both directly and through the performing arts. They participate actively in a wide variety of Museum programming and use interpretive resources in the galleries. They have the strongest art background. They like discussing the meaning of a work of art with friends, and they are interested in the artist's materials and techniques. Enthusiasts frequently visit the museum and, among the clusters, are the most likely to be members.

based on Pitman and Hirzy (2011)

New programming initiatives have included the establishment of a Center for Creative Connections, interactive exhibitions, a much-enhanced online presence with redesigned website and new smartphone tours, and late night events. The latter have included DJs in the galleries and bedtime stories for young visitors.

Using social networking to build relationships at Brooklyn Museum

Given its flexibility, relative cheapness and ability to project content worldwide, the web is rapidly becoming the main means of engaging users and potential users with museums. As part of this process, social networking represents a remarkable opportunity for developing closer relationships. In an exploratory study of how American museums are currently using social media (Fletcher 2010), 90.2 per cent of those who completed the survey use social media to target new and current visitors but concentrate on young professionals and families. Facebook was seen as the most effective medium, regardless of museum size, followed by Twitter.

Crucially, social networking is not marketing. It is a democratic forum in which people contribute independently as well as consume, becoming what have been called 'prosumers' (Kotler et al. 2010: 7). The most popular sites, such as Facebook, Twitter, Flickr and Wikipedia, allow users to engage actively in creating and extending their online experiences. This is reflected in the Fletcher survey, where most museums are using social media for one-way communication of events, etc., but those museums that described their social media efforts as successful or very successful were using social media as a basis for dialogue. The central questions for a museum seeking to engage with its users through this means are:

- Can we develop an effective and inspiring *social site map* to engage with our audience?
- Can we get our audience talking with each other *about us*?
- Can we use social networking to create a community of users?

As such, a museum seeking to use social media will have to confront its relevance to the audiences it seeks to reach and abandon trying to give users something *we* want them to talk about, as opposed to something *they* wish to discuss and share. It will have to value openly the contributions made by users. It will also need a strategy to sustain the dialogue and foster long term engagement. Most people using social media in museums would say that setting up accounts and profiles is relatively easy but 'using them effectively to establish and maintain audience relationships takes real time, commitment and ability to keep up with current trends' (MacArthur 2010: 58). Experience also shows that a social media policy is essential to provide guiding principles, appropriate safeguards and internal controls, as well as embedding social media across departments as a collaborative effort. Guidance on social media policies and a downloadable analysis of best practice can be found at www.socialmediagovernance.com.

Brooklyn Museum is the second largest museum of art in New York City, and one of the leading art institutions in the world. When its current director Arnold L. Lehman was appointed in 1997 he changed the mission for the museum to encompass diversity and the engagement of a broad audience. Its media strategy is a direct reflection of that mission and possibly the best example in the world of the sustained application of new media to diversify and build relationships with its users: 'We have now become the youngest and most diverse audience of any general fine arts museum in the country' (Bernstein 2011). Brooklyn itself is also 'home to the largest and most vibrant concentration of artists in the world' (Lehman 2010), representing a core community of interest for the museum.

In 2006 the museum decided to build on its existing online presence by using Web 2.0 to reach out to a younger audience demographic. Since then it has built up a presence on Facebook, Foursquare, Flickr, iTunes, Twitter and YouTube, among others, to raise awareness of the museum, attract new audiences, create communities of users and support learning. The introduction to the community section of the website emphasises its collaborative nature:

> The Brooklyn Museum believes in community and in the importance of the visitor experience. In this area you'll find a number of ways to connect with us: blogs, photo and video submissions, podcasts, and more. We look forward to hearing from you.
>
> www.brooklynmuseum.org/community

The museum is committed to making as much of its collection accessible online as possible. This has three distinct goals. First, to make the data available for researchers and scholars. Second, to provide a way a casual user could just jump in and start to navigate visually throughout. Third, to create an interface that is in keeping with the museum's mission and its community-oriented goals. The museum set out to use tagging in a slightly different way, again to emphasise its commitment to a community of users. Those who register to join the museum 'Posse' (http://www.brooklynmuseum.org/community/posse/) have their tags attributed to their own posse accounts:

> In this way, tagging becomes a social activity on our site. Now when Posse members contribute, their contribution is credited and we get to know more about the visitors who are helping us to apply terms to our objects. To date, the Posse has created over 45,000 tags on collection objects and 95% of the collection online has been tagged by Posse. In addition . . . we wanted to make it fun as well. Tag! You're It! is a tagging game that enables posse members to play against each other (using a tag-o-meter scale) and as a posse peep gets to certain levels in the game, "thanks for tagging" videos display as people march up the scale as reward for hard work.
>
> Brooklyn Museum (undated)

In 2007, the museum integrated its various blogs into its website (http://www.brooklynmuseum.org/community/blogosphere/bloggers/) to make them easier and more enjoyable for staff to publish and also more open and transparent for users. 'Authors, following a set of institutionally approved guidelines, write posts focusing on behind-the-scenes information not readily accessible to the public' (Bernstein 2008). The blog now has contributions from over fifty members of staff as well as having guest bloggers, which means users of the site get to know the staff and gain a much greater understanding of all aspects of the work the museum does. Visitors to the site can sign up so they are kept aware of future events and can also forward content to friends.

The museum has its own group on YouTube. Linked to its promotion of 'Target First Saturdays' (free programmes of art and entertainment from 5.00–11.00 pm on the first Saturday of the month and targeted at younger audiences), the museum invited visitors to make and upload to YouTube their own one minute video of the museum through their own eyes, with winners selected by a panel appointed by the museum. My favourite remains 'Art Thief' (http://www.youtube.com/watch?v=mxpSS12qdRA).

The museum launched 1stfans (http://www.brooklynmuseum.org/join/1stfans/) in 2009 to reach out to what Will Cary (membership manager) described (blog 5 December 2008) as 'a large group of Brooklyn Museum visitors that would like to be more involved with the Museum but do not view the traditional Membership structure and benefits as appealing'. It targeted those who attended First Saturday events or who only engage with the museum online. The museum markets 1stfans as 'a socially networked museum membership' – 'an interactive relationship with the Museum that will happen in the building and online' – so this is very focused on the experience of being a member of a community of users. It includes exclusive online content and other special benefits.

In 2008 the museum used crowd-curation in the conception and delivery of their Click photography exhibition. The idea for the exhibition was taken from James Surowiecki's book *The Wisdom of Crowds* (2004) and explores whether a diverse 'crowd' would reach the same conclusions as an expert jury. Artists were asked to submit electronically a work of photography on the theme 'Changing Faces of Brooklyn', along with an artist's statement. In the end 389 photographers submitted. All submissions were then posted online as anonymous and judged by online visitors based on their relevance to the theme and artistic quality – those voting could not see the cumulative scores. There were 3,344 evaluators, submitting a total of 410,089 evaluations. The voters came from 40 countries, but 65 per cent were local and 75 per cent of the evaluations cast were by locals (Bernstein 2011). The photographs were then displayed at a size scaled according to their juried ranking. They were also displayed online.

> Once mounted, the exhibition was a highly social space. The community of people who had been involved in making it – photographers and judges alike – came to share the experience with each other and with their own networks. Online the conversation continued. Users continued to make new comments post-opening . . . Visitors could surf the images that were "most discussed" . . .
>
> Simon (2010: 117)

The museum first piloted cell phone tours in 2006, finding the pick-up rate tripled that of on-site audio tours. The first mobile version of the website was released in March 2010, followed in July by apps for both iPhone and Android.

The museum is placing increasing importance on the interconnection between the web and the gallery itself. In developing a recent exhibition on 26 women artists, curators discovered there was little information online about them. Rather than just placing material on the museum's website, curators went where the audience was and uploaded on to Wikipedia. This material was then fed back into the exhibition space on iPads. Visitor studies revealed that people were using this material for an average of seven minutes, so it fostered really deep engagement (Bernstein 2011).

In seeking to meet its goals of authenticity and delivering content the way its users wanted, Shelley Bernstein, Manager of Information Systems, Brooklyn Museum, stated:

> Web 2.0 is about social connections and community, not about marketing or PR. The museum must fully commit to being in the community and offer content that people care about. When creating a platform for discussion, it must be sure to listen to what visitors have to say and respond when necessary. As much as possible, it must create projects that really mean something, both to the institution and to the participants; give visitors ownership over content; and allow visitors to use content in any way they see fit. It must also involve the curatorial presence in projects whenever possible.
>
> Bernstein (2008)

Reaching out to communities

> The majority of museums, as social institutions, have largely eschewed . . . a broader commitment to the world in which they operate.
>
> Janes (2009: 13)

The capacity and commitment of museums to reach out to their local communities is discussed in detail in Chapter 8 as it affects every aspect of museum provision. However, at this stage it is important to note what a mission to engage with local communities will mean in marketing terms. Are the standard marketing approaches equally relevant to the broader audiences museums are being encouraged to cultivate? The principles are the same – you must look to your objectives and to the nature, needs and wants of your target audiences. But the impact you seek can be much more difficult to achieve.

You are moving here into the realms of social marketing and attempting to change human behaviour. Rather than persuading the 'traditional' audience to visit more often or to go to additional sites, you are seeking to persuade non-visitors – many of whom

Figure 2.2 **Miners' Gala Parade, Coalville, Leicestershire, 2010**
Piloted in 2008 at Snibston Discovery Museum, it was the first Gala to be held in the area for 25 years. It was revived as a partnership between Snibston, the National Union of Mineworkers and the local community, and is now an annual event. Courtesy of Leicestershire County Council/Coalville and District Photographers Society.

feel strongly that museums and heritage sites are not for them – to come. Equally, as already discussed in Chapter 1, you are not aiming to get people to do something as a one-off but to make a permanent change in their behaviour.

The bottom line here is the nature of the product on offer and the relevance of this to the target audiences. There must be a willingness to change what is on offer or there is no point in starting this process. However, there are key aspects that marketing strategies can influence, outlined in Box 2.4.

Box 2.4 Developing a social marketing approach

Research the market – defining target audience needs and wants is central (it is likely to be called community consultation in this context). Market research/consultation can also play a marketing role – making contacts in local communities through whom information, etc. can be disseminated.

Customer ignorance is a major barrier. Make more people aware of what you have to offer – reassess where your literature is distributed; explore new media outlets, like community magazines, newspapers targeted at black audiences; look at the increasing role of the website, for example for people with disabilities, etc.; contact clubs, associations, churches, community centres, etc.; offer talks, etc.

Lack of motivation to visit is another key barrier. External image is crucial. The starting point is to change perceptions of your service. Ensure the marketing material is attractive, focused and accurate. Be sure your brochure looks socially inclusive.

Marketing alone is no answer – product change will be essential. However, do not make extravagant claims that cannot be delivered – focus attention, and the limited funds and staff time available, on the achievable and then build from that platform.

While gradually enhancing the main product, focus on balanced and interesting programmes that reflect the interests of the different audiences – temporary exhibitions, special tours, events for grandparents with grandchildren, etc.

Train staff to ensure the quality of contact they have with visitors results in good word-of-mouth recommendation to other community members.

Evaluate the impact of your marketing strategy or campaign and modify future approaches accordingly.

---

3 Welcoming and supporting the museum user

INTRODUCTION

> If everyone in the museum – and I mean everyone from cleaner to director – believes that their first and most important duty is to ensure that each and every visitor gets what they want from their visit then the museum will be [visitor] friendly. It's as simple and as hard as that. It's not primarily about the nuts and bolts, and the ticking of check lists. It's about attitude. Get that right and you're a winner.
>
> Ian Forbes, Director, Killhope North of England Lead Mining Museum, winner of the
> first *Guardian* Family Friendly Award (2004)

The ability of the museum to engage with its users must be viewed in the context of the entire relationship of the user with the museum – and the priority must be to develop this relationship for the long term. The nature of the museum experience is complex and largely intangible, as illustrated by Box 3.1 (overleaf). It is essential that the museum helps its users to navigate this complexity. Central to this is the need to create an environment that ensures users feel welcomed, relaxed and socially engaged. At the core of a successful museum experience we will find visitors who feel comfortable on-site, that they 'belong', that they are enjoying themselves and are able to socialise with family, friends and perhaps even strangers. This chapter looks at those elements of 'visitor service' that impact on the user experience, particularly:

- a central role for the visitor services team
- socialising the museum environment
- enabling users to customise their visit
- planning for change.

Meeting the specific needs and expectations of family visitors is discussed in Chapter 7.

If we want our visitors to be in the best possible frame of mind when they enter our exhibitions, take part in our programmes or attend our events, if we wish them to involve and engage themselves with our collections and have their understanding and appreciation enhanced, and if we want them to leave with positive memories, recommend the museum to their friends and return soon themselves, then we *must* ensure, through the provision of quality visitor services, that the right environment is created to make this possible. Thus, having stimulated potential users to visit our museums, as discussed in Chapter 2, the next stage in developing an engaging museum is to plan, create and sustain a visitor-friendly museum environment.

Box 3.1 The engaging museum: a holistic approach to the user experience

Core product
Collections
Collection documentation
Digitisation of collection data
Online presence
Site/building
Expertise

Underpinning ethos
Clear sense of direction
Culture of engagement
User focused
Commitment to building long term relationships
Commitment to reaching outwards
Proactive role in community
Collaborative and willing to share authority
Recognition of multiple perspectives
Commitment to placing the user voice alongside
   that of the museum
Online presence integral to service

Tangible elements
Extensive online and media provision
Social media presence
Levels of membership to meet differing
   needs
Visible presence of the user's voice on-site
   and online
Opportunities to volunteer
Orientation and signage
Paced and layered display content
Palette of interpretive media to meet the
   needs of all users
Temporary exhibitions
Regular events and activities
Handling collection
'Always something new'
'Something for everyone'
Education programme
Outreach and in-reach programmes
Guided and self-guided tours
Diversity of staff
Physical accessibility
Seating
Café/restaurant
Shop and restrooms
Opening hours
Pricing differentials
Marketing materials

Intangible elements
External image
Sense of welcome
Commitment to service quality
Responsiveness to user needs
Supportive, stimulating atmosphere
Sense of belonging
Safety
Inclusive
Informal
Empathy
Innovative
Appealing/interesting
Enjoyment/fun
Enriching
Supports social interaction
Seeks out the user's voice
Stimulating
Engaging
Participative
Incorporates multiple points of view
Encourages discovery
Encourages reflection
Supports learning
Sense of the special
Engenders a sense of achievement
Memories taken and meanings constructed

In 2001 the USA Visitor Services Association produced a list of needs common to visitors, which they termed the 'Visitors' Bill of Rights':

1. Comfort: "Meet my basic needs."
2. Orientation: "Make it easy for me to find my way around."
3. Welcome/belonging: "Make me feel welcome."
4. Enjoyment: "I want to have fun,"
5. Socializing: "I came to spend time with my family and friends."
6. Respect: "Accept me for who I am and what I know."
7. Communication: "Help me understand and let me talk too."
8. Learning: "I want to learn something new."
9. Choice and control: "Let me choose; give me some control."
10. Challenge and confidence: "Give me a challenge I know I can handle."
11. Revitalization: "Help me leave refreshed, restored."

Rand (2001: 13–14)

While museums are about 'real things' – real sites, real objects, exhibitions, programmes, etc. – the 'Bill of Rights' shows that it is the visitor engagement with these, with the wider museum environment, with museum staff and with other visitors that creates the user experience. For some visitors, the emotional, aesthetic and intellectual response to direct engagement with the site and/or collections will be all that matters. For the majority, the quality of their experience will depend on all aspects of the visit, a complex combination unique to the individual or to the social/family group. In this context, museums should be seen as part of the service economy, a role that most museums now accept. As such, they have many similarities to other service providers in the need to understand and respond to user demand, and to achieve user satisfaction at a time of rapidly rising expectations of service quality.

A CENTRAL ROLE FOR THE VISITOR SERVICES TEAM

Customer service may be the single most distinguishing factor of why visitors go to one museum more often than another . . .

Rubenstein and Loten (1996: 2)

Quality visitor services, including front-of-house staff and volunteers, play a vital role in encouraging the museum user to engage with and learn from collections. This affects *all* visitors, even those with specialist knowledge and interests. It is a rare visitor who does not have any interaction with staff. As Table 3.1 illustrates (overleaf), there is an inseparable link between visitor services and all other aspects of a museum's activities. Visitor services 'wrap around' the site, collections and exhibitions to humanise the museum and bring the visit alive. Visitor services and facilities are also essential to the task of 'making the intangible tangible', in terms of physically defining the quality of the visit. It is particularly important, however, for those who in the past have felt excluded from museums. If we take social inclusion agendas, disability access and cultural diversity strategies seriously, quality front-of-house staff are probably the most important

Table 3.1 **Museum visitor services**

Practical support	'Feel'	Staff/volunteer input	Site
Accurate, engaging, inclusive marketing	Quality	Polite	Attractive
Quality pre-visit information and website	Well organised	Efficient	Accessible
Good directions	Sense of arrival	Well dressed	Safe
Convenient opening times	Welcoming	Visitor-centred	Cared for
Physical and conceptual orientation	Supportive	Friendly and easy to approach	Clean
Information on contents	Child- and disability-friendly	Supportive	Well lit
Physical access – all aspects	Informal	Knowledgeable – and happy to assist	Good temperature
Restroom facilities	Relaxed	Entertaining	
Baby changing	Authentic and knowledgeable	Access to specialists	
Shop facilities	Trusted	Empowered to handle complaints	
Café with menu for all	Participative	Good telephone manner	
Comfortable seating	Imaginative	Enquiries – quick response	
Inclusive media	Inclusive	Customer service trained	
Allowed to take photos	Own pace	Diverse	
Group bookings	Not 'church-like'	Inclusive in their thinking	
Available to hire	Fun and lively	Good interpersonal skills	
Able to volunteer	Stimulating	Sensitive to visitor needs	
Audience research	Challenging	Disability trained	
Nothing out of date	Enthralling		
Reasons for any restrictions given	Comfortable		
	Social interaction		
	Busy and quiet areas		

element of all the key visitor services. If we truly seek to transform our museums, making them visitor-friendly, we must transform the front-of-house staff team which delivers so much of the service we provide.

One only has to think about who the average visitor encounters in the gallery – it is not the curator, education officer or designer but museum attendants, gallery assistants and docents. The encounter between visitor and staff member can make or break a visit. This is often referred to as a 'moment of truth', that point where a user comes into direct contact with a staff member (Carlzon 1987). Every writer on service quality makes this point:

> Another good way to judge a store: by its interception rate, meaning the percentage of customers who have some contact with an employee ... All our research shows this direct relationship: the more shopper–employee contacts that take place, the greater the average sale ...
>
> Shoppers tend to hate ... intimidating service. Also rude service, slow service, uninformed service, unintelligent service, distracted service, lazy service, surly service.

Probably the single best word of mouth for a store is this: 'They're so nice down at that shop.'

Underhill (1999: 37 and 160)

The quality of contact between staff and museum visitors will have the same impact as in a shop; in addition, the general visitor will view anyone in a uniform located in a museum gallery as a fount of all knowledge on the museum's contents. Most larger museums and heritage organisations now pay serious attention to visitor services and the appointment, training and management of front-of-house staff, as well as developing strategies for their engagement with the public. However, in many smaller museums, front-of-house remains in the dubious care of staff whose selection and training has received scant attention. It is not surprising, therefore, that poor visitor services provision is a problem that afflicts museums worldwide. This situation must change if museums are to face up to the challenges of the twenty-first century. It is time for all museum managers to wake up to the fact that front-of-house staff are central to the visitor experience. It does not matter how good the collections are, or how well they are displayed, or even how clean the restrooms are. The visitor experience will be detrimentally affected by an ill-trained, unhelpful or even rude member of staff; it will be substantially enhanced by a friendly, knowledgeable gallery assistant.

There needs to be an absolute emphasis on the human dimension of service quality and a realisation that enhancing the role, expertise and self-confidence of front-of-house staff is essential if service quality is to improve. This must include 'selling' the importance of visitor services to other museum staff, and ensuring that whoever has overall responsibility for front-of-house has a place on the senior management team. It also means investing heavily in the staff and volunteers, as outlined in Box 3.2, but this will repay itself many times over.

Box 3.2 Investing in front-of-house staff

- Reassess security cover to include a small number of well-trained, roving security personnel supported by CCTV, alarms and security screws, etc.
- Change the job descriptions of the other front-of-house staff to emphasise their visitor services role, while recognising that their presence continues to provide basic security cover.
- Provide customer service training across all the staff, beginning with senior management and including volunteers. Ensure all training (not just those on front-of-house) includes interpersonal skills – for example, active listening, assertiveness, interpreting body language, use of eye contact.
- Enable front-of-house staff to use their initiative to solve visitor problems, giving them the confidence to know when they can make decisions (e.g. in responding to a complaint) and when they must seek higher authority (e.g. in responding to an enquiry to which they do not know the answer). It also means managers being willing to surrender control!
- Ensure that the front-of-house staff are well informed about what is happening across the museum.
- Ensure training for front-of-house staff on the contents of new exhibitions.
- Introduce a system that recognises and rewards superb customer service by individuals and teams.
- Give front-of-house staff the opportunity to develop areas of expertise (a technique already well established in living history museums).

There is, of course, no need to reinvent the wheel. While there remains little published on service quality in museums, with only Adams (2001) of real relevance, there has been a gradual definition of relevant occupational standards. In the UK this occurred following the creation of the Creative and Cultural Sector Skills Council. In Australia there is nationally accredited training leading to Certificates in Museum Practice. In the USA, the evaluation of visitor service and public relations is an important element in the Museum Assessment Program Public Dimension Assessment operated by the American Association of Museums. Across the world, many individual organisations have produced their own quality manuals and service standards, supported by in-house training of staff and volunteers. At the National Trust, their *Informed Welcome* strategy sets standards, forms the basis for training and provides practical advice to the thousands of volunteers who provide the organisation's public face, as illustrated by the extract included as Box 3.3.

Box 3.3 Extract from National Trust *Informed Welcome*

During your time with us you will feel welcome
Positively friendly initial greetings
At every opportunity outline the central theme of the property
Tell stories – especially to children
Use humour when and where appropriate
Don't sound too scripted or stuffy
Talk to people in wheelchairs and then their companions
Find solutions and go the extra mile
Explain the reasons for rules and restrictions
Positive final goodbyes when people leave
Recommend other properties people might visit

We will listen to you in order to understand your expectations
Use active listening skills
Open body posture/mirroring the other person
When listening to a child, try to get down to their eye level
Spot indirect questions, e.g. 'I wonder who painted that picture' and respond to such
    invitations to join a conversation
Ask open questions
Your experience with us will be both positive and enjoyable
Tell people what they CAN do, not what they can't
Telling people what they can do gives them the opportunity to learn more about the Trust/
    property they are visiting

We are here for you and will identify ourselves
Simplistically – clear badging and branding
Also – referring to the Trust in terms that denote belonging, 'we' and 'us' rather than 'they'
    and 'them'

We will offer appropriate information, facilities and services that will enhance your enjoyment
Offering information about the following things:
Local history, culture, events and places of interest
Transport, e.g. cycle network, train and bus timetables
Places to walk and picturesque views

We will work hard to ensure that everyone can enjoy their time with us
Welcome disabled visitors and then their companions
Try to sit down when talking to someone in a wheelchair
Promote free entry policy for disabled people's companions
Consider multimedia options for enabling access to areas of properties that are currently
   inaccessible
Treat those with learning difficulties as you would other adults
Identify ways in which people with sensory impairments can experience the property –
   touch, smell, atmosphere and sounds
Identify objects that can be touched and invite people to handle them
Offer Braille, large print and audio guides where available
Offer children's guides and trails where available
Find ways for children to make discoveries and have fun
Also offer spaces where children can go to run around and let off steam
Use symbols wherever possible on signs around the property

National Trust (2004)

SOCIALISING THE MUSEUM ENVIRONMENT

The number one criteria [sic] of all my subjects – black and white, frequent visitor,
occasional visitor, or non-visitor – was feeling comfortable and at ease in one's
surroundings . . . and nearly all also valued social interactions.

Falk (2009: 49)

Socialising the museum begins with first impressions and carries on through every
aspect of the visit. Gurian (2006) speaks of 'Threshold Fear' in terms of the point at
which the unconfident visitor can turn away. This may begin with the external museum
image and continue with route-finding, the overbearing impact of the 'temple' archi-
tecture we associate with many museums developed in the nineteenth century, and
the charging point. In the latter element, she emphasises that it is not necessarily about
cost but about interaction with strangers – the charging point can become an entry barrier to an unfamiliar location (although, of course, a fee can prevent casual repeat use).
Gurian emphasises the need to identify, isolate and reduce these barriers. She feels it is
particularly helpful if 'novice' visitors can observe the process of entering from a distance first, through a glazed entrance, large lobby, etc.
    We must replace this fear with a sense of occasion, of welcome and of inclusiveness.
On a grand scale, Brooklyn Museum in 2004 and the UK National Maritime Museum

Figure 3.1 **Bringing the inside outside**
A welcoming exterior reaches out to users and helps bring Tel Aviv Museum of Art alive. Here young people study under *Root Treatment*, by Swiss artists Gerda Steiner and Jorg Lenzlinger. Courtesy of Yael Borovich.

in 2011 have reconstructed their entrances to create plazas and make their buildings more permeable, as a way of reaching out to welcome people in. Once inside, an informal atmosphere is essential. People must feel comfortable – an intimidating atmosphere will not only put many people off visiting in the first place, it will also discourage social engagement and discussion during a visit. 'The fact that the museum had a laid back environment where we could just talk and hang out was really good for us' (comment from a girls' high school pupil, quoted in Groundwater-Smith and Kelly 2003: 11).

Most visitors come in social or family groups, so their response to exhibits and experiences is frequently reflected in their interaction with each other – we must provide the time, space and opportunities for this interaction, including watching others. Plentiful seating is vital. It provides mental space, giving time for some reflection on what has gone before, and for social interaction in which to discuss each other's experiences and thoughts.

Readily available seating is also important in combating visitor fatigue. Finding ways to reduce museum fatigue is a major challenge for museums. With fatigue comes a decrease in the visitor's ability to engage, followed by a rapid decline in the quality of

Figure 3.2 **Foyer performance, Tel Aviv Museum of Art**
Larger events can bring a sense of excitement and reach new audiences. The museum hosts regular performances of music and dance. Courtesy of Yael Borovich.

the visitor experience; as a result, the exit becomes the most attractive element in the exhibition. Fatigue in a museum is both physical and mental. It is the result of the size of the museum or exhibition and related staying time, the complexity of circulation, the density and uniformity of display, overcrowding, noise levels and thermal discomfort (Jeong and Lee 2006). Museum fatigue is discussed in Chapter 4. Overcrowding is a core issue. People in themselves take up a lot of space, so a gallery that is anticipated to receive a lot of visitors will need to leave substantial room just for the audience and for audience circulation. Perceptual overcrowding occurs at a much lower density than actual overcrowding. Maximea (2002) suggests:

> In a very crowded timed exhibition, visitors would probably put up with 20 square feet [1.8 m^2] per person (including space for exhibits) ... More usual visitor densities for museum exhibitions range from 30 to 50 square feet [2.8 to 4.6 m^2] per person for discovery and contextual exhibitions (at peak times) to 100–200 square feet [9.3 to 19 m^2] per person for more expansive contextual and aesthetic exhibitions.
>
> Maximea (2002: 90)

Equally, providing facilities for visitors also adds to spatial requirements – 'dwell points', activity areas, study zones and seating areas all add to needs. Thus there are battles to be fought between visitor and exhibit requirements, and the results will be unique to each location. My view is that each element must be able to justify its existence against the objectives set and the agreed communications strategy. To date, in most museum galleries, visitor needs have invariably lost out. This imbalance needs to be rectified if visitors are truly to be encouraged to engage with collections. The solution is to combine improvements to the physical environment with appropriate pacing of exhibition content. This is a subject that will be returned to throughout this book, but it is worth noting here that an engaging museum, committed to user participation, collaboration and reflection, will require much more space for people than Maximea allows for.

CUSTOMISING THE VISIT

Our visitors want to use museums as *they* want, not as we dictate – and what they want are experiences they can tailor to their individual requirements. This is recognised in the National Trust's and Arts Council England's segmentation by motivation (see Chapter 1). Museums can no longer act as agents of mass communication but must offer an opportunity for individual users to create their own experiences, as outlined in Box 3.4.

Box 3.4 Customising the museum visit

- Make anticipation of the visit part of the experience through the image projected beyond the museum.
- Ensure high quality physical and conceptual orientation (including downloadable material pre-visit) so the visitor is empowered to create his/her own experience.
- Support self-directed exploration by providing different types of content and experiences so people can choose what interests them most and explore that in a way that they feel comfortable with and are stimulated by.
- Tailor content to meet individual visitor needs and learning styles.
- Support visitor engagement by providing opportunities for them to make cognitive, emotional and experiential connections.
- Encourage visitor participation by enabling people to share their opinions, to engage in dialogue with staff and other visitors, and to contribute their own content.
- Allow visitors to save aspects of museum content that they were particularly interested in and have these emailed to them for access after the visit.
- Enable people to follow up their interests after the visit and to continue to contribute their thoughts and content 24/7.

We can support visitors as they customise their experience by the ways we encourage them to engage with content. The role of docents and gallery interpreters is a key element in this, and these volunteers and paid staff are often incorporated into the front-of-house team and are the main person-to-person contact that visitors have with a museum – providing an overlap between visitor welcome and interpretive support. This is reflected in the extract from the National Trust's *Informed Welcome*, quoted above. In the USA, the American Association for Museum Volunteers and the Association for Volunteer Administration estimate there are almost 500,000 volunteers and docents serving in such a capacity at museums and similar sites (Cunningham 2004: ix).

In the era of the mobile phone, customising the visit is also likely to include taking pictures of it because Generations X, Y and M want to share their experiences with their friends on social networks. We want to encourage their enthusiasm. It is part of their normal behaviour and, if they tell their friends what a good time they are having, who can ask for better marketing? There is no good reason for banning casual photography in museums. See, for example, the 'It's time we MET' marketing campaign at the Metropolitan Museum of Art in New York (2009), based on a photography contest where hundreds of visitors submitted nearly a thousand photographs illustrating how they shared the visit with friends and family (www.metmuseum.org/metshare/timewemet). Picture a Museum Day, on 17 March 2011 (www.museumpics.com) was an international event aimed at encouraging people to photograph their museum visit and share the images on Flickr. More than 7,000 pictures were put up in 24 hours (#MuseumPics).

However, the starting point for customising the visit lies with orientation – both physical and conceptual. Audiences want to make up their own minds on where to go, what to do, what to look at, how long to spend, etc. By providing first class physical orientation, both at the entrance and within displays, we empower visitors to select for themselves, we show them we respect their ability to do this, and we minimise their effort in working out 'what is going on' so they can concentrate their attention on engaging with museum content. It is also important to recognise that people need differing types of orientation:

> For those who learn by reading … we provide maps, signage, brochures and other pamphlets. For those who want others to show them how to experience the Museum, we provide frontline staff … Lastly, for those who just want to forge ahead on their own … we try to make the experience as intuitive as possible.
>
> Leonard (2001: 1)

The relevance of physical orientation can best be seen when comparing the behaviour of first time and repeat visitors, and the amount of time and effort first time or rare visitors put into the issue of orientation. Yet this is the most basic of principles – good physical orientation not only helps visitors find their way around, it is an essential tool in empowering visitors to select for themselves what they want to see and do, a core building block in customising their visit (see Table 3.2 overleaf).

Museums are just beginning to recognise the potential to develop their websites to help users customise their visits in advance. This is particularly useful for large museums with a scale of contents that can overwhelm the casual visitor. On the website for the Louvre, people can create their own visit plans by completing a profile listing when they are coming, who with, what their interests are, what languages they speak, and so forth. The Louvre website also has a customised alert system for regular users to

Table 3.2 **Orientation for visitors: indicative visitor segments**

When	All visitors	Families in addition to what is listed under 'all'	Education groups	Partnerships and community groups
Pre-visit	Full site description on website to permit choices, including location map, and location map of nearest car park Opening times and transport options Pre-visit packs including information about how to access information in different formats Other visit information for disabled Good traffic signage	Pre-visit information on website to include children's page with food choice, changing facilities, etc. Provided under different age ranges	Associated material on website Education resource materials All year round access Free planning visits for teachers Access to relevant staff when planning Booking by phone or internet	Outreach by staff and volunteers to groups and potential partner agencies to explain opportunities Free planning visits Link person before/during/after Named contacts at property to follow up for visits/projects/etc. Resource materials All year round opportunities
Arrival	Warm welcome Clear signage – e.g. toilets Staffed reception point Orientation panel What is there to see and do? What options are there? How long will it take? Where can I have coffee? Who is there to help? Bulletin board – what activities are on today?	Clear menu of what is on offer for families and children Clear 'children are welcome and encouraged here' element to site welcome, including shop and catering	Greeter Link for accompanied teacher groups Information for self-teaching groups Separate access from public Somewhere to leave bags Dedicated lunch area Clear timetable defined	Importance of enthusiastic welcome – staff/volunteers to meet Clear arrangements re. access Separate access from public via Learning Zone if required Flexible evening options e.g. women-only events Somewhere to leave bags

During visit	Orientation with site map available throughout museum Clear site signage – a standard signage system is required for the whole site	Family leaflet/pack	Staff and volunteer support Designated education spaces and access to other areas	Staff and volunteer support Potential filming of projects Clearly identified rest areas Project/group specific
Departure	Encouragement to feed back and fill out evaluation Souvenir purchase Signposting to further information e.g. website and other relevant local sites Opportunity to be contacted in future, inc. sign up for emails	Child friendly staff in shop Souvenir purchase		Evaluation forms/ session 'Goodbye' – as thought through as the welcome – people feel thanked, valued, can come back
Post-visit	Invitation to join discount scheme for paying exhibitions and events Email contact with latest news Staff blogs Encourage recommendations and feedback Opportunities to contribute thoughts and content	Child-focused activities on website Children's club to join	Interactive website to feed back project work, etc.	Interactive website to feed back Media links – e.g. local press

advise them of exhibitions and events that are likely to be of interest (Fillipini-Fantoni 2003: 3).

Conceptual orientation is also essential, to minimise visitor effort in working out 'what is going on', so they can concentrate their attention on engaging with museum content. What is this museum/exhibition/activity about? What has it got to do with me, the visitor? How is it organised, thematically and physically? How long will it take? What can I, the visitor, expect to gain from it? There is nothing new about this – 'tell people what you are going to do, tell them when you are doing it, and tell them when you have done it'. Yet it is depressing how rarely this orientation is provided. Within an exhibition, activity or presentation, it should also be made clear to the visitor when he or she is leaving one section and entering another. Each section should form a coherent whole, and contain a defined hierarchy of material. Clarity is all. It allows visitors to concentrate their energies on engaging with collections and creating their own meanings.

Providing a conceptual framework also supports 'connectedness' – the ability of visitors to make connections between different parts of an exhibition. In evaluating the use of the Frogs exhibition at the Exploratorium in San Francisco, Allen (2002: 296) was surprised to discover that visitors made such connections at only 5 per cent of exhibition elements. She acknowledged Hilke's study (1988) that suggested the visitor's primary agenda was not to look for relationships within exhibition content but between content and their own knowledge/experience. However, she also suggested that connections will be much easier to make if visitors have a clear conceptual framework within which to seek them.

A programme of change

Developing quality visitor services as a core element of museum provision will require a change of culture and a change of heart at all levels within the museum. If senior managers fervently believe in high quality service, they must both personally take charge and communicate their enthusiasm to their employees – they should lead, inspire and motivate. They must be seen regularly at front-of-house encouraging and supporting staff ('walking the job'). There must also be a change of practice. There must be a detailed visitor services policy and training document. A senior manager must have direct responsibility for implementing the policy and developing 'an organisational culture emphasising sensitivity to visitor needs and a commitment to quality' (Johns 1999: 140). Museums must also appoint the right staff in the first place, who must like visitors and enjoy working with them as part of a team. They must be sensitive to the needs of different audiences – this improves with training and experience. They must want to develop their own skills. They should preferably be representative of the communities they serve.

Managers should also consider the following as the basis for a programme of change:

1 Invest in people to underpin quality.
2 Put a strategy in place for continuous improvement: define tasks, objectives for them, budgets and names against them, and the process of evaluating and moving on.
3 Put an evaluation strategy in place, establish an agreed means of defining how successful any changes are and of feeding this back into the overall strategy for change, altering it accordingly.
4 Maintain a good understanding of your audiences (existing and targeted) as this is essential. Evaluate the visitor experience – this must be a constant feature.
5 Ensure a key purpose of visitor services is to support the social nature of the museum outing.

Take time over all of this. Change cannot all come at once. Sensible targets are better than unachievable ones. However, priorities are important; for example, in staff training begin with basic customer care and listening skills, supported by disability and cultural diversity awareness. Support this with ongoing visitor survey work, and celebrate successes and improved responses. Never lose sight of the need to motivate staff – it can be the individual encounter between member of staff and visitor that can bring your site or collection alive.

Section 2
The twenty-first century museum

If . . . museums must move away from assumed public value and begin
to measure their impact, and if . . . museums must achieve impact for the
community instead of impact for the museum, then the impetus is on
museum education to rise to the challenge that lies before us and reposition
the museum in the eyes of the public.

Nolan (2010: 119)

Over the last two decades museums have gone a long way towards
transforming themselves from inward-looking, curator-driven and
collections-focused institutions to outward-facing, audience-focused
destinations. Museum learning and outreach teams have been to the fore in
this process. Now museums must face up to their next great challenges: in
converting audiences from casual one-off visitors into regular users, and in
re-establishing the relevance of museums to society as a whole in the twenty-
first century.

Both of these depend on the quality and variety of learning experience
that museums can offer. But these are not tasks that museum learning teams
can do on their own. It will require change to every aspect of the museum and
its activities. At its heart, however, will be the ideal of the engaging museum
as a source of inspiration and learning. This, in turn, leads to the ideal of
museums as places where meaning-making takes place, and where ideas can
collide positively, provoke thought and lead to both greater understanding
and ongoing active involvement online, on-site and within wider society.

This section begins by exploring current understanding of the nature
of informal and formal learning in museums and the implications for
the development of museums as learning environments. It goes on to
discuss two central issues in depth: the ability of museums to design for
conversation among adults and families, and to incorporate the many voices
of our users; and the social responsibility of museums to reflect multiple

perspectives and to support community engagement within civil society. It finishes with an Endpiece on what the future might hold for the permanent exhibition.

4   Informal learning

INTRODUCTION

This chapter explores museum practice that can support learning through *prolonged and meaningful user engagement*. It is based on the premise that prolonged user engagement is a desirable outcome in its own right. It should be a core objective for any museum as it is a necessary precursor to other desired outcomes, particularly learning. The chapter begins by briefly examining the influence of learning theories, and the increasing concern for the promotion of twenty-first century skills. It then focuses on the principles that underpin the concept of engaged learning in the museum, and their implications for museum practice. This will involve a major shift in attitude and approach by museums. For example, a new exhibition will be shaped by a commitment to engagement rather than the primary goal being to convey information – so emphasising the importance of the experience itself, not just the outcomes.

It must be acknowledged that not all who visit museums will want to become deeply engaged. Most current users of museums, after all, are on an infrequent social visit. But even here we can begin the process of transforming them from visitors to users by ensuring their visit is enjoyable, provides opportunities for social interaction, supports gentle, unpressured involvement and reflection, and encourages people to return.

THEORIES OF INFORMAL MUSEUM LEARNING AND THEIR IMPLICATIONS

Learning is both a *process* and an *outcome* – the process is about *how* we learn, the outcome is about *what* we gain from learning. For most of the world, the process is dominated by a hierarchical education system that is still largely based on the nineteenth century concept of the mastery of objective bodies of knowledge. This educational process is focused on the facts and information to be learned (with content defined by a curriculum), and designed to transfer these bodies of knowledge from the teacher (expert) to the student (beginner or 'empty vessel'). It takes place in set spaces (classrooms, lecture theatres) within fixed time slots. It is a highly structured view of education as a ladder, with incremental steps of knowledge that must be acquired and measured by testing at various stages. In this environment, students are motivated by the rewards (grades, diplomas, etc.) that follow the successful completion of tests.

In recent decades, this formal educational system has seemed increasingly at odds with a world where we can find almost any piece of information at the touch of a button and every self-motivated learner is on the web. Outside formal educational institutions,

priorities for both the learning process and outcomes have become more about enabling people, in a fluid and changing society, to know how to learn, adapt, interact,
gather information, think creatively and critically, solve problems, make meanings for
themselves and both communicate and apply the results. Along with digital literacy,
these twenty-first century skills, as outlined in Table 4.1, need not be place-located or
time-restricted, not least because of the impact of the internet.

Table 4.1 **Twenty-first century skills framework,
adapted for libraries and museums**

Learning and innovation skills
- Critical thinking and problem solving
- Creativity and innovation
- Communication and collaboration
- Visual literacy
- Scientific and numerical literacy
- Cross-disciplinary thinking
- Basic literacy

Information, media and technology skills
- Information literacy
- Media literacy
- Information, communications and technology (ICT) literacy

Life and career skills
- Flexibility and adaptability
- Initiative and self-direction
- Social and cross-cultural skills
- Productivity and accountability
- Leadership and responsibility

Twenty-first century themes
- Global awareness
- Financial, economic, business, and entrepreneurial literacy
- Civic literacy
- Health literacy
- Environmental literacy

IMLS (2009a: 2)

In this environment, learning is no longer seen as something that ends once formal
study has been completed. Rather, it is recognised as a lifelong pursuit and its continu-
ation is considered essential both to the contemporary information economy and to
personal wellbeing. Gone are the days when mastery of one field was an adequate job
requirement. Instead we now have demand for 'simultaneous mastery of many rapidly

changing fields', necessary for jobs that are less likely to be 'routine' and 'fact-based' and more likely to be 'non-routine; technical; creative; interactive' (IMLS 2009a: 1). Not surprisingly, the formal educational system is faced with the need to adapt rapidly to these changed circumstances. What is more, as the lines between formal and informal learning become less clear, formal educational institutions have slowly begun to recognise the need to work alongside other, complementary learning environments such as museums. The challenge for museums is to grasp this role.

Since their foundation, most public museums have followed an approach based on the same process of knowledge transfer as in the formal education system, but without the testing. The objective was to transmit the 'true' structure of science, history or art and enable 'learning at a glance'. This was initially achieved by placing specimens, artefacts or paintings in the 'correct' order to produce what Kirshenblatt-Gimblett has described as the illustrated lecture recreated as display:

> The written label in an exhibition was a surrogate for the words of an absent lecturer, with the added advantage that the exhibited objects, rather than appear briefly to illustrate a lecture, could be seen by a large public for a longer period of time.
>
> Kirshenblatt-Gimblett (1998: 32)

While display approaches have become more varied, exhibitions and associated programming and online content have continued to be seen by many museums as one-way communication to be unquestioningly received. Even science interactives and immersive environments have been designed to communicate specific content defined by the museums.

Museums, however, have found that they must increasingly respond to the demands of users who are no longer willing to be passive recipients of received wisdom but instead want more say in what they are allowed to know. These users insist they participate actively in the process of learning, seek to add their own contributions and to see the life experiences of their communities represented, and have plenty of alternatives if museums do not meet their needs. This position is reinforced by projections of the likely demands of future generations, as discussed in Chapter 1, and by increased understanding of twenty-first century learning requirements. The result has been a growing realisation by museums that they can no longer be one-way communicators of information. Instead, they must become enablers and mediators and must focus on the approaches involved in delivering this much more flexible and relevant learning agenda, as reflected in Box 4.1 overleaf.

Thus we have seen the abandonment of behaviourist learning theories that supported the concept of learners as passive recipients of museum wisdom and the embracing instead of theories that emphasise active involvement, particularly learning styles, constructivism and Gardner's ideas of multiple intelligences. Theories around *learning styles* become essential if one accepts the learner as an active participant in the process – this leads naturally to an acknowledgement that people will learn in different ways. The theory of *constructivism* is again based on a premise that learning is an active process, but focuses on the generation of outcomes – actively involved learners, reflecting on their experiences, will construct their own understanding of the world

---

Box 4.1 Developing museums for learning in the twenty-first century

Twenty-first century museums:

- have content co-created among diverse partners and audiences; they are accessible in multiple ways
- are a combination of audience- and content-driven
- focus on audience engagement and experiences
- have purposeful learning outcomes (content knowledge and twenty-first century skills such as critical thinking are visible, intentional outcomes of audience experiences)
- are a combination of tangible and digital objects
- are multi-directional (they co-create experiences involving institution, audiences and others)
- act in highly collaborative partnerships
- are embedded in community (they are aligned with and act as a leader on community needs/issues).

based on IMLS (2009a: 6)

---

we live in, building from what they already know. Involving users in such meaning-making leads to a further redefinition of learning as 'meaningful experience' rather than 'defined content outcome' (Hein 2011: 348).

Gardner placed value on different ways of knowing and gave the label of 'intelligence' to each. His theories have built on the constructivist concept of meaning-making to give museum learning validity as an optimum environment for what Falk and Dierking (2002) have called *free-choice learning* – unpressured and open-ended, impacting on the emotions as well as the intellect, involving all the senses, taking place in an environment that is safe for experimentation, and creating diverse stimuli and responses. Such active engagement has been shown to work with a wide variety of audiences, and can reflect a range of opinions, interests, needs and expectations.

Building from this, many museums have made the conceptual leap from speaking of 'education', a term now seen as too closely associated with formal study which is delivered to people, to referring to 'learning', more associated with the active involvement of the learner (Hooper-Greenhill 2003: 2). Reflecting this, UK museums have adopted the UK Campaign for Learning's definition of learning which still incorporates the acquisition of an independent body of knowledge as one core outcome, but focuses on change through experience:

> Learning is a process of active engagement with experience. It is what people do when they want to make sense of the world. It may involve increase in or deepening of skills, knowledge, understanding, values, feelings, attitudes and the capacity to reflect. Effective learning leads to change, development and the desire to learn more.
>
> Maxted (1999)

So, here we have a form of virtuous learning cycle where a broadening of the concept of learning outcomes and their impact results in the desire to learn more. The initial implications for museum display are straightforward: if museum users vary in where their interests lie and in their preferred methods of engagement, then museums must provide different entry points to content, develop exhibition design approaches that support different learning styles and promote active involvement, and ensure content is layered and represents multiple points of view to encourage meaning-making.

This marks an important advance in how museums can develop content to meet different learner needs, whether on-site or online. However, it still fails to reflect much of the approach to user learning which museums need to develop for the twenty-first century. In particular, museums must take into account the extent to which learning is influenced by the context (personal and social as well as physical) in which it takes place, that it is primarily a social activity, that it is underpinned by its cultural signifi-cance, that it requires an understanding of multiple perspectives and that it is increas-ingly collaborative.

Falk and Dierking (2000) developed their Contextual Model of Learning to emphasise that there is no single factor responsible for what and how people learn in a museum and what they take away from the experience. Instead they posited eight fac-tors as influencing learning, outlined in Box 4.2.

Box 4.2 Factors influencing learning by museum users

1   Motivation and expectations
2   Prior knowledge, interests and beliefs
3   Choice and control
4   Within-group socio-cultural mediation
5   Facilitated mediation by others
6   Advance organisers and orientation
7   Design
8   Reinforcing events and experiences outside the museum

based on Falk and Dierking (2000)

Based on her own research, Kelly (2007) proposed an alternative 6P model of museum learning, outlined in Box 4.3 overleaf.

While resonating with Falk and Dierking's work, Kelly's model is, in my view, par-ticularly effective in examining the implications of the different categories, not least in regard to the creation of a museum environment for learning and the related design of exhibitions, as can be seen in Box 4.4 on page 83.

Like Falk and Dierking, Kelly is a supporter of the application of the socio-cultural theory of learning that has become increasingly prominent in museum thinking in recent years. Based on the work of Vygotsky (1978), it emphasises the importance of social interaction and group dynamics. Individual interests and motivations sit along-side the environment in which learning takes place – combining the physical context

Box 4.3 The 6P model of museum learning

Person	Purpose	Process
Prior knowledge	Motivation	'Doing something'
Experience	Interests	Hands-on
Role	Enjoyment	Objects and tools
Gender	Change	Cognitive and physical
Cultural background	Choice	Surface and deep
Lived history		
Personal interest		
Personal change		
Meaning making		
Seeing in a different way		

People	Place	Product
Family	School	Facts and ideas
Friends, colleagues	Museums, galleries, cultural	Short and long term
Accompanying adults	Other cultural institutions	Outcomes
Libraries	Linking	Meaning making
Work peers	Internet	Change
Community	Environment/nature	
Professionals:	Life	
• museum staff		
• teachers		

Kelly (2007: 207)

and the social groupings involved. Individuals can be supported by others in their learning – what Vygotsky terms *scaffolding* – and this is particularly relevant both to how family learning takes place and to learning online.

In relation to this, the USA Museum Learning Collaborative (www.museumlearning.org) focused on the conversational nature of museum learning. Leinhardt and Knutson (2004: xiii) considered learning to be 'a form of conversational elaboration among participants'. They saw museum learning as influenced by the personal histories of the visiting group, the designed environment of the museum or gallery and 'the explanatory engagement of the group with objects, ideas and concepts in an exhibition'. Another contributor to the collaborative, Paris (2000: 201), emphasised the need for museums to create environments that encourage exploration, provide choice and facilitate collaboration. However, he placed particular importance on social interaction,

Box 4.4 Implications for museums of the 6P model

Person: making connections with their own lives; building on prior knowledge
- Provide a range of interpretive experiences for visitors, including interactive ones, even in exhibitions for adult audiences.
- Improve understandings of the variety of visitors' prior knowledge, experiences and interests through continual front-end evaluation.
- Enable visitors to make links from exhibitions to other areas of their lives.

Purpose: choice in how they behave, and what they discuss and learn
- Give visitors choice and control over their museum experience and their learning through providing multiple pathways through an exhibition and a variety of interpretive experiences suitable for both individuals and groups.

Process: the numerous ways that learning happens
- Create a stimulating learning environment.
- Enable visitors to engage in critical thinking and questioning, with exhibitions and texts that raise questions, point to some answers and address both facts and ideas.
- Present multiple points of view to enable visitors to reach their own conclusions and make their own meanings.
- Provide physical, active and lively hands-on experiences that engage the body as well as the mind.
- Make clear the relevance of the exhibition to visitors' learning goals.

People: the significance of social learning
- Design exhibitions that encourage conversation and promote group interaction but also allow for reflection.
- Recognise that different people in the group play different roles, and some individuals play more than one role at any one time.
- Support the learning needs of adults and children, and assist the learner-facilitator role for adults.

Place: museums should clearly differentiate themselves from other informal learning providers
- Museums should promote themselves as unique and accessible learning places where visitors can experience real objects.
- Show how museums complement other learning environments.
- Utilise the internet to provide deeper layers of exhibition content, accessible either on-site or off-site at the learners' own pace and discretion.

Product: visitors look for 'why' and 'how' information, as well as 'what'
- Recognise and reinforce that everyone learns in an exhibition.
- Use questions and intersperse short, quirky 'did you know?' facts' throughout an exhibition, while also providing deeper layers of written content.
- When presenting exhibitions based on their collections museums could:
  - provide information about how and why objects are collected
  - enable access to objects and other real material to use and manipulate.

based on Kelly (2007: 207–16)

Box 4.5 How social interaction stimulates museum learning

1   People stimulate each other's imaginations. Questions, comments and new ideas pique curiosity and encourage further exploration. Collaboration encourages discussion and social negotiation of ideas so that visitors explore alternative perspectives, methods and solutions.
2   Collaboration promotes teamwork and social cooperation. Social goals are more motivating than performance or ego-centred goals. Motivation is enhanced when working with others because there is an obligation to the group and a shared goal of learning together.
3   People work harder in groups, and productive social interactions promote positive concepts about the activity.
4   When people work together, they provide models of expertise that others can emulate. Children or novices can watch . . . learn through observation and modelling.
5   Peers provide benchmarks for monitoring one's own level of accomplishment . . . Watching others may persuade the observer that 'I can do that, too' or 'I'm pretty good at this'. Mentors, docents and tutors provide encouragement as well as models. Their support is often essential for maintaining people's effort and feelings of accomplishment.

based on Paris (2000: 205–6)

---

believing that it was a prime motivator of learning in a variety of ways, as outlined in Box 4.5.

His views are supported by other research which has 'shown that the quality of interaction visitors have with individuals outside their own social group – for example, with museum explainers, guides, demonstrators, performers or even other visitor groups – can make a profound difference in visitor learning' (Falk 2007: 4–5), while Kelly too sees much museum learning as 'a process of social engagement . . . elaborated through conversation' (Kelly 2007: 168). By encouraging conversation, therefore, museums can enhance group learning. Not surprisingly, family group learning is of particular relevance if exhibitions and programming are designed to support it.

Finally, there has been only limited attention paid to the role of museums as cultural learning institutions, sitting alongside other forms of arts provision and participation. At their best and most dynamic, museums can play a major role in the lives of individuals and communities through their powerful qualities as sources of creative inspiration and cultural engagement. Museums hold their collections as the cultural memory of humankind. Through inclusive collecting and representation they provide an essential element in the construction of both individual and community identity and in promoting tolerance and understanding. By embedding themselves in their communities and co-creating content with community partners, they can ensure the multi-perspectival approach to their content and programming that is essential in twenty-first century society, and can support communities in a wider engagement with civil society. Engagement with communities is explored in Chapter 8.

DEVELOPING THE MUSEUM TO EMBRACE ENGAGED LEARNING

It is through direct engagement with objects that museum users can gain their most powerful learning experiences, resulting in:

- change through experience – the ability of cultural learning to make a difference to the lives of individuals and communities
- the stimulation of creativity and imagination
- an increase in or deepening of skills, knowledge, understanding, values, feelings, attitudes and the capacity to reflect
- greater understanding of others
- new confidence and individual growth, and
- underpinning by a different learning ethos to that of the current formal educational system – one more in tune with the realities of twenty-first century learning needs.

Such engagement has an important role to play in the diverse societies in which we now live, and has strong links to community-based art and museum outreach through its belief in empowerment through participation.

The deep and prolonged engagement required to make such a difference rarely happens by chance. Much of it depends on what users bring with them, and on their ability to make connections between museum content and their own lives. But museums can also have a major influence on the individual and group experience. To do so, museums must acknowledge that there are practical implications in terms of how they are structured, and how they develop their collections and public provision to support and promote engaged learning. The rest of this chapter is devoted to an attempt to define general principles for supporting learning in an engaging museum, outlined in Box 4.6.

Box 4.6 **Principles for supporting learning in an engaging museum**

1 A museum focused on learning through prolonged engagement is not possible without a transformed management and staff.
2 Creating a museum that supports prolonged engagement is both an art and a science.
3 Learning through direct engagement with objects lies at the heart of the engaging museum experience.
4 Prolonged engagement means capturing and holding user attention.
5 If we want our users to give engaged attention, we must ensure they feel welcomed, relaxed and socially engaged.
6 Engaged attention depends on users who are actively involved.
7 Engaged attention requires impact on the emotions and senses as well as on the intellect.
8 Regular gallery activities and programming ensure there is 'always something new'.
9 For prolonged engagement to occur, the museum must encourage and support conversation, group interaction and user-generated contributions.
10 The museum, by working with its users, can build learning communities based on inclusion, dialogue between multiple perspectives and enhanced understanding.

---

1 A museum focused on prolonged engagement is not possible without a transformed management and staff

> Changing the interpretation and design of exhibitions, improving the readability of labels, and improving standards for collection care are examples of first-order change [where the system itself remains unchanged]. Second-order change ... changes the system itself. Second-order change questions the premise that things *should be* a certain way – and it is the basic premise, not the way the premise is actualised, that is viewed as the problem in need of change.
>
> Munley et al. (2007: 88)

For the museum to focus on users as active learners and equal participants, and prioritise prolonged engagement over information delivery, it must recognise that both its role and that of its users will be transformed, as summarised in Tables 4.2 and 4.3.

Table 4.2 **The changing role of the museum**

From	To
Authority figure	Partner
Deliver knowledge	Support learning
Design static exhibits	Create flexible learning environments
Provide information	Pose questions
Present programmes	Create learning tools and provide forums
Finite set messages and meanings	Multiple messages and meanings

Table 4.3 **The changing role of the museum user**

From	To
Part of mass audience	Individual or social group
Being told answers	Asking questions
Absorbing information	Collaborating on a 'journey of discovery'
No or little control of learning	More choice and control of learning
Passive recipient	Active contributor

both tables based on Munley et al. (2007: 85)

Persuading users to commit to such a change will depend on their interests, motivations, life experiences and, particularly, their perception of relevance and the recognition of their contributions. This is discussed below. For the museum, it means a transformation in its philosophy, organisation and practice. As such, it must be driven by a committed governing body and leadership, a focused staff structure and a collective sense of purpose. This requires 'second order change' – transforming the system itself. At organisational level it requires a vision, a different museum culture and a business model that concentrates resources on the development and support of regular users (while still continuing to welcome one-off visitors). It means embedding the museum within the life of local communities and ensuring continuous evaluation and improvement of content. For individual staff, it is likely to involve sustained training to enable the development of new skills and attitudes relating to mutual understanding and the collaborative process. Unless the organisation is supportive and empowers staff to initiate change, to think creatively and experiment, and to consult with users, individual staff development is unlikely to happen.

There are few published accounts of the change process in museums. Abraham et al. (1999) provide a strategic overview of the processes used to manage change in 24 museums in Australia, Canada, the UK and USA. In a later article they concluded that:

> The effective management of change in museums is characterised by patient and considered leadership ... able to translate external needs to internal vision and then to employee action, integrate tasks, structures, processes and systems at the technical, political and cultural levels and integrate management practices to build internal and external unity.
>
> (Griffin and Abraham 2001: 336)

David Fleming, Director of National Museums Liverpool, suggests that refocusing a museum service requires root and branch organisational change, including:

- A *new vision* with a focus on audiences and the social role of museums
- If necessary, a *new senior management* to provide coherent leadership
- *Planning* embedded at all levels, from corporate to individual job plans
- A *new staff structure* to promote teamwork and cross-departmental working
- A *new style of involvement* of staff in decision-making
- Greater *political and media awareness*
- An elevated value for staff *training and development*
- Promotion or recruitment of '*change agents*' within the staff to act as missionaries
- Raised *ambitions*
- Discouragement of factionalism and disrespect for the work of others
- Encouragement of risk-taking and innovation
- All of this underpinned by careful financial management.

> Fleming (2005)

And this process of change can never stop. Museums must respond continuously to remain relevant to the ever-changing society in which they exist (West and Chesebrough 2007: 140).

2 Creating a museum that supports prolonged engagement is both an art and a science

There is no simple set of rules that, if followed, will result in more meaningful user engagement. It is a creative process. Yet, to have any real potential of succeeding, an engaging museum will be continually planned, worked at, evaluated, refined, reflected

---

Box 4.7 A strategic planning framework

Where are we now?   Where do we want to get to?

How do we get there?   What resources will we need?

How will we know if/when we have got there?

---

on and further developed. Because every aspect of at least the public face of the museum is involved, the process can best be defined as masterplanning. As in any strategic planning process, I prefer to start with a simple framework, illustrated in Box 4.7 and previously noted in Chapter 2.

For the development of display and online content and associated programming, I rely on a process of interpretive planning which is focused on well-defined outcomes for the museum and its users. There are alternative ways of devising the interpretive plan. Because it has worked for me for many years, I take an approach based on Veverka (1994), outlined in Box 4.8, but placing users first. The interpretive approaches adopted should be developed as the most appropriate response to the answers you define to the questions what/why/who/how, but will also be influenced by other factors. As an 'appropriate' response, it must also be possible to *evaluate* its effectiveness.

Box 4.8 A model for interpretive planning

WHO are you targeting the presentation at? – the target audiences, their needs and expectations. What do they want to know about? What do we want them to talk about?

WHAT do you wish to present? – such as specific site/resource issues, themes, etc.

WHY do you wish to develop/change the presentation? – by identifying specific objectives and *outcomes*. What are the *benefits* for the user, for the site/collections, for the organisations, and how are these benefits to be *evaluated*?

HOW do you intend to present the museum? – the *interpretive strategy* and *gallery concepts* to achieve the objectives set and the outcomes required.

based on Veverka (1994: 32)

It is essential to continue to set goals and measurable objectives and to ensure that these are directly related to ongoing research of users and non-users. The central question when developing new ideas and approaches should be 'What would our users make of this?' Formative evaluation, including piloting, the use of prototypes and resulting adaptation, should be an integral part of the process (see, for example, Borun and Dritsas 1997, and Borun et al. 1997). As the USS *Constitution* Museum has shown (www.familylearningforum.org), piloting ideas and draft content with users can only improve the end product for all.

The evaluation of learning outcomes is discussed in Chapter 5. Other forms of summative evaluation should include:

Practical impact: How long are users spending in our exhibition? For example, using Beverley Serrell's '51% Solution' (Serrell 1998: 2):
- Do 51 per cent of the visitors move at a rate of less than 300 square feet per minute?
- Do 51 per cent or more of the visitors stop at 51 per cent or more of the exhibit elements?
- Can 51 per cent of a random sample of visitors express attitudes/concepts related to the exhibition's objectives?

Flexibility: Can user contributions be incorporated on-site and online? Given that content will continue to change after opening, both due to user contributions and the need for regular adaptation, can the site cope with this?

Institutional: How is what we are doing affecting the museum itself? Is the museum as an institution transforming itself so that it can truly change? Is there a willingness to share authority?

3 Learning through direct engagement with objects lies at the heart of the engaging museum experience

> Most visitors come to museums specifically to see the objects on display and to read the labels in exhibits. Visitors spend most of their time looking at, and presumably thinking about, the objects and labels in exhibits, and leave with images of them.
>
> Falk and Dierking (1992: 67)

This issue will be explored in depth in Chapter 6, but is introduced here. What makes learning in museums different is the depth and quality of the individual or group encounter with the 'real thing'. Every element of the engaging museum should be there to support this encounter and resultant reflection and meaning-making. Every stage in the exhibition process is relevant to making this happen:

> The nature of people's interaction with objects depends upon the qualities of the object ... the personal significance the visitor gives to it, the exhibition environment (crowded, hot, stuffy, dark, quiet, animated), the context of the object in the exhibition (how it is placed and what it is related to), and the value attributed to the object (and how it is interpreted) by the exhibition or institution.
>
> McLean (1993: 22)

I have been as guilty as any other curator of concentrating on the overall theme in the development of an exhibition rather than focusing on the stories the available collections can tell. Idea-driven exhibitions such as city history museums are particularly subject to this problem, with the collections displayed to illustrate and authenticate the story rather than being at the epicentre of the story being told. They will be discussed in detail in the book's Endpiece.

For all the talk about the multiplicity of object meanings, most visitors need help to bridge the communication gap between themselves and the object(s). There is no 'right' way to display objects and no sharp distinctions between alternatives. The challenge for the engaging museum is to develop ways that support users to observe, discuss, analyse, interpret and eventually make meanings for themselves.

4 Prolonged engagement means capturing and holding user attention

Attention is a remarkable attribute: an ability to concentrate on one element among a myriad of competing attractions. Unless we can do this, normally subconsciously, our daily lives would be unbearable. Attention is essential to user engagement with collections or other content in the museum. Bitgood speaks of three levels of attention within a continuum, as outlined in Table 4.4.

Table 4.4 **The three levels of attention**

Capture	Capture is achieved either by the museum grabbing the user's attention through a powerful stimulus (like a loud bang), or alternatively the user scanning an exhibition until coming across something that could be of interest. Users can be easily distracted at this stage.
Focus	Focusing requires paying attention to one thing at a time and ignoring others. Because of the multiple elements and objects competing for attention in most exhibitions, users often need some guidance to decide what is considered important. This level of attention involves only a few seconds of shallow processing, and attention can still be easily distracted.
Engage	Engagement involves deep sensory-perceptual, mental and/or affective involvement with exhibit content. It generally requires concentration and a sufficient amount of time to engage (more than a few seconds). Engagement includes personal interpretation of exhibit content (often called 'meaning making'). The outcome may also include a deep, emotional response such as aesthetic appreciation, feeling close to nature, or anger at industries responsible for polluting the air and water.

based on Bitgood (2010)

Crucially, the capacity for deeply engaged user attention is limited, and it dissipates with time and effort (Bitgood 2000: 33). The challenge for museums is to maximise the attention capacity of our users. This involves:

- promoting relevance to users through finding a 'content hook'
- minimising the impact of 'museum fatigue'
- designing for engaged attention
- seeking to revitalise attention through 'pacing'
- planning to support sequential attention.

Promoting relevance to users through finding a 'content hook'

Stimulating engaged attention is the Holy Grail for museum exhibition authors and designers. To an extent it is outside our control, dependent on the agendas our users bring with them, the nature and motivations of the group they come with, and their physical and mental state on arrival (which can be partly our fault if signage is poor). But it depends particularly on the ability of the museum to convince users of the relevance (or other benefit) of content to their own lives. Bitgood (2010: 7) speaks of this latter element in terms of 'potential utility divided by costs' – our users will balance the perceived relevance and benefit against the time and effort involved in gaining the benefit. To focus on relevance, you must know your audience, know your subject, and find connections that bring the two together – these connections provide the content hook.

The content hook builds on Tilden's first principle (see p. 99) that the user will not engage unless he or she perceives the content to be relevant to his or her needs, interests and understanding. We each bring our past with us: our experiences, interests, prior knowledge, etc. We each have our own feelings, attitudes and perceptions about museums and heritage sites. Based on 12 years of visitor research at the Smithsonian Institution, Doering (1999) could speak of an 'entrance narrative' that accompanies each user, with potentially three distinct components:

- a basic framework, namely the fundamental way that individuals construe and contemplate the world
- information about a subject matter or topic, organised according to that basic framework
- personal experiences, emotions and memories that verify and support this understanding.

If we want to encourage users to engage deeply with our content and gain from the experience, we must use that entrance narrative and the need for personal relevance it reflects as a positive element in the approach we take to presenting content. In effect, we must seek to personalise content by relating it to the users' own lives, experiences, interests and knowledge – new information and ideas will be relevant and interesting to our users if connected to them and their own experiences. This is not only about people relating to people. As Webb makes clear, it also reflects how often we respond to things because of how we feel about them – our emotional response to them – rather than from some kind of objective viewpoint (Webb 2000: 21).

Minimising the impact of 'museum fatigue'

The mental and physical fatigue, often called 'museum fatigue', that our users face during their visit (mentioned in Chapter 3) is something to which even museum professionals can succumb. We start off viewing every element of an exhibition but gradually speed up and by the end are rushing through. Although it will vary between individuals and circumstances, we run out of energy, our attention wanders, we lose our concentration.

The first challenge is to minimise unnecessary effort, to allow users to concentrate their attention on what matters – the collections and other content. As discussed in Chapter 3, poor orientation (where are we, what is this all about) will dominate user attention. Enabling users to select and locate easily what is most important to them – as well as to discover intriguing material they might not have otherwise considered exploring – means they can concentrate their energy on creating a museum experience that matters to them. In addition to poor orientation, other key causes of museum fatigue include overcrowding, heat and noise, a lack of seating and other physical factors relating to the site, for example long corridors to traverse.

The second challenge is to ensure clarity of vision in content development that leads to the structuring of content around distinct themes. This makes physical and conceptual orientation possible, saving a huge amount of effort in trying to discover what the exhibition is about and why it is relevant. It also allows users to focus on those elements that most meet their needs. It will reduce the risk of stimulus overload – too many objects, too many media elements, powerful alternative stimuli, all competing with one another – which can make focused attention very difficult. It should prevent that most frustrating of attention wasters, the separation of the object from its associated label. Finally, good planning should also reduce distraction from other members of the visiting group, or other visitors, by providing a palette of exhibit approaches that can help to engage all members of user groups. There is, of course, a major difference between distraction and welcomed social interaction.

Designing for engaged attention

Exhibition concept and design are essential to stimulating and supporting engaged attention, as outlined in Box 4.9.

Seeking to revitalise attention through 'pacing'

The most effective means of revitalising user attention, after structuring and limiting content, is through 'pacing' within displays:

> The concept of pacing is proposed as a means of reducing both physical and mental fatigue for the museum visitor. Specific issues related to pacing include: the creation of diversity and contrast throughout the museum; the effect of crowds and circulation; and the provision of appropriate resting places and other amenities.
>
> Royal Ontario Museum (1976: 37)

Too many museum displays, even when they contain a wide array of modern media, are single pace and 'mood'. A change of mood stimulates visitors. Effective displays seek to change mood and to appeal to different modes of apprehension, from the

***Box 4.9* Designing for engaged attention**

- Create a gallery space that invites exploration.
- Give users choice and control over their exploration through, for example, multiple entry-points to content or even different routes.
- Create a circulation route that ensures every important exhibition element has an equal chance of capturing attention.
- Ensure clear distinction between thematic elements, for example through differing colour schemes.
- Immersion techniques, such as living history environments, can be a powerful tool in engaging the senses and imagination.
- Give space and prominence to key objects, for example through lighting.
- Minimise the need to shift attention back and forward between object and associated information.
- Provide easily accessible layered content to support deeper exploration
- Provide opportunities for participation.
- Build in staff-led engagement as a regular feature, for example through object handling.
- Design to support conversation and other user interaction around content.
- Help users to ask their own questions that lead to further exploration and discoveries, including collaborative study.
- Provide multiple points of view to encourage thought and personal meaning-making.
- Provide opportunities for users to contribute content and to read and respond to the contributions of others.

based on Bitgood (2010)

experiential to the contemplative, at different times. Contrasts between exhibitions and non-gallery spaces can be equally helpful in recharging the user's batteries and reigniting their interest. Good interpretive planning should ensure that content is paced, provides a range of experiences, meets the differing needs of visitors and balances the roles of the different elements. One way of ensuring this happens during the design stage is to create an experiential matrix, as outlined in Table 4.5.

***Table 4.5* The experiential matrix (indicative)**

Gallery /area	A	B	C	D	E	F
Contemplative						
Experiential/immersive						
Interactive						
Activity area						
Dwell point						
Seating/research zone						

While an experiential matrix can provide an essential reference point to ensure variation in content through galleries, experience design is best expressed as a map, or bubble diagram, illustrating the flow of visitor experiences.

Planning to support sequential attention

While recognising that users cannot and will not concentrate on every element of an exhibition, we need to support their ability to focus and engage steadily throughout the content: 'the most effective design manages attention in a sequential rather than simultaneous searching process since it will increase the chance that each element captures attention' (Bitgood 2010: 6).

The approach taken should also ensure that an exhibition finishes on a high note rather than fizzling out – we need our users to leave on an emotional and intellectual high, supportive of the work we are doing, likely to follow up their visit through online provision and to return in the near future, and willing to act as ambassadors on our behalf to other potential users.

5 If we want our users to give engaged attention, we must ensure they feel welcomed, relaxed and socially engaged

The ability of the museum to engage with its users must be viewed in the context of the entire relationship of the user with the museum – and the priority for the museum must be to develop this relationship for the long term. The image projected by the museum and its success or otherwise in creating an environment that ensures users feel welcomed, relaxed and socially engaged, are both underpinning elements. These were explored in Chapters 2 and 3.

6 Engaged attention depends on users who are actively involved

The key curatorial question for me to address had suddenly shifted from, What is this exhibition about? to Who is this exhibition for? Changing the dominant emphasis from content to audience challenged me to rethink my approach to all aspects of the exhibition development process . . . My primary obligation was no longer to present an argument, or tell a story from a singular perspective for people I assumed were much like me, but rather to understand a diverse audience and provide them with opportunities for multiple insights, experiences, and meaning making. This realisation transformed the entire nature of exhibition development . . .

Rawson (2010: 49)

Prioritising active participants rather than seeing our users as passive recipients will ensure that the museum:

- focuses on physical access for all
- enables users to personalise their learning experience
- places emphasis on planning for participation and social interaction
- promotes its ability to relate, provoke and reveal
- uses new technology to the best advantage
- incorporates space and time for thinking and reflection.

Focuses on physical access for all

Enhancing physical access for those with disabilities is now a legal responsibility in most Western countries. However, it is the medical model of disability – the concept of impairment, no more than a description of physical, sensory or mental difference – which has dominated the disability legislation passed since the 1990s. Examples include the Americans with Disabilities Act (ADA) 1990 followed by the publication of the ADA Standards for Accessible Design in 1994, the Australian Disability Discrimination Act 1992 and the UK Disability Discrimination Act 1995 (DDA – amended 2005). This is a severely limited approach compared to the developing body of knowledge and practice around what has come to be known as the 'social model of disability', as illustrated by Box 4.10.

Box 4.10 Models of disability

The **medical model** (now outmoded) identifies disability as an illness or condition affecting an individual. The onus is on the individual to deal with the consequences, locating blame or responsibility around the person with the disability, leaving them to manage solutions.

The **social model** identifies barriers within society which create disability for individuals. These can be physical, organisational and attitudinal. Responsibility for solving or removing the barriers is shared by all those involved in any situation or interaction.

Delin (2003: 18–19)

Legal responsibility has meant that museums, among other things, have had a requirement to take every reasonable step to ensure equality of physical access for all. This includes not only being able to enter a building and follow the same route as everyone else but also, for example, incorporating seating, improving lighting and stopping reflections in cases, providing opportunities to handle collections, increasing the font size of text and providing information in a variety of accessible formats, including perhaps sign language, and ensuring website accessibility. Museums have been able to work towards accessible standards as exhibitions have been replaced, while the conservation requirements of historic buildings have on the whole overridden the needs of those with disabilities.

The reality is that physical access has improved at museums, but all too often this has involved the application of accessible elements to already developed proposals rather than incorporating access into planning and design from the outset. However, those museums that have taken the social model of disability to heart have gone much further, using access audits to define barriers across provision and to put strategies in place to remove them. Such barriers are likely to include a lack of senior management commitment, the need for staff training, shortage of funding, a lack of representations in museum content of people with disabilities, and the failure to appoint people with disabilities to posts in the service. Commitment is key to this – not only accepting the moral, ethical, and legal duty to provide access to those with disabilities, but taking into account the capabilities and the needs of all visitors. Some museums have appointed advisory panels of people with disabilities to support change.

One core need is for physical access to become an integral part of exhibition design from the outset, rather than being added as an afterthought. In 1997, the North Carolina State University Center for Universal Design brought together a working group of architects, product designers, engineers and environmental design researchers to establish Principles of Universal Design, outlined in Box 4.11, to guide a wide range of design disciplines, support the design process and educate both designers and the wider public in the design of products and environments to be usable by all people, to the greatest extent possible, without the need for adaptation or specialised design.

Box 4.11 Principles of Universal Design

1 **Equitable use**: The design is useful and marketable to people with diverse abilities.
2 **Flexibility in use**: The design accommodates a wide range of individual preferences and abilities.
3 **Simple and intuitive use**: Use of the design is easy to understand, regardless of the user's experience, knowledge, language skills, or current concentration levels.
4 **Perceptible information**: The design communicates necessary information effectively to the user, regardless of ambient conditions or the user's sensory abilities.
5 **Tolerance for error**: The design minimises hazards and the adverse consequences of accidental or unintended actions.
6 **Low physical effort**: The design can be used efficiently and comfortably and with a minimum of fatigue.
7 **Size and space for approach and use**: Appropriate size and space is provided for approach, reach, manipulation and use regardless of the user's body size, posture or mobility.

Connell et al. (1997)

Improving access for those with disabilities already makes good business sense. In the UK, for example, almost 15 per cent of the population has a disability, according to the narrow medical definition in the Disability Discrimination Act 1995. In improving access for those with disabilities, museums can also make a major difference to the experience of disabled people's friends, families and carers, who make up a further 25 per cent of the population. The importance of Universal Design for families with young children is discussed in Chapter 7, but it can have relevance to many other group visits. For example, in research by Yorkshire Museums Council, it was discovered that physical access was a particular concern within the Asian community, who often visited in extended family groups: 'Visits would be made with elderly relatives and young children. Wheelchair, pushchair and accessibility for the infirm were considered very important in contributing to the quality of the visit' (Woroncow 2001: 3).

What is more, as Chapter 1 made clear, people are living longer. In the USA, Baby Boomers and seniors now number over 100 million – and many disabilities are age related. People have increasing difficulty walking, or standing for long periods, while some 90 per cent of people with impaired vision are over 60, and 60 per cent of those with hearing impairment are over 70.

The continued improvement of physical access will be an essential task for museums for the foreseeable future.

Enables users to personalise their learning experience

I liked the way that the resources seemed to appeal to every different level of person coming to a museum. There were things for little kids, and parents, and people who have a vast knowledge of art as well as novices.

Focus group member, Denver Art Gallery

The ambition for museums should be to develop approaches that will support the learning of all audiences – children, families, novices, sophisticated users. To achieve this, museums can no longer act as agents of mass communication but must instead enable users to adapt their visit, on-site or online, to meet their specific needs. This works on two levels: *customisation* and *personalisation*. In *customising* the visit, our users seek to experience museums as *they* want – in ways they can tailor to their individual requirements (see Chapter 3). They come when they want, leave when they want and engage with what they want.

Alongside this comes the potential for users to *personalise* their learning experience. We already know that museum users learn in different ways and that their reactions to different media will vary. They display uneven previous knowledge and levels of interest about the subject matter. Museums can support their learning by allowing for contrasting learning styles and building upon the pre-existing experience and knowledge levels of their users. The challenge is to establish an approach to presentation from which each user can select, as he or she prefers. At its most basic, this means focusing on what has become known as the VARK model, a simplified version of Kolb and Gardner's theories, illustrated in Table 4.6. If your exhibitions incorporate a palette of interpretive approaches that cater for these four learning styles, you will have provided an outline framework for most users that you can then build on. Additional support should include multiple points of entry, as discussed previously, and a *layering* of material, meeting individual needs and ensuring the availability of different levels of information. It is also an important means of providing multiple perspectives and enabling users to develop their own opinions on issues.

Table 4.6 **The VARK model**

Visual	Likes to see, read
Auditory	Likes to hear, discuss
Read/Write	Likes to read
Kinaesthetic	Likes to do

But museums can now also look at giving users the ability to adapt their visit to create their own unique learning experience. New technology is taking personalisation of learning in the museum much further. It has long been known that if children can record, edit and make comments on their activities in a museum, they remember much more (Wolins et al. 1992). One area where the use of mobile technology is growing is in the provision of opportunities for users to do this by creating *personalised learning trails* through the capture and sharing of audio, photographs and text (Walker 2007: 1). A case study in relation to formal education users – MyArtSpace/OOKL – can be found in Chapter 5. There is real potential for this approach to be adapted for informal museum users, particularly families. The development of personalised learning trails through museum websites also represents a considerable opportunity (Fillipini-Fantoni 2003).

Museums must also be able to cope with the contemporary reality that the needs and expectations of our potential users are changing rapidly, and that the design of displays and other provision must be flexible enough to respond to these changes. Rather than setting out to create long term displays which then do not change for ten years or more, change should be built in to the displays. It *must* be possible to alter content on a small and large scale, easily and cheaply, and to incorporate user contributions as a normal element.

Places emphasis on planning for participation and social interaction

In practical terms, user participation can vary from reflective engagement to 'hands-on' involvement with interactive exhibits, both on-site and online. But it can also go beyond providing opportunities for engagement with what the museum has provided to incorporate user-generated content and collaboration with the museum. Nina Simon's book (2010) *The Participatory Museum*, which can be accessed at www.participatorymuseum.org, a website that also provides hyperlinks to many of the articles the author referenced, provides an essential manifesto for the development of opportunities for participation in and with museums, providing principles for participation, participatory models and case studies. She also examines the impact of a sustained approach to participation on the museum as an institution.

The evidence suggests that the exhibits that most effectively support user engagement are those that encourage social interaction, discussion and involvement within and beyond the groups involved. These are discussed in detail in Chapters 6 and 7.

Participation also means enabling and encouraging users to comment on and contribute content to exhibitions. Incorporating opportunities for user feedback is an important element in recognising exhibitions as a three-way conversation. It becomes more meaningful still if user comments are then displayed for all to view and discuss in turn:

> Eighty-six percent of Australian War Memorial visitors, eighty-nine percent of Canadian visitors and eighty-nine percent of the Australian Museum sample agreed or strongly agreed that museums should be *Places that should allow their visitors to make comment about the topics being presented.* Participants wanted museums to provide opportunities for visitors to have a say through feedback forms, suggestion boxes, tours, lectures/seminars and discussion groups with guest speakers, with the option to opt out if you wanted to . . .
>
> Kelly (2003: 9)

The social web has transformed participation, opening up opportunities for social interaction at any time. Its very basis is about collaboration and making connections.

> If the culture that the web is creating were to be reduced to a single, simple design principle it would be the principle of With. The web invites us to think and act *with* people, rather than *for* them, on their behalf or even doing things *to* them. The web is an invitation to connect with other people with whom we can share, exchange and create new knowledge and ideas through a process of structured lateral, free

association of people and ideas. The principle underlying the web is the idea of endless, lateral connection.

Leadbeater (2009: 5)

Sustained engagement almost certainly relies on the museum building such online participative relationships with its users:

- providing access to collections and content worldwide
- experimenting with multi-layered content
- instilling the expectation of participation in potential users, both of the physical site and of its online presence
- helping to slowly transform the museum from a single-voiced authoritative institution into a collaborator that actively seeks user-generated content and works to develop communities of interest.

User contributions to content, on-site and online, are discussed in Chapter 6 below.

Promotes its ability to relate, provoke and reveal

Revealing the meanings behind museum collections remains a critical objective of engagement. The challenge is to stimulate emotional and intellectual participation by users through ensuring content is relevant to their lives, and provoking thought so that they seek to explore more deeply. By raising questions and encouraging critical thinking, users can be encouraged to make their own discoveries leading to personal meaning-making. This is the underpinning philosophy of interpretation, encapsulated in the principles defined by Freeman Tilden in his book *Interpreting Our Heritage*, published in 1957. Tilden was the first writer on interpretation to seek to set down specific principles to follow, as shown in Box 4.12, seeing these as much more important than a definition of interpretation itself.

Box 4.12 Tilden's six principles of interpretation

1 Any interpretation that does not somehow *relate* what is being displayed or described to something within the personality or experience of the visitor will be sterile.
2 Information, as such, is not interpretation. Interpretation is *revelation* based upon information. But they are entirely different things. However, all interpretation includes information.
3 Interpretation is an art, which combines many arts, whether the materials presented are scientific, historic or architectural. Any art is in some degree teachable.
4 The chief aim of interpretation is not instruction, but *provocation*.
5 Interpretation should aim to present a whole rather than a part, and address itself to the whole man rather than any phase.
6 Interpretation addressed to children (say, up to the age of 12) should not be a dilution of the presentation to adults, but should follow a fundamentally different approach. To be at its best, it will require a separate program.

Tilden (3rd edn 1977: 9), my emphases

These remain the underpinning principles for interpretation today. Beyond relation, provocation and revelation, principle 5 is about making connections – with other parts of the exhibition, with users' own lives and experiences and with the wider world. It is through such connections that we can begin to make a real difference to people's lives.

Uses new technology to the best advantage

The speed of technological change worldwide is breathtaking. What is particularly remarkable, however, is that this has been matched by the rate of public take-up of the new opportunities offered. Starting with the most obvious, by 2010 almost 2 billion people had access to devices that connect to the internet, a fivefold increase since 2000. What is more, while in 2000 Asia, North America and Europe were on an almost equal footing, today usage in Asia – and particularly China – has surged ahead. But all regions are growing rapidly. Nigeria, for example has seen growth of 21,891 per cent, albeit from a low base level, to 44 million (Pingdom 2010).

Almost 5 billion people worldwide now use mobile phones (Internet World Statistics 2010). The growing commitment by museums to smartphone apps is a direct response to the speed at which the public are acquiring this more advanced telephone technology. A survey of 1,600 visitors at the Smithsonian Institution in 2010 (OP&A 2010) found that 52 per cent had internet enabled phones and 30 per cent had a phone that could play apps.

New technology should be an integral part of museum provision and therefore incorporated in the museum's masterplan. Not surprisingly, the chief barriers to its use in museums are funding, internal resources and staff knowledge/expertise. However, museums are increasingly recognising the need to prioritise this field. The most apparent impact is that the number of people visiting museum websites is estimated to have exceeded the numbers visiting museums in person as long ago as 2002 (Hawkey 2004).

The use of social media to build relationships with users was discussed in Chapter 2. Potential uses of new technology for formal educational provision are explored in Chapter 5. Developing personalised learning trails and building online participative relationships with users were discussed earlier in this chapter. The challenge here is simply to note the potential ability of new media to enhance informal user engagement and learning, and to bring collections to a wider audience. This is clearly part of the role of social media usage and a major function of wider internet provision. Kelly makes a telling comparison between the principles of constructivist learning in museum exhibitions and the tools of social media, illustrated in Table 4.7.

For on-site users, mobile technology is playing an increasingly major role in enhancing engagement and access. The American Association of Museums 2011 Mobile Technology Survey revealed that:

- 42% of USA museums currently provide visitors with an opportunity to use mobile technology during their visits. The majority of these are still audio only, either through devices provided by the museum or cell phone downloads.
- Art museums are the most common users of mobile technology, followed by history museums.
- Emerging mobile technologies, such as smartphone apps and multimedia (including augmented reality, QR codes, etc.), are currently present in less than

Table 4.7 **Comparisons of constructivist exhibitions and social media**

Constructivist exhibitions	Social media
Free choice	Free choice
Many entry points	Many entry points
No specific path, no beginning, no end	No specific path, no beginning, no end
Based on prior knowledge and experience	Based on prior knowledge, experience and interests
User-controlled	User-controlled
Usually visited in own time and as part of structured educational experience	Usually visited in own time and place, may be part of structured educational experience as well as leisure
Present range of points of view and perspectives, museum seen as authority	Present range of points of view and perspectives, yet authority can be questioned or unclear
Provide materials that allow users to experiment, conjecture and draw conclusions	Interactive websites can provide programmes and information that allow users to experiment, conjecture and draw conclusions
Used for leisure, entertainment and learning	Used for leisure, entertainment and learning
May be difficult to remain up-to-date	Usually up-to-date, constantly changes

Kelly (2008: 2)

five percent of museums. However, one third of mobile and non-mobile museums plan to introduce new mobile technology platform(s) in 2011, and the fastest growth will be in the area of smartphone apps.

- For 83% of museums, 'increased visitor engagement' was the most common goal.

AAM (2011)

And this is before we consider the opportunities offered by Augmented Reality (AR) and other technological advances (see, for example, Hellman 2010). One has to assume that these will first become mainstream in sectors other than museums and galleries. There will always be leaders in the field – in particular Brooklyn Museum continues to show the way (see Chapter 2) – others, however, are also active. For example, the Streetmuseum iPhone and Android app created by the Museum of London using AR is remarkable in leading users around London to locations where it will overlay historical photographs on live video footage of the contemporary scene (www.museumof london.org.uk/Resources/app/you-are-here-app/index.html).

Museums cannot do everything. The crucial issue is prioritisation, focusing on what can best engage target audiences. But given the speed of change, and the enormous potential for new media to support learning and engagement, all museums must be aware of the need for relevant strategies.

Incorporates space and time for thinking and reflection

The underpinning concept of an engaging museum is that it is a place that stimulates creative thought and supports reflection. The design of the user experience, on-site and online, is key to this. All the elements involved have been discussed already and/or will be explored in depth later in the book. However, it is worth summarising them, as outlined in Box 4.13.

Box 4.13 Designing for thinking and reflection

- Encourage social interaction and conversation.
- Develop multi-user, multi-outcome exhibits.
- Ask questions.
- Enable people to watch and learn from each other.
- Provide enablers in the galleries
- Provide opportunities to practise an activity or skill.
- Provide opportunities to contribute to content.
- Provide feedback and/or rewards to motivate further engagement.
- Provide additional layered content on-site and online.
- Provide related programming.
- Provide appropriate seating.

based on Russell (2005)

Seating is the one new aspect introduced here. Museum users need regular areas of seating where they can collapse (mentally as well as physically) for a short time before moving on. This links back to the role of orientation within displays. Allowing a break enables people to select what to concentrate on next. This is a much neglected area within museums. Space is precious, so is given over to display. It is also a constant battleground with designers, many of whom seem to have an in-built objection to seats cluttering up their spaces.

But the provision of seating areas is not just about rest and recuperation. In fact, Gilman's view was the opposite of this:

> We are at sea on the question of the best way to provide seats in a museum until we catch sight of the truth that their foremost office is not to restore from fatigue, but to prevent its advent. They are most useful, not when they afford the greatest ease and when they most exempt the visitor from the temptation to go on examining things, but when they afford just enough ease to make it comfortable to go on looking and are conveniently distributed among the exhibits for this purpose.
>
> Gilman (1918: 270)

I too view seating as an *active* part of an exhibition. In developing opportunities for users to engage, we must not think only of active participation. *Reflection*, in allowing the learner to think about and make sense of his or her experiences, is an essential part of engagement and central to the process of learning. Seating gives an ideal opportunity to provide mental space for some reflection on what has gone before. This can be enhanced by the provision of relevant support material and books, in case people want to explore an element in more depth while comfortably seated. It also provides a space in which to discuss each other's experiences and thoughts. I always recommend that seating be placed around circular tables rather than in lines. Sitting in a close circle, or facing each other, encourages conversation.

7 Engaged attention requires impact on the emotions and senses as well as on the intellect

What is the nature of the experiences that will bring people to museums, historic sites and other places of informal learning? People's motivation will have much more to do with the *feeling* component of the experience than the informational one. If we are to provoke thought, reveal meanings and promote prolonged, meaningful engagement we must go beyond knowledge transfer to engage the senses and emotions.

The appeal to the senses and emotions does not come only from the most magnificent aspects of sites or collections. It is as likely to arise from a detail, something which affects us directly on an individual level – the smell of a peat fire, the volume of noise from a textile machine in operation, the sight of a mummified baby, touching a cat's paw-print on a Roman tile. Engagement requires the use of the senses and the stimulation of emotions; this, in turn, substantially enhances the quality of the visit. Yet even today in most museum presentations the user is sensorially deprived – left with visual contact and little other involvement:

> The European tendency has been to split up the senses and parcel them out one at a time to the appropriate art form. One sense, one art form. We listen to music. We look at paintings. Dancers don't talk. Musicians don't dance. Sensory atrophy is coupled with close focus and sustained attention. All distractions must be eliminated .
>
> Kirshenblatt-Gimblett (1998: 57)

So much museum display and online content is still conceptualised and organised within a narrow academic view of how people communicate – words, supported by images and visual access to objects. The introduction of modern information technologies does not in itself change the situation – as always, it is how the medium is used. Compare this with the real world, where human beings use all their senses to relate to and interconnect with each other in a multitude of ways (see, for example, Finnegan 2002).

I would not seek to downplay the importance of sight. After all, the impact of images can be powerful and long-lasting (especially if our emotions are involved). Colour can have powerful effects on mood and behaviour. However, there are strict limits to what the visual can reveal and, even within those, people are highly selective in what they look at and read. Our other senses – sound, smell, touch and, if possible, taste – can add enormously to a visitor experience and therefore to understanding:

> Sight is the least personal of the senses. Today in the West it is also the most powerful. The deployment of sight requires a certain focal length, a distance, from its target:

otherwise things are 'out of focus'. The other senses, on the other hand, require proximity. Touching, tasting and smelling need us to be close to things, and are in that way senses which require intimacy and which enable familiarity. They involve the body more, through demanding an immediate close presence.

Hooper-Greenhill (2000: 112–13)

We hear sounds even before we are born. Smell is immediately evocative both in the real (for example, of a coal fire) and in the imagination (discovering that travellers to mid-nineteenth century towns in England could smell them before seeing them). Touch provides direct physical interaction – physical contact is an essential part of humanity. We think of only four types of true taste – sour, sweet, salt and bitter – but this belies all the sensations that taste can impart to us and the memories and insights that these can evoke. It is rare that we can incorporate items to taste within exhibitions (such as soda farls cooked over a peat fire at the Ulster Folk Museum or clam chowder at Old Sturbridge Museum). However, between 80 and 90 per cent of what we conceive as taste is actually due to our sense of smell – it is this that helps us to develop the mouth-watering flavours we associate with favourite foods today. Text, copies of historic menus and smell can allow us to contrast past preferences with those of today and give an alternative insight into past lives.

But are there more than the five traditional senses to consider? Should we be looking also at something which combines them, yet is more than a sum of their parts – something that links the senses directly to the emotions? Museums and heritage sites most commonly present and engage users with a *sense of place*, of somewhere rooted in the past yet integral to community identity today, of the locatedness that people feel for where they live:

A 'home town' remains a special place for a lifetime. It has something to do with a first exposure to life, the place where we first come to know the world . . . The landscapes and places of childhood are the sensory implants through which we view the rest of the world forever.

Archibald (1999: 15)

Linked to this is a *sense of history*. Here also, it is through combining the 'traditional' senses with emotion that the past is really brought to life for museum users. The opportunity to listen to period music in the long gallery of a historic house, to touch something made or used by another human being thousands of years ago, to listen to the 'normal' sounds in or sniff the smells of an eighteenth century living history site. A written text can never provide an adequate substitute.

Finally, I frequently wonder whether also to define our response to *music* as an additional sense. Music seems to be unique to humans. We know its importance stretches back well into prehistory. Every culture creates and responds to music. Our response to music appears to be both physical and emotional. The same piece of music can affect us differently at different times. The appropriate use of music can transform a user's reaction to a site or display.

The potential use of the senses to draw you in to a particular time and place can be illustrated at any living history museum – yet this is ignored in most traditional museums, where generic cases and display media leave the user divorced from sensory context. Compare this with the Sensing Chicago gallery at Chicago History Museum, targeted at children but relevant to all. Each sense is given its own space where you can see yourself in the past, engage with the sounds of Chicago by finding sounds that go with projected images, and take an olfactory exploration of the city through a map embedded with different scents. Not surprisingly, the evaluations have been highly positive (McRainey 2010). This is discussed further in Chapter 6.

8 Regular gallery activities and programming ensure there is 'always something new'

Museums and galleries have long been aware that an effective temporary exhibitions programme and a vibrant activities and events programme are essential in attracting both regular and repeat users. In a programme of exit surveys carried out at the Australian Museum, Sydney, between November 1999 and January 2001, 'experiencing something new' was the highest rated factor given for visiting museums and galleries in general, with 77 per cent of those interviewed rating this as high or very high in terms of reasons for visiting. 'Experiencing something new is also closely aligned with entertainment, learning and worthwhile leisure, other factors scoring highly in the survey' (Kelly 2001: 9).

While temporary exhibitions and special events can be planned independently of individual displays, it is equally essential that space for a regular programme of activities should be seen as part of individual gallery interpretation from the planning stage. These should be a mainstay in terms of providing opportunities for users to participate and for encouraging repeat visits as there is always something 'new' happening.

Gurian (2006: 141) speaks of three categories of staff-led programmes. I would actually expand this to define six types of supported activities:

1 The provision of activity sheets and backpacks that visitors can use to support their engagement. These are increasingly common, and normally focused on children and families. The potential for adult usage has barely been explored.
2 The presence of enablers in the galleries who interact with visitors on an individual basis when appropriate. To date, this approach has been developed most effectively in children's museums and interactive science centres.
3 Short tours, talks or demonstrations by gallery staff, related to specific exhibits. Gurian speaks of this approach as both changing visitor flow and focusing attention on elements of the displays that otherwise might be ignored.
4 'The introduction of some additional program into the space by using materials that do not remain in the space when an interpreter is not present' (Gurian 2006: 141). I define these as 'normal' gallery activities – as variable as an art trolley, object-handling sessions, storytelling and living history.
5 Enquiry-based structured educational project work.
6 Larger scale events.

Clearly the final programme will be a balance across the range, dictated by site feasibility and audience availability. However, little of it will be possible unless the potential is recognised at design stage, so spatial and other requirements can be allowed for – you cannot separate design and layout from later support activities. Examples of this include:

- leaving space at reception for a bulletin board to list the activities on each day, and possibly to locate a display of activity backpacks. This location can also act as a meeting point for guided tours;
- making object-handling activities a regular feature in a gallery will be much easier if you have built in storage and a space where the activity can take place;
- some of the most effective living history activities and other types of performance I have seen have taken place in spaces deliberately created in front of display cases;
- drawing is one of the best ways to encourage children to study objects and an Art Trolley makes this possible. *But* – they need space to lie down;
- activity sheets and backpacks, targeted at families, again require space in front of relevant exhibits – and also require flexibility in layout so different exhibits can be highlighted over time;
- spaces are also needed where school and other groups can gather, or where story-telling can take place.

This means, for example, the building-in of multipurpose activity areas and leaving adequate space in front of 'child friendly' exhibits.

Planning for these activities will include:

- the provision at the museum reception of support materials, activity packs, etc., for use by family groups
- the development of handling collections for use in the galleries by the general public, supported by an enabler
- the presence of docents and/or gallery assistants as enablers throughout the museum, supporting visitors and running a daily programme of activities within the galleries linked directly to the displays, including object handling
- a timed programme of activities throughout the day, with visitors able to see what is happening, and when, as they arrive. This could be run with one gallery assistant moving to different locations, but it is a wonderful opportunity to stimulate a range of staff and encourage them to develop, evaluate and improve the programme continuously.

Spaces for these activities must be built in to the displays as 'dwell points'. These have a range of functions, from school project work to planned activities for informal users, linked directly to the displays in their immediate vicinity. Dwell points have an additional function in encouraging social interaction. They support and encourage involvement in informal group interaction. They are a neutral territory, where visitors can see activities going on before making a commitment to join in, so people feel comfortable and unthreatened. They must be comfortably furnished and include 'activity generators' at all times, not just when there is a planned activity in progress. Chairs should be clustered around a (preferably) circular table for easy eye contact.

The museum should also consider a specific programme of events through the year. These could be small scale, like storytelling, or major events such as concerts. It is crucial to consider the potential for these in advance of building and design work.

9 For prolonged engagement to occur, the museum must encourage and support conversation, group interaction and user-generated contributions

This is the subject of Chapters 6 and 7 below.

10 The museum, by working with its users, can build learning communities based on inclusion, dialogue between multiple perspectives and enhanced understanding

This is the subject of Chapter 8 below.

5   Museums and formal learning

INTRODUCTION

Museums for a New Century (AAM 1984) described the history of museums and schools working together as 'perhaps the most longstanding and successful example of the interest and ability of museums to join forces with other institutions in working toward common goals' (quoted in Fortney and Sheppard 2010: x). This 'enduring collaboration' continues to provide a remarkable learning experience for pupils. So, let us start with some thoughts on the positive impact museums are having on the formal educational sector. In 2010, museums in the USA provided more than 18 million instructional hours to American students and educators, ranging from professional development for teachers, to travelling exhibits to schools, and the traditional field trip (Bell 2011). Meanwhile the period from 1997 to 2010 was a golden age for museum education in England, thanks to sustained central government funding, with levels of school participation more than doubling. And these were not just visits by schools and children from wealthy areas. Over 30 per cent of visits were from schools in areas where child poverty is highest (RCMG 2006: 9; RCMG 2007b: 1).

Museum partnership with formal education plays to the strengths of both. It is central to the concept of the engaging museum on three main counts:

- The quality of the museum experience can ensure active prolonged engagement with collections and other content, with pupils in control of their own learning.
- The quality of the museum experience can transform pupils' attitudes to their subjects and to learning in general.
- The museum experience of a formal school visit frequently overlaps with continuing informal engagement with the museum itself and with its online presence. For many pupils this includes revisiting with their families.

This chapter begins by looking at the central need to get the basics right in supporting structured educational visits. It then concentrates on five other aspects of museum provision of increasing importance: creativity, digital literacy, civil engagement, early childhood education and complementary learning, before concluding with the issue of evaluation. The reason for this focus on what is currently non-standard provision away from the 'bread and butter' work is that, even without the steep funding cuts that have followed in the wake of the 2007–8 financial crisis, museum educators must face up to the need for major change in their relationship with formal education and plan now to ensure future relevance.

The key issue is the intense concern over the way formal education systems worldwide are currently preparing young people for work and for life. State education as we know it today was developed in the nineteenth century to meet the needs of a world being transformed by industrialisation. The primary purpose was to provide a trained workforce for an industrial economy. Even at the time of the 1944 UK Education Act, when the modern education system in England was introduced, it was estimated that the workforce consisted of about 80 per cent manual workers and 20 per cent clerical and professional (NACCCE 1999: 18). Since then, and particularly since the 1980s, countries across the world have been engulfed by economic, social, technological and cultural change. Work and life patterns have been transformed out of all recognition. Yet, while the social and cultural experiences of children would be unrecognisable to their peers of, say, 50 years ago, schools have failed to keep pace with this change:

> Some commentators point out that the classrooms of today would be easily recognisable to the pioneers of public education of the 1860s: the ways in which teaching and learning are organised, the kinds of skills and knowledge that are valued in assessment, and a good deal of the actual curriculum content, have changed only superficially since that time.
>
> Morgan et al. (2007: 14)

The current, discipline-based formal education system is simply not designed to deliver adequately the twenty-first century skills discussed in Chapter 4, which include cross-curricular approaches, adaptability, thinking creatively and critically, working together and communicating or expressing oneself effectively. It continues to let down those who do not have traditional academic capabilities. It is also geared to mass delivery within a fixed timetable, while the demand is increasingly for personalisation that enables each child to reach his or her full potential. As a result, there is now enormous pressure for rapid change to meet changed circumstances. Formal systems must also come to terms with a growing recognition that they cannot do everything. As the lines between formal and informal learning become less clear, structured educational institutions have slowly come to accept that they must work collaboratively with other, complementary learning environments, including museums. This need for partnership is made particularly pertinent as learning is no longer seen as something that ends once formal study has been completed but instead is recognised as a lifelong pursuit, essential both to the contemporary information economy and to personal wellbeing.

In the long term, these pressures on formal education will affect the viability of museum provision for schools *negatively* in two ways:

- The use of new technologies within teaching has been described as 'the most striking difference between the twenty-first century classroom and its twentieth century counterpart' (Schlageck 2010: 17). With the increasing emphasis on training pupils in 'digital literacy', museums risk being left behind if they cannot make technology-driven project work integral to their offer.
- With pressure from employers and governments to adapt what schools are teaching to ensure the pupils emerging are 'employable', the formal educational sectors are narrowing their focus on to literacy, maths, science and IT, jettisoning or marginalising the arts, culture and history. The failure of the arts to speak with one voice has

helped to ensure that cultural learning, including that in museums, has a low status with governments, employers and the formal educational system, something associated with leisure time rather than for its creative skills development and transformative powers.

But these negatives are outweighed by the *positive* opportunities on offer:

- Museums and new technologies were made for each other, in terms of their innate support of free choice learning and creative thinking.
- Museums will increasingly need to play a supplementary role in ensuring the arts and cultural learning remain available to school age children as well as to adults if such provision is downgraded in the school timetable.
- Over the next 20 years, many of the key innovations in education are likely to take place *outside* the formal education system, particularly through participatory media. Museums have a remarkable opportunity here to further complement formal learning and to collaborate with communities of learners. See, for example, www.future ofed.org.

FORMAL EDUCATIONAL USE OF MUSEUMS: GETTING THE BASICS RIGHT

[Pupils] perceived the museum environment to be visual, engaging, 'more alive', contextualised, fun, multisensory, imaginative, arousing emotion, that it gave a connection to real life; a place where pupils were given opportunities to explore new skills through interplay, hands-on and minds on learning.

Johnsson (2004: 6)

The structured educational visit, or 'field trip', sits at the heart of the museum–school relationship. Its nature has changed over time, particularly as it has become increasingly focused on matching curricular needs. However, whatever changes the future holds, the visit is likely to remain a successful experience for school pupils, particularly those, normally up to the age of 11, who are taught in the same class group throughout the year. Their teachers find it relatively easy to organise visits – for example, primary school aged children currently make up 80 per cent of school visits to museums in the UK. School pupils know what they expect, and teachers know what they need, from the museum experience. The last 20 years have proven conclusively that museums can deliver this, highlighting the positive role museum visits can play in supporting structured education, as outlined in Box 5.1.

***Box 5.1* Ways museum visits can support structured education**

Museums can:

- provide a unique learning experience for pupils which brings classroom teaching to life and supports sustained engagement with content
- enhance delivery of the curriculum through enquiry-based project work and through working independently out of school
- inspire pupils through direct engagement, including physical access, with remarkable collections
- support different learning styles
- help pupils develop new knowledge and experience
- through enquiry-based learning, enable pupils to use key skills such as questioning, observing, comparing, investigating, predicting, reporting – and pupils can control the enquiry and learning process
- help pupils to develop transferable skills and concepts
- help pupils to develop twenty-first century skills such as digital literacy, open-mindedness, creative problem solving, critical thinking, communication and team-working, and foster their creative abilities
- offer opportunities for pupils to learn about their local communities
- offer opportunities for cross-curricular links
- offer opportunities for pupils to develop positive attitudes to their subjects and to learning more widely
- help develop children's social skills and build relationships with teachers and their peers
- provide an enjoyable and memorable learning experience, and
- change pupils' attitudes to learning

…all in a secure and stimulating environment.

What is more – thanks to ongoing evaluation – we can *prove* all of this. The evaluation of museum education is discussed later in the chapter. However, one key research result which underpins this chapter but is often underestimated in importance, is the major impact museum experiences can have on pupils' *attitudes* to learning. Osterman and Sheppard cite an unpublished two year study in Cleveland, Ohio, to reflect this:

> The teachers consistently desired that students' experiences be highly positive and memorable. They acknowledged the need to tie museum visits to learning standards, but felt that the key to a successful field trip was giving students an exciting and rewarding experience. Once the student interest was aroused, the teachers felt far greater success in focusing on the factual and conceptual learning back in the classroom.
>
> Osterman and Sheppard (2010: 3)

Yet many problems remain that prevent museum education services achieving their full potential. Some of these – particularly transport costs, trends in national educational policy, increasing difficulties in finding adult volunteers to accompany the trip, the practicalities of bringing older pupils and the decision making of individual schools – are largely outside museum control. Others very much depend on what the museum itself offers. Let us look at this from the point of view of the teacher. In the USA, the No Child Left Behind Act (2001) placed greater accountability on student academic achievement and teacher performance. Teachers must now monitor field trips in terms of purpose, student performance, preparation and support, including usefulness and relevance to academic goals (Marable-Bunch 2010: 11). Similarly in England, teachers must evaluate every museum visit both from their own point of view and from the per-spectives of their pupils, and provide evidence of that evaluation for external inspec-tion. This documented evaluation will include:

- evidence of pre-visit planning, including pupils' work and views
- quotes and interviews from pupils on the visit
- samples of work completed as a result of the visit – is the quality of pupils' work better after the museum visit? and
- an assessment of pupil learning set against learning objectives for the visit.

Without an outstanding evaluation and ease of planning, the visit is unlikely to be repeated. Museums *must* plan their educational provision from the point of view of what schools want, not from their own agendas. It is up to museums to make certain they get the basics right, so that any evaluation is outstanding. This means:

- helping teachers with problematic planning issues, including risk assessments
- ensuring a close fit with the curriculum and other teacher priorities
- supporting the teacher to ensure a quality museum experience
- providing education resource materials that assist effective outcomes
- providing access to 'expert enthusiasts'
- ensuring an enjoyable and memorable experience.

Helping teachers with problematic planning issues, including risk assessments

Teachers must deal with all the practical issues around a visit, from risk assessments to coach hire. They must get approval from the head teacher and all the parents, acquire adult helpers and potentially fundraise to pay for the visit. These can be difficult and time-consuming.

However, there are some areas where the museum can share the burden. For ex-ample, teachers must prepare a risk assessment, following guidance from their local educational authority or board, prior to any out-of-school visit. The teacher who acts as group leader for the trip has individual responsibility for safe practice and for ensur-ing that on the trip they take good care of their own and others' safety, and must also ensure the correct ratio of adults to children. This is an onerous task, yet much of the risk assessment can be carried out by the museum and made available to teachers, making the planning of the trip much easier.

Ensuring a close fit with the curriculum and other teacher priorities

When the objectives and expected outcomes of museum resources mirror academic standards, curricula requirements and skill-building activities, they are more likely to be used in the classroom.

Marable-Bunch (2010: 10)

The first priority for the museum is to ensure its schools provision – whether a visit programme, outreach, or online provision – will meet the specific needs of the current school curriculum. In the UK, 90 per cent of teachers state that work at the museum was directly linked to the curriculum (RCMG 2006). History remains the largest subject category for school visits to UK museums, with science & technology and art & design also important.

However, there is growing evidence that more teachers are using museums to work across the curriculum (27 per cent in the research for RCMG 2006 compared with 3 per cent for RCMG 2004b), although history continues to play a strong role in cross-disciplinary work. Contextualisation can be particularly important here, connecting their learning to 'real world' situations: 'when students see the value of what they are learning, they are more motivated and become more actively engaged' (Ocello 2010: 47). This also supports the development of their thinking and reasoning skills, and a growing understanding of the application of the knowledge they have acquired.

As school curricula change in response to current pressures, there may well be a reduction in single discipline focus. Museum educators must keep a close track of changes in the curriculum and in the priorities of their local schools, and listen to what teachers are telling them about their needs and concerns.

Supporting the teacher to ensure a quality museum experience

Children learn best in museums through carefully planned, enquiry-based project work, not worksheets or guided tours (although at times these are unavoidable, for example on safety grounds) – and relevant project work can be developed for children certainly from the age of 4 upwards. In practice, teachers planning school visits to a museum require detailed schemes of work defining learning objectives linked directly to the curriculum, suggested enquiry-based learning activities through which these can be achieved, and the means by which the learning outcomes can be assessed. Experience shows that the best way to develop such project work is for the museum to do so in collaboration with teachers, including the production of high quality educational resources (see below) as an essential tool in helping teachers to prepare pupils for a visit and for use on-site.

Even so, the role of the individual teacher in turning this into a quality museum learning experience for pupils is considerable:

- pre-visit planning with museum staff
- ensuring a close fit with the curriculum, as discussed above
- using pre-visit activities from the resource materials to introduce museum exhibits as evidence, pose questions and present examples as well as attempting to ensure all pupils arrive at the museum with a similar background level of understanding

- helping the pupils develop their research questions for the visit
- ensuring adequate differentiation within activities, to meet the needs of children of different abilities
- carefully planning the whole visit, breaking the pupils into groups (with adult support if necessary) and ensuring the relevant reference materials and equipment are available
- helping the pupils on-site locate and record evidence and try to find the answers to the research questions they had set
- encouraging intuitive guesses and suggesting further questions by which these may be tested
- drawing out cross-curricular links
- structuring the post-visit 'reporting back' by pupils that builds on the visit and enables the recording of evidence of outcomes.

Persuading teachers to do all this work and bring pupils on a visit will only happen, and be sustained in the long term, if the museum is providing what schools need, making it worth the effort and expense for a teacher to take pupils out of the classroom. The priority is therefore on the individual museum to make a sustained effort to encourage and support school use.

Museums can provide a remarkable level of support for an enquiry-based approach to learning through providing access to a range of 'real' sources of evidence; by developing detailed schemes of work and building relevant enquiry-based projects into their displays; by providing designated education spaces and facilities and expert staff; and by developing related resource materials for use in school, as outlined in Box 5.2.

Box 5.2 Building structured educational project work into museum display

- Ensure a warm and welcoming atmosphere for school groups.
- Embed enquiry-based project work that is directly linked to the curriculum within the gallery experience, ensuring interaction and involvement.
- Incorporate 'dwell-points' within displays – spaces where groups could work on tasks together.
- Leave space in front of key exhibits for groups of pupils to engage with them together.
- Provide a designated education space (or spaces) adjacent to the display for related tasks to be carried out, for example object handling or dressing up.
- Produce high quality education resource materials to support the displays – containing pre-visit, during visit and post-visit work all directly based on curricular-specific schemes of work.
- Make available an education officer or trained volunteer to lead their work on-site, where possible.
- Develop an interactive website to support feedback.

Providing education resource materials that assist effective outcomes

Pressure on the school timetable has meant that a programme of school visits has become increasingly rare. A single trip is now the norm, so the provision of, and easy access to, high quality, copyright-free education resource materials has become an essential tool both in helping teachers to plan for a visit and for pupils to use on-site. Museum education resource materials should include relevant project work to be done in the classroom before the visit – this should be effective in its own right as well as being a preparation for the visit. There must be good quality materials for on-site projects, and proposals for follow-up work. I always produce and pilot such materials with teachers to ensure they match school requirements.

An education resource pack is unlikely to be used cover-to-cover by a teacher, but will be cherry-picked. The activities in the pack should each stand alone and be capable of direct use without the teacher having to make alterations unless s/he wishes to. In reality, many teachers will use the activities directly on the first occasion and adapt them to meet specific class needs subsequently. However, the pack will not be used at all if the teacher does not feel confident in using it. This is why it is best to start with the tried and tested, particularly for teachers of under-12s, who are less likely to be subject specialists. Images are the most effective starting point and are also inclusive – written materials can exclude some pupils with poor reading attainment levels. It is essential to make sure the pack is picture-rich (with images of at least A4 dimensions). After having used those, the teacher may be willing to brave the use of documents, etc. A hard copy resource pack should be loose leaf, for ease of use by teachers and ease of change by the museum. Also, the museum need only produce a few copies at a time, with no high up-front printers' costs.

In many museums, resource packs are now being supplemented or replaced with material, downloadable from the web, that can include content for use on interactive smart boards. Developed with teachers, this can be tied into lesson plans timed to class period length. In my view, the same principles remain: the material must be enquiry-based, built around the goals of the learning programme, and user-friendly (for pupils); it must consist of or be based on authentic sources, and be copyright-free for educational purposes. Websites have the additional great advantage of allowing the development of relationships between a museum and individual schools and classes, giving the museum the potential for much better feedback on the quality of the visit (based on the quality of the project work completed afterwards). See also the discussion of museums and digital literacy below.

Providing access to 'expert enthusiasts'

Many teachers lack confidence in using museums as a teaching resource. In the UK this is particularly the case for those working with science-based themes (RCMG 2004a: 12), although it clearly applies to anyone who has no previous experience of the process. Giving teachers a personal introduction to the museum and some hands-on training can increase confidence and ensure a better understanding of how best to incorporate a museum visit and resources into their teaching. Having a museum educator, a subject specialist or a creative practitioner to support the teacher, or lead sessions, can make a huge difference to the pupil experience and build the teacher's expertise for the long term.

A museum educator can introduce the techniques involved in using objects as evidence:

> Ann ... showed us how to look historically, question historically. She brought in the artefacts – an elephant skull, a pinnacle (from a roof), a child's shoe. We worked in groups. She gave us guidance on how to use them. The relationship with the children was so positive, it was lovely to see, to react to their reactions ... We made new comparisons. We looked at it from different angles – this is now built into the way we shall look at artefacts.
>
> Theresa Winters, head teacher, Shirwell Primary School, Devon,
> quoted in RCMG (2002: 6)

Access to 'expert enthusiasts' becomes more important for secondary school pupils (aged 11–18). For example, teachers readily acknowledge the need to 'bring science alive'. When a qualitative study asked 38 secondary science teachers 'How can natural history museums effectively support science teaching and learning?',

> the strongest themes to emerge were that natural history museums can effectively support science teachers by providing access to resources not available at school, offering opportunities for students to meet 'real scientists', and engendering a sense of awe and wonder about the natural world.
>
> (Collins and Lee 2006: 2)

When the teachers were asked to rank nine activity formats, the top three all involved museum scientists, as outlined in Box 5.3.

Two quotes from teachers summarise the importance they place on giving their pupils direct access to museum scientists:

Box 5.3 Teachers' ranking of museum activity formats

Overall rank	Activities
1	Fun science shows with practical demonstrations
2	Debate with scientists engaged in active research
3	Talks/lectures from scientists engaged in active research
4	Focused tasks using museum collections and specimens not normally on display
5	Focused tasks using museum galleries and displays
6	Practical experiments
7	Interactive tours
8	Activities involving group presentations from students
9	Free exploration

Collins and Lee (2006: 5)

What I really like is the opportunity to come and hear speakers who are active, intelligent, from my point of view, women biologists, who don't look like your archetypal [scientists] ... delivering biology with enthusiasm and commitment; [students may think] 'this is where I could go next with my A-level'. That's what I like here.

When students ask 'how did you get into this field, what qualifications did you have?' It's good for them to hear somebody who's really working in it. She's a really nice, exciting person, talking with enthusiasm, that's what they need ... talking to scientists about the route that took them there, so they can imagine doing that.

(Collins and Lee 2006: 6)

Similarly, Contemporary Gallery Education is focused on the central role of the creative practitioner as educator and facilitator, and on a belief in empowerment through participation in the creative process. This provides a remarkable opportunity for pupils to work directly with a practitioner on the 'imaginative process of problem-solving': experimenting, taking risks, reflecting, re-visiting, engaging in experiential learning, with the creative process 'thus seen as a dialogue between the artist and the work' (Pringle 2006: 8).

Ensuring an enjoyable and memorable experience

Ask yourself of each school visit:

- Were pupils engaged and involved?
- Where relevant, did they listen and respond positively?
- Did they remain 'on task' for prolonged periods?
- Did they speak enthusiastically among themselves and to others about their experience?
- Can we see any difference in their confidence, esteem and attitudes to learning?

It does not matter how directly related to curricular requirements a school visit has been, the museum element will fail if it does not fulfil the key tasks of giving children an experience that is both really enjoyable and memorable. Generally children see the museum as a place for learning. They want to contribute actively to their own learning, not be passive receivers of information. They want specifically to touch and smell objects, research their own questions, dress up in character, and play in the museum:

All the children wanted more 'hands-on' and engagement with objects and exhibits. They wanted sessions to be tailored to their age group. They wanted to be able to play more in the museum (a special play room), do role-play, draw and generally contribute to the experience. They wanted plenty of time in the museum. The pupils wanted more information about the objects, where they come from and how long they had been in the museum. They also wanted to know more about the museum itself and who collected the objects. Pupils emphasised the importance of being able to afford an item from the gift shop or bring something back from the museum that they had made.

Johnsson (2004: 10)

And, of course, a pupil who goes home enthusiastic about the visit will encourage his or her family and friends to come – important free marketing, but also key to continuing learning, with the family as a core learning institution (see Chapter 7).

MUSEUMS, THE ARTS AND CREATIVE LEARNING

At a time when the formal education system is under intense pressure to develop pupils' 'human resources', such as adaptability, thinking creatively and critically, developing and acting on new ideas, working together and expressing themselves effectively, I am at a loss to understand the growing marginalisation of the arts and humanities within the curriculum. Creative education is fundamental to developing these abilities *and* the motivation and skills required to execute them in practice. It is transformative, inspiring young people and raising their self-esteem.

Five principles underpin the importance of museums and galleries to creative education:

Figure 5.1 **Creativity in action, Tel Aviv Museum of Art**
Each week, some 1,500 children, youths and adults attend classes in painting, drawing, ceramics, sculpture, photography, video and computer art. Courtesy of Yael Borovich.

1   Creativity is not a separate ability that is enjoyed by only a minority of people. It is present in us all and is developed when our creative capacities are exercised on a regular basis. The collections held by museums and galleries can provide the inspiration and motivation to stimulate creative activity.

2   In an inclusive society, there should be a core belief that all children and young people can be creative and should have access to creative experiences. Museums and galleries are key locations for providing such access, as part of wider cultural provision.

3   Museums and galleries are cultural gateways, holding collections that represent the cultural memory of humankind, important for the development of an inclusive and tolerant society and of a sense of identity. Through these collections, pupils can engage with the creativity of the whole of humankind, past and present.

4   The nature of creative learning, as outlined in Box 5.4, lends itself to the free choice learning process in museums and galleries. Museums are places of imagination exploration, debate, democracy, understanding and reflection. The museum experience is a dynamic one – and pupils are more likely to be motivated, engaged, challenged and excited by the creative, expressive, reflective and emotion-based activities that museums can offer.

5   Museums believe that pupils are empowered through participation and through taking responsibility for their own learning. Both are essential to creative education.

Box 5.4 The nature of creative learning

- A process, not an event
- Grounded in imagination
- Dynamic – each phase impacts on the others
- Flexible – there is no set entry point or sequence
- Iterative, not linear – pupils revisit various phases during the process
- Social and collaborative – the creative process is most powerful when pupils exchange and build on each others' ideas
- Builds quality – although there may be more than one right answer to a creative problem, some solutions are stronger or clearer than others. As a result, the creative process requires that pupils engage in critical as well as imaginative thinking
- Results in original work. As well as the generation of new ideas, it requires the technical skills in the medium in which the work is being created, whether this is piano playing or furniture making.

based on Silverstein and Layne (2010: 4–6)

We know teachers recognise the potential of museums for stimulating creativity. In Generic Learning Outcome evaluation in the UK (discussed later in the chapter), 94 per cent of teachers rated museums important or very important for Enjoyment, Inspiration and Creativity (RCMG 2006).

The creative nature of the museum experience for pupils is reflected in their ability to define their own areas of enquiry for a museum visit:

When given a say in their museum experience, planning aspects of their visit, selecting topics to be studied and working together in small groups, students respond with greater enthusiasm. Purpose, choice and ownership work especially well for older students.

Osterman and Sheppard (2010: 3)

Giving pupils direct, multisensory access to collections stimulates their imaginations and sense of curiosity, develops critical thinking skills and leads to greater engagement and personal discovery. This in turn results in additional creative responses as participants seek to express their feelings and communicate their findings. Other approaches may involve working with an artist educator or making contributions to gallery content, for example by writing object labels or recording responses to exhibits. It may even mean co-creating galleries with museum staff. New technology and Web 2.0 open an enormous range of possibilities, some of which are introduced when discussing digital literacy below. The opportunities are as endless as the meanings collections hold.

Creativity need not be specific to each discipline. For example, in the UK, teachers of primary school children are encouraged to take creative, cross-curricular and whole-class approaches to developing writing and language. There is growing evidence from case studies of how museum collections can inspire imaginative writing and, through this, help children develop their writing skills. From 2007 to 2009 11 museums partnered 15 primary schools in the north-east of England (pupil ages 4–11) to explore how a museum experience could inspire writing and cross-curricular teaching, raise attainment and provide a resource for the delivery of the Primary Framework for Literacy. At the end of the project evidence showed:

- 75% of sampled children improved their writing during the project
- 26% of sampled children improved their writing by two or more sub-levels (far more than would normally be the case)
- Pupils were able to write longer pieces with more descriptive detail
- Teachers noted that the museum visits had inspired their children
- Comments showed that boys in particular became more engaged in writing
- Children said they found writing easier when it was based on real experiences – 82% of children surveyed said they were 'good writers' at the end of the project.

Renaissance North-East (2010: 4)

For a good account of tried and tested techniques to deliver literacy-based sessions in museums, see Renaissance North-West (2008).

Creativity is not a subject in the school curriculum, but the teaching and honing of creative skills should be an essential function of formal education. When pupils discover their creative strengths it can transform their sense of achievement and self-esteem. It is also an essential part of meeting the key challenges for education in the future:

- To develop in young people the skills, knowledge and personal qualities they need for a world where work is undergoing rapid and long term change.
- To enable young people to make their way with confidence in a world that is

being shaped by technologies which are evolving more quickly than at any time in history.

- To provide forms of education that enable young people to engage positively and confidently with far-reaching processes of social and cultural change.
- To develop the unique capacities of all young people, and to provide a basis on which they can each build lives that are purposeful and fulfilling.

based on NACCCE (1999: 18–25)

MUSEUMS AND DIGITAL LITERACY: SCHOOLS PROVISION

Practices of 'digital literacy' are likely to be important throughout young people's lives as the development of technology and media continues to affect how people work, how they socialise, communicate and spend their leisure time and how they learn and share knowledge.

Digital literacy is therefore coming to the attention of educators as they recognise that not only does the teaching profession have a role in preparing children for a digital world, but that a sustained engagement with technology and media is *now integral* to the development of knowledge across disciplines and subjects.

Hague (2010: 3), my emphasis

Digital literacy is about more than being able to search effectively on the internet, or even to make informed judgements on the authenticity and accuracy of the content on individual websites. Rather it is about 'the ability to participate in a range of critical and creative practices that involve understanding, sharing and creating meaning with different kinds of technology and media' (Hague 2010: 3). Most museums continue to see modern technology in terms of a remarkable new range of tools that can support teaching and learning on-site and online. But the impact is much greater than this:

Online technologies are more than just tools, more than just facilitators. They change the way that we are able to do things so radically that they create behaviour that would not be possible without the tool and therefore the behaviour and the tool become inseparable.

Finnis (2009: 82)

The underpinning mission of museums – to engage people, and enable them to make connections and meanings, through the collections they hold – may not have changed, but new technology is transforming how this is achieved. New technology provides museums with the opportunity to allow pupils unprecedented virtual access to their collections, and can support investigation in depth and in ways that were hitherto impossible. But for this to happen, museums must grow beyond an online Web 1.0 approach (that is, online versions of linear, single-voiced exhibitions with authority retained solely by the museum), with perhaps a few games attached, to create content for structured educational use that supports the development of twenty-first century skills. They must appreciate the way content online is already being shared, sorted, classified, collaboratively rethought, reclassified, republished and reused, and recognise that this will become the norm for pupils developing their own projects. They must understand that the on-site museum learning experience can also be transformed, and that new technologies can enable students to engage much more fully with collections. And they must make sustained engagement with technology and media *integral* both to school visits and online provision. Otherwise museum collaboration with schools has a limited future.

New technology used well can bring classroom, museum and online content closer together, integrating museum learning into school learning in a way that encourages and enables pupils to ask questions, collect evidence and think critically and creatively. With the support of teachers and museum personnel, this technology can guide pupils through their research and reporting while still allowing them to co-design their own projects and create their own interpretations through active enquiry. Meanwhile, the speed at which constant, fast broadband access is being made available worldwide means that, suddenly, museum material can be globally accessible. The museum online, while different, is becoming as important as the museum on-site. We can develop learning materials for the world and can support committed learners inside and outside the classroom in ways that both build engagement for life and integrate digital skills.

I fully recognise that iPad and smartphone technology and use are developing rapidly, and will be a core element in future museum education. However, the speed of change is so rapid that in the following case studies I have ignored the technology and software to focus on what I believe to be examples of innovative schools provision that:

- retain the focus on the collections
- are participative
- play to the strengths of museum learning (providing choice and control for the learner), using these to enhance the formal learning process
- enhance digital literacy
- where relevant, ensure direct linkages between classroom and museum to create as near as possible a seamless learning experience
- are learner-centred
- are great fun and memorable – placing enjoyment as a key element in learning.

Using technology on-site

Case study: Samsung Digital Discovery Centre, British Museum (www.britishmuseum. org/samsungcentre)

Giving the children media tasks really focused them on going around the gallery and made the visit very purposeful.

Primary school teacher, Multimedia magic session

Museums have long been able to offer specific facilities on-site that individual schools could not develop and support. For large museum services, digital provision should become part of this offer – not for use on its own, but integrated into engagement with collections. This will not be cheap, and the budget must be sustained to keep pace with developments in the technology. This case study is an important example not only because of the quality of experience it ensures for schools and families, but because it is

Figure 5.2 **Children gather data in the Early Mediaeval gallery, British Museum**
The children research the museum's collections as part of the Sutton Hoo learning workshop at the
Samsung Digital Discovery Centre. Courtesy of benedictjohnson.com.

based on an ongoing relationship between the British Museum and Samsung Electronics which gives the museum continuing access to the latest developments.

The Samsung Digital Discovery Centre at the British Museum opened in March 2009 and has a core digital learning programme which exclusively targets young audiences. Staff work with children aged 5–19 in the context of school and family visits to the museum. The Centre serves 10,000 children and adults annually. Its provision of laptops, digital still and video cameras, smartphones, flatscreen TVs and audio equipment is renewed every one or two years by Samsung. It currently offers, free of charge, nine different kinds of sessions for pupils from foundation stage through primary to secondary school. The workshops are focused on using digital technology as a support for exploring the museum collections. They include:

- **Sutton Hoo Headline** The Sutton Hoo ship burial was excavated in 1939, and was probably the burial of a prince or king from the first half of the seventh century AD. It contained the most remarkable set of Anglo-Saxon objects ever found, which are on display in the museum's Early Mediaeval gallery. In this full-day workshop, children work in small teams to create video news reports about the objects found at the burial ground. They first visit the gallery to collect data on the objects using smartphones. In the afternoon, they access their saved data over the web to compose a news report. Through use of a green screen and background images from the archaeological site, reporters appear 'on location'. Children research, plan, script and film the report themselves. Finished videos are posted online on Vimeo where they can be accessed back in the classroom for follow-up activities. An example can be viewed at http://vimeo.com/samsungcentre/torriano2011

- **Multimedia Magic** Prezi is a Web 2.0 presentation tool that allows you to create an interactive sequence of images, words and movies that can be accessed online or downloaded for offline viewing. In this ICT and media skills-based workshop, children follow a Prezi trail on handheld computers through the museum's Ancient India gallery. They use digital cameras to capture photographs, voice recordings and video interviews relating objects to their personal experience. Returning to the Centre, children work in pairs on laptops using the Web 2.0 tool Glogster to create web-based posters with the media they collected. Posters are accessible online and can be printed out to make a colourful classroom display. The workshop is unique in that it is marketed to teachers as an ICT-skills activity and does not cover predictably popular history curriculum topics such as ancient Greece or Egypt. This is a big win for the museum, because it introduces children to rich yet unfamiliar areas of the collection that they would otherwise not see.

- **Painting for the Afterlife** The British Museum has 11 wall paintings from the tomb-chapel of Nebamun, a wealthy Egyptian official, dating from c. 1350 BC. They are some of the most famous works of art from Ancient Egypt. On an interactive whiteboard, children explore a 3D reconstruction of the tomb and examine three paintings in depth. Framed by Visual Thinking Strategies the whiteboard facilitates careful looking. After the group discussion, children work in small groups to create photographic collages inspired by Nebamun's paintings in Vuvox, another Web 2.0 tool. Taking advantage of links between Vuvox and the photo sharing site Flickr, the museum built a free and easily updatable database of image assets that children can use in their collages. After their work in the Centre, children visit the gallery to see the original paintings.

These and other school workshops emphasise both traditional subject areas such as history, English, art, religious education and citizenship *and* ICT skills. Integrating ICT into on-site learning activities boosts children's engagement, builds confidence working with technology, caters to different learning styles and helps extend the museum visit. All media and artwork created in the Samsung Centre workshops are sent back to school on CD, DVD or as links in an email. This provides teachers with an easy way to follow up the museum visit by asking students to present their creations. Viewing and discussing work in the classroom reconnects children to their experience with objects in the museum galleries and re-enforces what they have learned. The museum publishes a variety of online resources which teachers can use to support the workshops.

Case study: OOKL/MyArtSpace (www.ookl.org.uk)

A cheaper solution for museums in developing project work is to link mobile technology to a school's own digital provision. Whether the mobile technology used for museum learning involves individually owned smartphones or museum-supplied equipment, the central issues for learning strategies are the same, as outlined in Box 5.5.

Box 5.5 Issues for learning strategies involving mobile technology

- Having clear learning goals – both curricular and in terms of the culture of learning
- Having an authentic purpose for the use of the devices
- Integrating the use of the device to the other available technologies
- Ensuring close collaboration between school and museum when planning the project
- Supporting the production of student work in a variety of media – with lessons planned to support both use of the media and production of content
- Enhancing the ability of teachers to use the materials
- Ensuring both teachers and pupils appreciate the relevance of the digital content
- In practical terms for the school, preferably having one device per pupil, and never more than one per two pupils – and ensuring the devices have adequate memory capacity
- Overcoming practical issues for the museum, including copyright and wireless internet capacity.

based on Faux et al. (2006)

In this case study, the mobile devices linked very effectively both to the other technologies (museum exhibition, printed media or online data) and to different spaces (classroom, museum and virtual). They also acted as a bridge to the *personal* space where pupils collect and create items of personal interest. What in the end was most remarkable was the success of the projects in bridging the museum–classroom gap by facilitating the teacher's design of pre- and post-visit lessons, enabling students to create artefacts in the museum and have them readily available for further work afterwards in the classroom, and extending the museum context into the classroom.

OOKL is a private sector company, now operating worldwide, that combines mobile phone and web-based services to support learning between schools and cultural venues. From February 2006 to January 2007 the technology was deployed at three sites in England: the D-Day Museum (a museum in Portsmouth that interprets the D-Day Allied landings during the Second World War), Urbis (a museum of urban life in Manchester) and the Study Gallery (an arts centre in Poole). Throughout this year-long trial, over 3,000 school students used the service on organised visits from local schools.

The approach brought together pre-visit, during-visit and post-visit activities. Pre-visit, the teacher used resource materials provided by the relevant museum to set research parameters for the visit, centred on key questions. On arriving at the museum, the pupils were given a multimedia mobile phone preprogrammed with MyArtSpace software enabling them to take photographs with the phone's camera, record audio commentaries, and take notes. They could also 'collect' objects by typing in a two-letter code shown on a printed card beside the exhibit. This started a multimedia presentation on the phone, using audio and images to describe the museum exhibit. After collection, they were shown a 'Did you know?' screen that offered extra information, and then prompted them to type in their reasons for choosing that object. They were also shown a list of who else had collected it. Crucially, after each action, the content was automatically transmitted over a phone connection to the MyArtSpace website, which built a personal record of their visit. This could later be accessed from home or in school. Once back at school, they could organise the material they had collected into online 'galleries'.

Evaluation of the project (Sharples et al. 2007) showed its positive impact on student engagement. At the D-Day Museum, for example, for a conventional school visit time spent in the gallery increased from 20 to 90 minutes.

Evaluation of another project, at Kew Gardens in London, concluded:

> The mobile phone was a tool that aided engagement as children observed and then recorded their observations in a number of ways … They were self motivated and willing to share their experiences, reflect on the task and, in some instances, they also justified the content they had recorded. They worked like scientists because they were investigating and collecting evidence.
>
> Johnson (2007: 5)

Developing online provision

Case study: The Le@rning Federation (www.thelearningfederation.edu.au)

Museums hold diverse collections. What would happen if someone invested in the infrastructure, and persuaded lots of individual museums to overcome issues around copyright and come together collaboratively to assemble joint content and make it available to schools for free, for ever? This is what is happening with museums in Australia and New Zealand, through The Le@rning Federation (TLF).

TLF was established in 2001 as an Australian government initiative, supported by the central and state governments, and by the government of New Zealand. It is now managed by Education Services Australia and has a remit that goes well beyond museums. All resources are mapped to current state curricula and to the developing national curriculum in Australia. Crucially, the project has developed an interoperability framework, standards and specifications that ensure all education systems and schools can access the resources within their standard operating environments.

TLF has been working with museums on a project and policy level since 2005. Projects have been completed with 26 cultural and public organisations to identify, license and describe in curriculum terms over 5,500 digital items from these institutions' collections. These items have been published through the TLF repository, called the Exchange, and distributed to schools. In 2007 the Council of Australasian Museum Directors (CAMD) agreed to establish a collaborative process across the museum sector to further standardise specifications for digital content. Later that year TLF and CAMD agreed a pilot project to forge stronger links between the museum and education sectors. The project ran from 2008 to 2009, involving three museums (Museum Victoria, National Museum of Australia and Powerhouse Museum, Sydney) and 15 schools:

> The online environment, known as Scootle Sandbox and adapted from Scootle, allowed teachers participating in the Trial to create and manage collaborative learning activities using the digital resources they had selected. These activities were designed to facilitate a dynamic learning environment for students that would support interaction, collaboration, cross-disciplinary thinking and the use of digital media.
>
> Curriculum Corporation (2009: 2–3)

Collaborative learning was central to the project, reflecting international research (Crook et al. 2008) which indicates that the communication and collaboration made possible by the use of Web 2.0 technologies can improve educational outcomes in the areas of enquiry, literacies, collaboration and publication:

> Positive responses within teacher and student surveys quantified that the online learning environment provided was engaging (80 per cent of teachers and students), assisted collaboration (79 per cent of teachers and 84 per cent of students), was effective (79 per cent of teachers and 87 per cent of students), stimulated learning (79 per cent of teachers and 77 per cent of students), assisted students to achieve learning outcomes (72 per cent of teachers and 81 per cent of students) and was easy to use (80 per cent of teachers and 89 per cent of students).
>
> Curriculum Corporation (2009: 5–6)

SCHOOLS AND CIVIL ENGAGEMENT

> . . . for all schools to be actively engaged in nurturing in pupils the skills to participate in an active and inclusive democracy, appreciating and understanding difference.
>
> DfES (2007: 1)

What does it mean to be a member of a community? What responsibilities come with that? How do divided communities come to terms with the past? How can we develop more tolerance and understanding within communities? What can we do if we feel deeply that something needs to be changed? How can communities make a difference on the big issues facing the world today? How do we ensure that young people engage passionately with the world? How do we equip young people for life in a global and culturally diverse, democratic society? Civil engagement is not just about having a voice, it is also about how you use that voice *and* about being willing to listen to others. So, how can we encourage the process of dialogue and communication within society?

Given the dramatic fall in civil participation within Western societies in recent times, good citizenship should be an essential component of the formal education system. Education for civil engagement also involves the development of higher end skills that should enhance the wider academic achievement of all involved (Dávila and Mora 2007). While citizenship education is nothing new – schools across Western societies have been involved in it for many years – citizenship has been a statutory component of the schools curriculum in England since only 2002. It is currently conceived within three strands: social and moral responsibility, community involvement and political literacy. There are three main expected learning outcomes:

- knowledge and understanding about becoming informed citizens
- developing skills of enquiry and communication, and
- developing skills of participation and responsible action.

These outcomes are reflected in the case studies below. They reveal the importance of museums as key out-of-school contexts for civil engagement, on two main grounds:

- Museums are natural, open environments for alternative teaching methods that are essential to the development of the skills required for civil engagement, such as debate/discussion, role play, engaging pupils with issues in the real world, and enabling pupils to have their voice heard and their opinions respected. Here pupils rather than teachers can be in control of their own learning and can get actively involved.
- Through their collections, museums provide contextualisation for key issues. In particular, in order for young people to explore how we live together today and to debate the values we share, it is important they consider issues that have shaped the development of contemporary society – and to understand them through the lens of history.

Case study: Campaign! Make an Impact, UK

'Campaign! Make an Impact' is a programme developed by the British Library in collaboration with local museums and archives and a number of schools to show how children and young people can be inspired by the past and to support them in finding their own voices and the confidence to change the future. Children and young people learn about historical campaigns through museums, libraries and archives collections and then create their own ideas for campaigns on current issues they feel passionate about. Guidance encourages each project to use a three-step approach:

- Study a historical campaign.
- Look at ways of creating a successful campaign by exploring media, listening to experts, researching the impact of different forms of communication and making links between historical examples and modern ways to campaign.
- Plan a new campaign and develop this across a number of curriculum areas.

Preliminary findings (McLarty 2010) suggest that, while venues and schools believe it is too early to define impacts, a few areas stand out, particularly an increase in young people's confidence. The young people involved are starting to see that anyone can create a campaigning idea and work to make a difference, and that these opportunities are not limited to those who are rich and famous. In one museum in north-east England, a respondent claimed:

> It does help people make the connection. They [pupils] can see that this was just other people like them, not celebrities, just people who decided to put a committee together.
>
> McLarty (2010: 14)

Case study: RACE: are we so different? Science Museum of Minnesota, USA (Virtual tour of exhibition at www.understandingrace.org/about/virtour.html)

I believe this exhibit to be an outstanding effort in every way . . . hopefully providing the catalyst for the most important, sensitive and often avoided conversation of all on the meaning of race in this country and the impact it has on all of us.

Burnett (2007)

The RACE exhibition was developed at the museum in collaboration with the American Anthropological Association to encourage audiences, particularly middle and high school children, to explore the science, history and everyday impact of race. It ran from January to May 2007 and has since been on a tour across the USA. The museum describes the exhibition as:

> Focusing on the history of the very idea of race and the effects of this idea throughout the history of the USA, *RACE* allows visitors to explore at their own pace how views of human variation have developed in the USA and in their own communities and lives.
>
> Key topics explored include economic disparity and opportunity, health and medicine, schools and the use and misuse of science in race.
>
> The exhibition uses interactive displays, video, theatre and simulated environments interspersed with views from leading commentators on race and everyday people.
>
> Science Museum of Minnesota (2007)

From the outset, the exhibition was seen as an opportunity for people to explore issues of race and discrimination, and gain a better understanding of how race has affected both the history of the USA and individual lives. The first-hand accounts of everyday people were particularly important in helping visitors identify with the exhibition. Alongside the exhibition development process, the museum built a comprehensive programme plan that included working with schools, theatres and a series of public forums. The members of a community advisory board also helped promote the exhibition among their own communities.

A central ambition was to encourage and enable discussion in a non-threatening environment as a means of continuing the learning experience. A private room was set aside adjacent to the exhibition for use by schools and adult groups. The museum adopted the approach of 'Talking Circles ... facilitated discussions for groups of 20 or less ... in which all participants are invited to reflect on their experiences in learning about and experiencing race as a factor in their lives and communities' (Jolly 2009: 90). More than 4,000 people in visiting groups participated during its original display at the Minnesota Science Museum, a 'valuable, non-confrontational way to explore difficult issues in a safe environment'.

The Talking Circle process was developed by the Minnesota Department of Corrections for use in the restorative justice process, and taken from Native American traditions. The technique allows everyone to speak and to listen in a safe and respectful setting. Participants sit in a circle with no tables; the facilitator starts the discussion with the 'Talking Piece'; only the participant holding it can speak as it is passed from one person to the next in the circle. The facilitator can ask the group to switch to a more free-flowing discussion at the facilitator's discretion and the group's consensus. School sessions last 45 minutes. The museum provides a downloadable teacher's guide as a support resource (www.understandingrace.org/resources/for_teachers.html) and also works in partnership with Tolerance Minnesota, an initiative formed to prevent prejudice in schools and communities.

Case study: Re-enactment of a German Democratic Republic (GDR) classroom, Leipzig

Some think it was like living in a social paradise ... Paradoxically it is the east German young people who know least because their parents are reluctant to talk about the past.

Elke Urban, curator, East German School Project

Increasing numbers of young Germans, born after the reunification of the country in 1990, know little or nothing about life under communism. In Leipzig, home of the 'peaceful revolution' that eventually led to the downfall of the communist German Democratic Republic (GDR), a museum in the former Stasi (secret police) headquarters seeks to counter this lack of knowledge by not only providing a tour of the Stasi building itself – a chilling experience – but also incorporating a 45-minute communist classroom session. This is the only school museum in Germany to tackle communism through re-enactment.

The re-enactment is a powerful, emotionally draining tool for engaging young people. The classroom is decked out with Communist Party flags, with a monochrome portrait of Erich Honecker, the last GDR leader, on the wall; the slogan 'We love the German Democratic Republic' is on the blackboard. The curator, Elke Urban, who was a teacher in the GDR, plays the role of Frau Müller, the teacher, wearing an austere dress made out of the East German nylon fabric Dederon. She deliberately creates a totalitarian atmosphere. In a session witnessed by Tony Paterson, from *The Independent* newspaper, all but one of the pupils were asked to don the blue neckerchiefs of the communist Young Pioneer youth group. 'Frau Müller' barked at a pupil who was wearing a jacket emblazoned with the letters USA, made everyone sing the Young Pioneer marching song, and spoke enthusiastically of an upcoming trip to an East German border-guard regiment.

> The most disturbing aspect ... was the pupils' reaction to "Steffen", the schoolboy who had volunteered beforehand to play the single dissident pupil who refused to join the Communist Youth. Steffen was first subjected to a barrage of criticism from Frau Müller and then deliberately ignored every time he put his hand up to answer a question. The other pupils began to ostracise "Steffen" themselves and accused him of disrupting the class. Although they were encouraged to stand up to the system before the session, none of the pupils rallied to Steffen's support.
>
> Paterson (2008)

Each classroom session is followed by an open and often heated discussion about the experience. On this occasion Elena Margones, one of the 18-year-olds in the role play, said: 'The pressure to conform was so great that, although I felt Steffen was being treated unfairly, I didn't dare say anything.'

Case study: Peace and Reconciliation Gallery, Herbert Art Gallery and Museum, Coventry, UK

Coventry's role as an international city of peace and reconciliation stems from its experiences during the Second World War and continues today, encompassing many of the city's diverse communities. The gallery aims to encourage awareness and empathy, and to facilitate debate around themes of conflict, peace and reconciliation. However, exploring these themes in a gallery environment offers a number of challenges. These are complex themes which encompass multiple equally valid viewpoints and unresolved debate. There are also difficulties in finding cultural objects that can help fully explore these areas. Focusing on personal experiences has proved crucial. They provide a familiar and accessible entry point for audiences and allow the museum to present a range of perspectives. Through these accounts visitors can access and engage with themes on a deeper level, making personal connections with the stories told.

To tell this story fully and encompass this variety of viewpoints it was important for the museum to work with many local groups and organisations. They helped develop both the content and concept for the gallery, and identified key stories. These groups included Peace House (an organisation supporting refugees and asylum seekers), Coventry Refugee Centre, the Centre for Peace and Reconciliation Studies at Coventry University, and Coventry Cathedral. The museum also built relationships with, and was able to draw loan items from, national and international museums including the Imperial War Museum, the Stadtmuseum in Dresden and the Warsaw Rising Museum. Elements of the gallery are changed regularly, reflecting the museum's growing relationship with local communities, and there is a full public programme of related talks and events.

The gallery and associated schools project were developed in association with the local education authority, and initially focused on children aged 10–11. It aimed to create an immersive experience that would

- develop an increased awareness of the impact of conflict on people, particularly children, in a historical and contemporary context
- develop greater knowledge of the nature and location of current global conflict
- introduce some of the skills used in negotiation and conflict resolution
- create greater awareness of local people working to support those affected by conflict and help create opportunities to make an impact themselves.

In a full day at the museum, children spend the morning using an interactive conflict-resolution computer game in the gallery, making collective decisions on action using interactive voting pods, followed by discussions on why particular decisions were made. The afternoon session, led by experts from CORD, a locally based organisation working in post-conflict areas around the world, culminates in a film based on the experiences of young refugees coming to the UK, with the children then able to interview one of the refugees.

Based on this initial project, the museum has developed core sessions for schools' use in what is a remarkable, thought-provoking environment.

EARLY CHILDHOOD EDUCATION

Children were asking their own questions and answering each other's. The words came tumbling out. They were almost falling over themselves in trying to get their ideas out.
Early Years practitioner quoted in Renaissance South-West (2008: 3)

In the past, provision for under-5s learning in mainstream museums has been highly inadequate. Now is the time to change that. With growing recognition that the early years of life are the most critical for learning, early years education has risen up the political agenda and the numbers of initiatives continue to expand. Governments are putting increasing levels of funding into this area. In the USA, for example, Schlageck (2010: 18) estimates there was $2 billion of extra stimulus money in 2010.

There is a strong case for the role of museums in early childhood education – a case that has been made for many years by the children's museums movement, not least in the USA (see www.childrensmuseums.org). The difference now is the growing evidence of what can be achieved by more mainstream museums. For example, Danko-McGhee and Shaffer, in arguing for the importance of aesthetic experience for toddlers, state that:

> Looking at art and encouraging conversations about it can support not only visual perception skills, but also literacy skills in young children ... Teachers can serve as good role models ... by using descriptive language as they talk about art works with young children.
>
> Danko-McGhee and Shaffer (undated: 2)

Active learning and the development of cognitive and communication skills are key to early learning. In summer 2007, five museums across the south-west of England carried out and evaluated a range of projects that sought to engage children from toddlers to 4 years of age. Each project:

- followed children's interests
- focused on providing opportunities to communicate
- offered active learning experiences, including the chance to be creative
- lasted a number of weeks
- documented children's learning journeys, using logs, diaries and stories.

The result was a substantive insight into the power of objects to engage very young children:

Investigating: investigating comes first. Children ask questions and gather information using all of their senses.

Communicating: children begin to express their ideas and feelings through words, sounds or signs. They listen, apply their reasoning and offer explanations.

Representing: children quickly move to representing their ideas. They might choose to draw or make, to play imaginary games, sing songs or make up stories about an object.

Recalling: encounters with objects can provide potent memories for children to recall and share. A museum visit can produce plenty to talk about, and objects back in the home setting can encourage exploration to continue: 'Izzy loved it. She told my gran all about the animals and the Exeter Puzzle Jug' (Parent of child aged 3, quoted in Renaissance South-West 2008: 6)

Provision need not only involve short term projects or informal visits. The Smithsonian Early Enrichment Center (www.seec.si.edu) has been in operation for over 20 years. Its lab school, serving children between the ages of three months and 6 years, is seen as a leader and innovator in the field of museum-based learning for young children (SEEC 2009). It is also committed to share its expertise on a national level by building partnerships with other museums and schools through its educational outreach programme.

COMPLEMENTARY LEARNING

Complementary learning refers to the idea that school and life success requires an array of learning supports. To be most effective, these supports should complement one another, moving out of their silos and working together to create an integrated, accessible set of community-wide resources that support learning and development.

Heather Weiss, Director of Harvard Family Research Project, quoted in Russell (2006)

If over the next 20 years, as I suggested at the beginning of this chapter, many key innovations in education are likely to take place *outside* the formal education system, complementary learning will be a crucial area of development. School pupils already make use of museum websites. Many parents who home-educate their children make heavy use of museums. Many museums already organise out-of-school clubs. But these all represent examples of museums continuing to operate in the safe environment of their individual 'silos'. The alternative is to come together to provide a coordinated programme of complementary learning opportunities. Two principles underpin the need for museums to commit to a complementary learning agenda (see Harvard Family Research Project 2005):

- Both school and non-school contexts are critical to children's learning: 'children need the whole community and not just schools for learning and success in school, out of school, and in adult life after finishing school' (Russell 2006). Parental involvement programmes and out-of-school programmes provided by bodies like museums, libraries, arts organisations and sports teams can both provably enhance academic achievements and reduce risky behaviours. But each organisation providing such programmes currently works in isolation.
- To be most effective, learning opportunities and contexts should complement each other. The organisations involved need to work together towards a consistent range of outcomes that create a continuum of learning opportunities and build on the strengths of multiple learning contexts.

Case study: New York Out-of-School Time Initiative

The comments below are based largely on Russell et al. (2009).

More than 500 municipal leaders surveyed by the USA National League of Cities ranked after-school programmes among the most pressing needs for children in their communities (Wallace Foundation 2008: 1). The USA federal government is currently spending about $3.6 billion annually for out-of-school time learning, while the US Department of Education reported in 2008 that 56 per cent of schools sponsored after-school programmes, involving around 4 million children (Schlageck 2010: 19).

Many museums are involved in out-of-school time programming. In the USA, the

Institute of Museum and Library Services is one source of funding for art and cultural activities in out-of-school programmes, providing grants to institutions like the Exploratorium in San Francisco and Huntington Museum of Art, West Virginia. It also seeks to identify best practice, as outlined in Box 5.6.

Box 5.6 Best practices in museum and library youth programmes

At institutional level, sustainable high-quality programmes:

- Ensure continuity of programme staff
- Conduct needs assessments and evaluations to strengthen the programmes
- Provide ongoing support and training for staff
- Incorporate new sources of funding as programmes evolve
- Embed programmes within the institution's mission
- Commit leadership.

At the community level, programmes are most likely to be sustained when they:

- Connect deeply with community-wide local efforts
- Partner with community-based organisations and other cultural institutions
- Identify and cover gaps in available programmes
- Build awareness of the programme and its impact on participants and the community.

Griffin (2010: 2)

However, is it possible to go beyond this and take a complementary learning approach that leads to collaborative and co-ordinated project development, bringing together schools, parents, participants and programme providers, and building on the strengths of multiple learning contexts? Johnson and Rassweiler (2010) provide a good introduction to the development of collaborations for learning that connect museums, schools and communities, emphasising the importance of building on existing relationships and skills, and finding the right match where benefits overlap across partners.

The Wallace Foundation has been supporting out-of-school time initiatives in five USA cities: Boston, Chicago, New York, Providence and Washington DC. Rather than using individual venues, the idea was to test city-wide approaches, each with funding sustained over a number of years, and their ability to plan, co-ordinate and deliver high quality out-of-school time programming (OST) for more young people, especially those with highest needs.

The New York Out-of-School Time Initiative was launched in 2005 as a comprehensive public system providing young people in high need neighbourhoods throughout New York City with access to high quality programming after school, on holidays, and during the summer, at no cost to their families. Each OST programme is operated by a non-profit organisation and is located in a school, community centre, settlement house, religious centre, cultural organisation, library, or a public housing or parks facility; in 2007/8 79 per cent were located in state schools. During the 2007/8 school year, more than 81,000 youth participated in one of 622 OST programmes city-wide, at a cost of over $100 million. Over three quarters of participants were either African-American or Hispanic/Latino. Some 84 per cent were entitled to free or reduced price lunch. The programme providers were also in close communication with the relevant schools in their areas about learning objectives and methods, as well as reaching out and engaging families through parent liaisons and special events.

There were three goals for the initiative:

- provision of safe and developmentally appropriate environments for youth
- support for their academic, civic, creative, social, physical, and emotional development, and
- response to the needs of New York City's families and communities.

These goals were underpinned by recognition of the need to provide rich and varied content-based activities, including academic skills enhancement, cultural exposure and enrichment, sports, recreation, community service, leadership development and exposure to new and engaging experiences – see Box 5.7.

Box5.7 Percentage of programmes offering types of activity, by grade level

Activity category	Elementary age range	Middle	High
Academic enhancement	100	99	84
Arts and Culture	94	97	68
Recreation	92	97	68
Life skills	64	67	57
Community building	51	48	52
Career and work	15	24	50

Russell et al. (2009: 8)

The evaluated impacts of the initiative have been highly positive, with enrolment exceeding targets and with a strong sense of belonging and social development among participants. There has also been improved academic motivation, school attendance rates and, to a lesser degree, academic benefits. Partner organisations also benefited, with most reporting that the initiative increased their organisation's capacity to reach out to serve more youth and families (83 per cent), provide staff training and technical assistance (73 per cent), partner with a state school (71 per cent), partner with cultural organisations (65 per cent), partner with city agencies (63 per cent), offer programming on weekends and holidays (59 per cent), and provide a career ladder for OST staff (57 per cent) (Russell et al. 2009: vi).

Such involvement should not be entered into lightly. You must be clear on your objectives and recognise them as part of the shared vision for the collaboration. You must also be realistic in recognising the huge differences between organisations and the large amount of staff time that will be involved (Johnson and Rassweiler 2010). However, museums must be a part of this type of development as their commitment to the academic and social development of young people grows. Schools too must recognise the benefits of such provision. Structured learning can no longer be seen as something that only takes place in a classroom during school hours and in set homework. There is a compelling argument for closer working relationships to create the 'continuum of learning opportunities' that is essential to complementary learning.

EVALUATING THE IMPACT OF MUSEUM LEARNING

It is up to all who work in the arts to spell out more clearly both what cultural learning entails and why it is important to society. We must also provide the *evidence* to prove it. In the formal educational system there are well established and accepted methods for the assessment of learning, including essays, multiple-choice tests and examinations. These can be formative (allowing the teacher to give feedback on progress) or summative (assessing overall achievement). There are many problems with such kinds of assessment, but they are the norm in the formal educational system. They will continue to have a role in an educational environment where there are both clear learning objectives and defined outcomes, *and* where learning is measured on some ladder of achievement. But learning outside a formal education structure is rarely like this. It can be highly elusive and is very difficult to measure in terms of where it occurs, how it progresses and what its outcomes are, both short term and in the longer term. Measuring such learning will never be simple.

In the UK, the sustained central government funding that flowed to museums between 1999 and 2010 came with a caveat: museums and galleries had to demonstrate the effectiveness of the investment. Every funding agreement was underpinned by learning targets. What began initially as a tokenistic measurement of numbers of participants then developed into what were largely advocacy documents (e.g. Arts Council England 2006). However, there was also a growing body of more detailed studies into how most effectively to define and measure the learning taking place and its impacts. Pringle (2006) includes a useful overview of approaches to measurement, but note that this is from a Contemporary Gallery Education perspective. For UK museums, the Inspiring Learning for All (ILfA) framework now underpins both learning provision and evaluation (www.inspiringlearningforall.org.uk). This grew out of a Learning Impact Research Project (LIRP) at the Research Centre for Museums and Galleries, University of Leicester (Hooper-Greenhill 2004). LIRP took as a starting point the broadly constructivist UK Campaign for Learning definition of learning which recognises the complexity and ongoing nature of learning:

> Learning is a process of active engagement with experience. It is what people do when they want to make sense of the world. It may involve increase in or deepening of skills, knowledge, understanding, values, feelings, attitudes and the capacity to reflect. Effective learning leads to change, development and the desire to learn more.
> Maxted (1999: 14)

Building from this, LIRP defined five user-centred Generic Learning Outcomes, or GLOs, that became central to the ILfA framework:

- knowledge and understanding
- skills
- attitudes
- enjoyment, inspiration and creativity
- action, behaviour, progression.

The Research Centre for Museums and Galleries (RCMG) was then able to use GLOs, and a breakdown of outcomes within each one (as shown in Box 5.8 overleaf) to evaluate learning in four major studies through questionnaires to pupils and teachers. The first (RCMG 2004b) looked at the three Phase 1 hubs funded under Renaissance in the Regions; the second (RCMG 2006) analysed all nine hubs, with a remarkable total of 2,669 teacher responses and 47,395 pupil responses across the two studies. Their reviews of the Strategic Commissioning Programme (RCMG 2004a and RCMG 2007a) added a further 503 adults and 9,415 pupils.

The surveys showed substantial increases in the numbers of schools using museums, including 32 per cent of visits coming from areas where children were at risk of social exclusion and 12 per cent of the total being special schools (RCMG 2006). This same study showed 86 per cent of teachers in the survey areas had visited a museum in a professional capacity in the previous two years, with almost half that number new to using museums as learning resources. Some 64 per cent had used museum online resources and 40 per cent had borrowed loan objects. There were very high approval ratings by both teachers and pupils. Coles notes that:

In response to questions to young pupils:

- 94 per cent agreed that they had enjoyed the visit
- 90 per cent agreed that they had learnt some new things
- 87 per cent agreed that a visit was useful for school work

For the older pupils, the results were almost as impressive:

- 87 per cent agreed that they had learnt some interesting things
- 82 per cent agreed that museums are good places to learn in a different way to school
- 73 per cent agreed that the visit had given them lots to think about
- 58 per cent agreed that a museum visit makes school work more inspiring
- 55 per cent agreed that they might visit again.

Coles (2009: 98)

Most teachers believed the learning outcomes resulting from using museums were very high:

Box 5.8 Generic Learning Outcomes

Knowledge and understanding
Knowing about something
Learning facts or information which can be: subject-specific; interdisciplinary/thematic; about museums, archives, libraries; about myself, my family, my community, the wider world
Making sense of something
Deepening understanding
Learning how museums, archives and libraries operate
Giving specific information – naming things, people or places
Making links and relationships between things
Using prior knowledge in new ways

Skills
Knowing how to do something
Intellectual skills – reading, thinking critically and analytically, making judgements
Key skills – numeracy, literacy, use of information and communications technology
Learning how to learn
Information management skills – locating and using information, evaluating information, using information management systems
Social skills – meeting people, sharing, team working, remembering names, introducing others, showing an interest in the concerns of others
Emotional skills – recognising the feelings of others, managing (intense) feelings, channelling energy into productive outcomes
Communication skills – writing, speaking, listening
Physical skills – running, dancing, manipulation, making

Attitudes
Feelings and perceptions
Opinions about ourselves, for example, self-esteem
Opinions or attitudes towards other people
Attitudes towards an organisation, for example, museums, archives and libraries
Positive attitudes in relation to an experience
Negative attitudes in relation to an experience
Reasons for actions or personal viewpoints
Empathy, capacity for tolerance (or lack of these)

Enjoyment, inspiration and creativity
Having fun
Being surprised
Innovative thoughts, actions or things
Creativity
Exploration, experimentation and making
Being inspired

Action, behaviour, progression
What people do
What people intend to do (intention to act)
What people have done
A change in the way that people manage their lives including work, study, family and community contexts
Actions (observed or reported)
Change in behaviour
Progression – towards further learning, registering as a library user, developing new skills – the result of a purposive action which leads to change

MLA (undated)

Increase in knowledge and understanding	95%
Skills	94%
Attitudes	92%
Enjoyment, inspiration and creativity	89%
Action, behaviour, progression	81%

While knowledge and understanding linked to specific curriculum requirements remained of key importance, teachers were also explicit about the causal link between enjoyment and learning, and spoke of emotional engagement that was to some extent inspirational (RCMG 2006). This type of response is reflected also in ongoing monitoring using GLOs across the English regions (see for example MLA Renaissance West Midlands 2010).

Most of this type of evidence is testimonial in nature, and it is very difficult to make any direct links to improvement in standard assessment tests and examinations. There is a similar lack of quantifiable evidence resulting from school visits to science museums and hands-on centres (Braund 2004). RCMG has attempted in later research to link the impact of museum visits directly to attainment in assessed work. Research for *Engage, Learn, Achieve* (RCMG 2007b) involved nine schools across the east of England visiting five museums and one archive, which supplied assessment marks for 762 pupils. The marks for the museum-based assessment were compared with up to three previous pieces of work. Based on the teachers' assessment criteria, 60 per cent of pupils achieved a higher grade for their museum-based assignment. Coles (2009: 98) points to a programme in north-west England called Write On that achieved a 35 per cent improvement above expected levels in pupils' literacy performance.

However, these examples remain rare and do not take into account other variables that might influence results. Yet the GLO evaluation approach is a huge advance on what preceded it, and the sheer scale and positive nature of the responses from teachers, pupils and parents is, in itself, compelling evidence of impact. Paralleling this, Rennie and McClafferty (1996) provide an overview of the major effect that museums can have on pupils' *attitudes* to learning science. As large numbers of teachers and pupils make clear consistently, school visits to museums engage pupils with their subjects. Museums are stimulating and joyful places for learning.

It is important to note that GLOs were intended as a starting point for more detailed study. They have the great advantages of being non-prescriptive, flexible and learner-centred, enabling the gathering and analysis of evidence of different forms of learning. But they are essentially passive, focusing on the *outcomes* rather than on the active processes involved in the learning itself. Focusing on outcomes can also place too much emphasis on the short term effect of the visit itself rather than looking at influence on progression over time. Linked to this, GLOs are almost exclusively used to reflect the impact of a single museum visit because that is the norm for usage of museums by schools.

While GLOs are a UK example, the outcomes-based approach to evaluation is becoming the norm worldwide. It is promoted, for example, by the Institute for Museum and Library Services in the USA. However, there is an alternative approach. If we seek, instead, to evaluate the active process of learning, Griffin suggests we look for *behaviours that suggest learning is taking place*, as outlined in Box 5.9 overleaf. I see this as core to the engaging museum – active learning linked to prolonged engagement. It could be applied equally to adult informal learning, but given that there is rarely a need to assess this, the approach seems more appropriate for evaluating pupil engagement during museum visits and projects.

Box 5.9 Behaviours that suggest learning is taking place

a. *showing responsibility for and initiating their own learning:*
- know what they want to look for/making choices
- writing/drawing/taking photos by choice
- talking to themselves
- deciding where and when to move

b. *actively involved in learning:*
- standing and looking/reading
- exhibiting curiosity and interest by engaging with an exhibit
- absorbed, close, concentrated examination
- persevering with a task such as drawing

c. *purposefully manipulating and playing with objects and ideas:*
- handling exhibits with care and interest
- purposefully 'playing' with exhibit elements/using hands-on exhibits as intended

d. *making links and transferring ideas and skills:*
- comparing exhibits
- referring to their prepared questions
- comparing/referring to previous experiences

e. *sharing learning with peers and experts:*
- talking and pointing
- pulling others to show them something
- willingness to be pulled to see others' interests
- group members talking and listening
- asking each other questions
- talking to adults /experts (e.g. teacher or museum staff)

f. *showing confidence in personal learning abilities:*
- asking questions of displays
- explaining to peers
- reading to peers
- comparing information with another source

g. *responding to new information or evidence:*
- evidence of changing views
- evidence of discovering new ideas

Griffin (2002: 4–5)

The behaviours shown in Box 5.9 are best evaluated through observation and by listening-in on conversations, at times supported by interviews. In reality, most GLO evaluations of school visits now also involve consultation with teachers and observation of pupil behaviour. The latter, reflecting Griffin's analysis of evidence of active involvement in learning, adds further depth to the GLO evidence that learning is taking place.

Pringle (2006) sought to take this a step further by representing the learning process in a contemporary art gallery diagrammatically to 'highlight the complex, inter-related nature of the teaching and learning experience in the gallery', as illustrated in Figure 5.3.

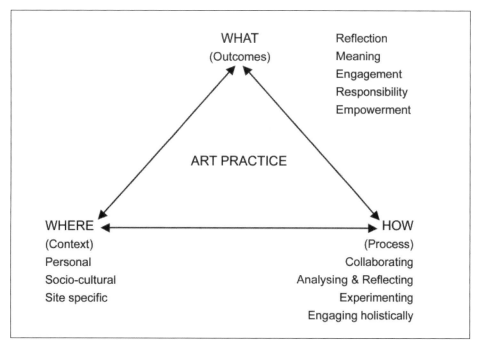

WHAT
(Outcomes)

Reflection
Meaning
Engagement
Responsibility
Empowerment

ART PRACTICE

WHERE
(Context)
Personal
Socio-cultural
Site specific

HOW
(Process)
Collaborating
Analysing & Reflecting
Experimenting
Engaging holistically

Figure 5.3 **Contemporary gallery education learning framework (based on Pringle 2006: 23–4).**

She used the term *mapping* as a means of evaluation, in 'a deliberate attempt to move away from the limiting practices of measurement and assessment'. She uses the specific nature of Contemporary Gallery Education (CGE) to support this view:

> CGE positions the learner as an active, engaged participant in an individual and collaborative process of learning. CGE is concerned with empowering the participant whilst encouraging them to take responsibility for their own and other's learning. This has implications for how this process is understood. Likewise, arts education projects frequently aspire to promote cultural inclusivity and individual empowerment. Those that do must involve participants in establishing the criteria for evaluating the work ... Participants need to be actively involved in the mapping process, not just the subjects of someone else's investigations.
>
> Pringle (2006: 26)

This led her to advocate 'personal meaning mapping' (PMM) as one way of measuring 'how a specified learning experience uniquely affects each individual's understanding or meaning-making process'. PMM was developed at the Institute for Learning Innovation, University of Maryland (see Adams et al. 2003). PMM data is collected as follows:

- Participants write down any words, ideas or thoughts they may have relating to a particular image or concept prior to engaging in an education activity or visiting an exhibition.

- This is followed by a discussion with an interviewer who encourages the respondents to articulate their understandings and develop them further. This is also written on the same piece of paper.
- After the event, the same process is repeated.
- The data is then analysed according to criteria relating to each research scenario. (For example, one dimension could measure the extent of knowledge by examining the nature of the vocabulary used).

Pringle (2006: 27)

There are clear difficulties in carrying out PMM on a large scale, but its use could add further depth to evaluation, building on GLOs and observation of process.

So, here we have the problem: the nature of museum and gallery learning is complex and therefore must be assessed in a complex fashion. This flies in the face of an establishment that wants simple answers. It is also an expensive and time-consuming exercise. However, it is an essential tool in selling what we do. It also enables us to evaluate the effectiveness of our work. Evaluation can only become more of an issue as time passes.

CONCLUDING THOUGHTS

Within the next 20 years, the formal education system as we know it will be transformed. If museums wish to retain an important role in supporting structured education, they must think and plan strategically for that future. This means looking at the nature of the traditional museum visit, embracing new technology, recognising the importance of out-of-school-time learning, building opportunities on-site for older pupils and continuing to develop online resources. It means sharing authority with partner organisations and opening content to the opportunities that Web 2.0 brings. This chapter could do no more than introduce some of the issues.

As I write, however, museum learning teams are being decimated as a result of austerity cuts in public expenditure. Years of expertise are being lost. Successful programmes are being tossed away. Yet museum audiences, including schools, expect a continually improving and relevant experience. If museums cannot continue to develop to meet changing school needs, the schools will not come. The UK, from being a case study from 1997 to 2010 on the positive effects of sustained new funding for museum learning, now looks like it will become a new case study on what happens when that funding is removed. How do you balance austerity with the need for dramatic change and development?

6   Conversations around collections

INTRODUCTION

> The engaging museum is not embodied in *its collections, displays and programming* but lies in the encounter between *these* and the audience, and among the audience themselves. *A museum exhibition* is not simply the result of self-expression by the *curatorial team* of a preconceived idea but the result of communication with the audience and other partners in the process. The *museum's* role is not just to proclaim but to listen, interpret, incorporate ideas and adjust . . . For the *museum, an exhibition* becomes more valuable the more it encourages people to join a *dialogue* around it and to *construct new meanings among* themselves. *An engaging museum* is based on constant feedback and interaction, people talking, arguing, debating around the *collections, displays and programming* . . .
>
> adapted from Leadbeater (2009: 8), my alterations shown in italics

This quote, adapted from Leadbeater's discussion of participative art, is central to the mental image I have of the user's voice speaking from the heart of the engaging museum – the buzz of conversation and discussion among museum audiences as they encounter and respond to the objects and other content within the museum, as they interact with each other, and as they contribute their own knowledge, stories, experience and ideas. In such a museum, staff will recognise the museum visit as a conversation between the collections, the users and the museum rather than viewing users as empty vessels to be filled with didactic content. As discussed below, this is not a denial of museum expertise. Rather, it recognises the benefits to all, including the museum, of sharing how much our users bring with them. It also acknowledges the highly social nature of museum learning and thus reflects Leinhardt and Knutson's (2004: xiii) model of museum learning as a 'form of conversational elaboration among participants'.

Conversations in a museum are both personal and mediated. They are personal in the sense that they are 'in a face-to-face setting with no formal constraints on who may talk or what they say' (Leinhardt and Knutson 2004: 82). They are mediated in that the museum has selected display content and associated interpretation. But their starting point is not specifically created participative exhibits. Rather, these conversations begin with the encouragement and support of users to focus their attention on museum collections; users then discover for themselves, interact around those collections alongside other family or social group members (and possibly other visitors), and ultimately develop new understandings – much more minds-on than hands-on. These conversations will lead to reflection and discussion; from that will flow meaning-making and, for some, the desire to contribute to content. A word of warning, however:

we cannot expect such depth of conversation around the user response to all objects and content. We are dependent here on users reaching the stage of engaged attention discussed in Chapter 4 – and the conversations themselves, not least in their brevity or expansiveness, reveal the extent to which users are engaged.

So, what will our users be talking about? The theory of museum display taught in museum courses across the world acknowledges the complex range of meanings that individual objects possess, and the even greater complexity involved when objects are grouped together in exhibitions; it speaks of the capacity of objects to 'speak for themselves', given the right circumstances, and to generate debate among those who encounter them, with the museum as the mediator. It emphasises the selective nature of display – the meanings highlighted through the choice of objects and of how they are grouped for display, the selection of the information and messages to accompany them, etc. – while currently also teaching that visitors select for themselves from what is on offer and create their own meanings. So, how can we best mediate the encounter between our collections and our users to provoke thought most effectively, thought that in turn will stimulate debate and reveal meanings?

Nina Simon (2010: 127–81) commits chapter four of her book *The Participatory Museum* to what she defines as 'social objects', describing them as having 'an ability to spark conversation', as ones that 'lend themselves naturally to social experiences'. They 'allow people to focus their attention on a third thing rather than on each other, making interpersonal engagement more comfortable'. They 'are transactional, facilitating exchanges among those who encounter them'. Her classic example of a social object is her dog: 'When I walk around town with my dog, lots of people talk to me, or, more precisely, talk through the dog to me' (Simon 2010: 127–9). She speaks of four types of social objects, outlined in Box 6.1.

Box 6.1 **Nina Simon's four types of social objects**

Personal: objects people have a personal connection to, that generate an immediate story to tell.
Active: objects that directly and physically insert themselves into the spaces between strangers, for example, animal behaviour in a zoo.
Provocative: an object that is a spectacle in its own right.
Relational: these objects explicitly invite interpersonal use by requiring several people to use them at once, for example telephones or game boards.

based on Simon (2010: 130–2)

She devotes most of the chapter to 'designing platforms for social objects', focusing on 'providing tools for visitors to engage with each other around objects' (Simon 2010: 133), outlining a range of approaches and case studies. In addition to looking at online provision such as Flickr, she explores five design techniques for use within museums, outlined in Box 6.2.

Box 6.2 Nina Simon's five design techniques for social objects

1 Asking visitors *questions* and prompting them to share their reactions to the objects on display
2 Providing *live interpretation* or performance to help visitors make a personal connection to artifacts
3 Designing exhibitions with *provocative presentation* techniques that display objects in juxtaposition, conflict or conversation with each other
4 Giving visitors clear *instructions* on how to engage with each other around the object …
5 Offering visitors ways to *share* objects either physically or virtually.

Simon (2010: 138)

This is an important analysis, essential reading and packed with ideas and examples. While there is little if any of it I disagree with, the primacy of the object within the conversation often seems to get lost, while there is only limited discussion of the needs of different audiences. I have already discussed audiences and their needs and motivations in previous chapters. Here I would like to reflect on the nature of museum collections and the meanings they hold. I would also like to explore how museums can encourage and support users to engage with and discuss those objects.

OBJECTS OF MEMORY

In a book like this I could not begin to explore the full range of meanings attached to objects, nor do I have the expertise to do so. As a historian, I will focus on those relating to memory.

Objects are the 'only class of historical events that occurred in the past but survive into the present. They can be re-experienced; they are authentic, primary historical material' (Prown 1993: 2–3). Such objects represent the visible and touchable outer world of the cultural memory of past societies. In deciding what objects to select and preserve museums are not only acting as a cultural memory store for humankind, but also defining what is or is not history. In the way they display and interpret that material evidence, they construct and transmit meanings. Today there is an ongoing conflict in history museums between a desire to present a single-voiced linear narrative of the past and an ambition to act as places of pluralism and inclusion which recognise the contributions all in society have made – this is discussed in Chapter 8.

Furthermore, the perspectives teased out by museums do not stand on their own. They must sit alongside the rich diversity each individual brings to the objects. Objects gain meanings in the context of human thoughts, feelings, fantasies and memories, but these responses are also *provoked by* objects. The interrelation of contemporary responses with objects can serve both as content and as a two-way process, which both contextualises objects and provokes new thoughts (Nakou 2005: 2). Thus, visitors to museums are not passive recipients. Rather, in the process of engaging with the collections and associated interpretive material on display, visitors add new content to their existing knowledge and understanding; they construct their own meanings. Increasing digital access to museum collections and documentation has added further to this democratisation of meaning-making. History is thus selected, constructed and transmitted by museums and then, in the process of being experienced by museum users, it is transformed into 'something else – their own understanding of the past, a type of "historical sense" independent of the professional historian's ideal' (Watson 2010: 205).

Having said all that, in principle objects serve cultural memory in at least one of four main ways (Black 2011: 418–21):

1 *Objects that reflect the society and culture that produced them*: such objects evoke a sense of time, place and society beyond individual memory. They can play a powerful role in defining a community's memories of its collective past, its social practices, its attitudes and beliefs, etc. In terms of defining and transmitting cultural memory, the issue is not what memories these objects hold but rather which memories/meanings are selected for transmission and how the selection process works.

2 *Objects that are created for their memory role, or have that role foisted upon them*: these include those directly associated with rites, ceremonies and customs, themselves linked to memory; those produced directly as commemoratives (of individuals or events) or souvenirs (of places); and those collected or retained, by individuals, families or communities, for the memories they are associated with.

3 *Objects that trigger remembering*: when people use museums, they bring their life experiences with them. Often, their encounter with objects in the museum brings back vivid recollections, half-remembered places and emotions which would otherwise have remained forgotten.

4 *Objects that retain evidence of the craft traditions that produced them*: I am referring here to the passing on of traditional skills and techniques, acquired by each new practitioner through watching craftspeople, practising under their guidance and studying examples of their craft. In the case of the latter, the object memory lives on after the maker and user, and becomes a vital link to the craft in its own right. Today many of these objects are held in museums.

My strong view is that, rather than thinking in terms of Simon's 'social objects', we should consider all objects collected by a museum to have the capacity to stimulate conversation. But these conversations are likely to vary depending on the type of cultural memory the object serves, or is presented as serving. The most important thing is that these conversations are meaningful – that they involve people bringing diverse perspectives to their encounters with collections, that the people having these conversations respond to those collections and share their responses and perspectives with each other and with the museum, and that they take away enhanced understandings as a result.

MEDIATING CONVERSATIONS IN MUSEUMS

While users will select for themselves which objects to talk about, the museum can mediate in a number of ways to encourage and influence such conversations. The remainder of this chapter explores ways museums can prompt and support conversation around and about their collections.

'Inducing visitors to stay . . .'

> We have surmised that the great need of the public was preparation of mind for what is shown; and we have accordingly multiplied labels and catalogues and guides; and of late years have developed a new museum service in the guise of personal companionship by docents, instructors, and demonstrators. All these things help. Nevertheless, what is more needed is that the works of art themselves shall have the opportunity of making their impression.
>
> To do this they require, among other things, time . . . From this angle, the problem of the use of the museum by the public becomes a problem of inducing visitors to stay . . .
>
> Gilman (1918: 274–5)

Visitors come to museums with their own agendas, often including the amount of time they have available, which we might be able to influence but certainly cannot control. Yet, if we want our users to have meaningful conversations about our collections, we must persuade them to spend the time needed to engage, reflect and respond. This means persuading them, through the quality of the museum experience, to stay longer than anticipated and to return more often.

I refer once more to the holistic nature of the museum visit. We must ensure that every aspect of our public face is directed to inducing people to stay and to come again regularly. When it comes specifically to the quality of their engagement with museum content and programming, 12 years of visitor research at the Smithsonian Institution led the visitor studies team to categorise the experiences their research suggested visitors found most satisfying, placing 14 key types of experience under four main categories, outlined in Box 6.3. All these experiences can lead to or directly involve conversation.

***Box 6.3* Four types of satisfying experiences**

1 *Object experiences* – being moved by beauty:
 - seeing rare/uncommon/valuable things
 - seeing 'the real thing'
 - thinking what it would be like to own such things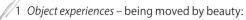
 - continuing my professional development.

2 *Cognitive experiences* – enriching my understanding:
 - gaining information or knowledge.

3 *Introspective experiences* – reflecting on the meaning of what I was looking at:
 - imagining other times or places
 - recalling my travels/childhood experiences/other memories
 - feeling a spiritual connection
 - feeling a sense of belonging or connectedness.

4 *Social experiences* – spending time with friends/family/other people:
 - seeing my children learning new things.

based on Doering (1999: 83)

Interpretive planning

I say throughout this book that the primary role of exhibitions and associated activities is to engage users directly with collections and related content – to gain attention, to hold it and to encourage reflection, conversation and meaning-making. By making user engagement the first priority, the initial 'big picture' development of an exhibition concept should begin *not* with 'What do we want our visitors to leave knowing?' but instead with four other questions:

- Who are our users?
- What will our users think of this?
- What do we want our users to talk about?
- Can we ensure the collections are at the heart of this process?

Having answered these questions, the museum will then select its main theme and sub-themes, and build content around these, using the main messages to provide the underpinning for conversation. The Victoria & Albert Museum in London is the UK's national museum of art and design. When the museum decided to redisplay its British collections, the run of 15 display areas were broken up chronologically into three main periods, Tudor and Stuart, Hanoverian, and Victorian, but the same themes were then applied to each period:

- What were the styles?
- Who led taste?
- Fashionable living
- What was new?

So, with the representation of the history of design in Britain as the main objective for the British galleries, these themes provided a framework for exploration and conversations.

Designing object display for conversation

Below the 'big picture' of interpretive planning, every stage in exhibition development is relevant to the generation of conversations – from the establishment of hierarchies in presentation to the final selection of objects for display. This also includes the display approaches and contexts deemed most appropriate, the selection and use of associated interpretive support and design media, and finally the placing of an individual object on display and the attachment (or not) of an associated label. Object positioning and sequencing, lighting, colour, labelling, etc. will all influence visitor behaviour:

- Giving an object *space* will emphasise its importance – isolation encourages attention because it encourages visitors to perceive the objects as important and therefore worth engaging with and talking about. Large, isolated, spotlit objects will most easily attract attention. Objects crammed into cases will lose individuality. Lighting and gallery colour, and even music, can of course add dramatically to the occasion:

Several visually striking pieces were showcased by being placed by themselves on enormous walls or by having a lot of empty space around them. Others were placed so that they were framed by doorways as the visitor surveyed the galleries ... visitors were able to see most of the artwork at close range without the interference of plastic. There were no railings. Labels were unobtrusive and low so as not to overwhelm the eye. The walls had been painted saturated shades of cool colours ... while African music played in the background.

From a description of the exhibition Soul of Africa in Stainton (2002: 217–18)

- Linked to this is the significance of the most prominent *sight lines* – focal points that can be viewed from distance or from a number of locations within an exhibition. Can you select key objects that illustrate the exhibition's core objectives and place these on major sightlines? This can both help draw people through the exhibition and focus their attention.
- Selective *grouping* of objects can support messages, and encourage the visitor to recognise associations and connections, for example from providing new insights into influences on artists to exploring development of pottery over time.
- Representations or re-creations of original *contexts* can support visitor understanding, particularly by enabling them to relate to their own lives and experiences. Hooper-Greenhill (1994: 75) cites a study at the Royal Ontario Museum showing that when visitors were given a choice as to how a group of decorative art objects, furniture and sculpture were displayed, they preferred either a room setting or a thematic presentation. It is no surprise that furniture stores use contextualisation through setting up room displays to encourage sales. People want to relate what they are viewing to their own lives – if they can imagine the objects in the context of everyday living, sales will increase.
- *Competition* can remove attention from the objects and dramatically reduce the likelihood of people engaging with and talking about them. This competition can come from the design media being used as well as from other objects. If you want people to focus on the objects, you must remove or minimise distracting factors.
- Creating *'conversation spaces'* within the gallery, including seating, and enabling 'people watching' between groups, can help people learn from and engage with each other. Museum visits by adults are rarely made alone, although more so in art galleries. As discussed in Chapter 4, the evidence suggests that the exhibits that most effectively support user engagement are those that encourage social interaction, discussion and involvement within and beyond the groups involved. This, in turn, both broadens and deepens people's engagement and understanding. So we must think in terms not just of self-referencing but also of group-referencing and group dynamics.
- Representing *multiple viewpoints* will help users feel they too have the right to develop and talk about their own ideas. This is an essential element in the process of personal meaning-making. Wilton describes the incorporation of user contributions in a temporary exhibition at the Museum for African Art, New York – Exhibition-ism – which 'confronted visitors with the processes involved in creating an exhibition and used its exhibited objects to argue that Western museum practices contradict the ways in which art and artefacts are used and understood among African communities':

The objects in this room were made available for a range of invited visitors to offer suggestions about display, labels, organisation: the same objects were arranged, rearranged, displayed differently, interpreted differently. This was an overt statement about the changing meanings which can be associated with objects dependent on the way they are collected and presented. And it was an overt statement that museum visitors have different visions and expectations – they are not necessarily passive onlookers.

Wilton (2006: 65–6)

As the most common example of the latter, a space to display and read comment cards, and respond to other people's comments, can encourage dialogue. This is discussed further below.

- Building *activity spaces*, or 'dwell points', into the exhibition creates locations where staff, gallery assistants and docents can engage and interact with the audience. This is discussed further below.
- In praise of the humble *label*. In seeking to engage users directly with objects and stimulate conversation around and about those objects, the label is likely to have a more important role than wider contextual texts – it will be the first port of call for those seeking further information. The most effective labels will be placed in

Figure 6.1 Touring the store at the Museum of the University of St Andrews
A guided tour of the store gives the museum and local people an opportunity to discuss its role and explore its collections. Courtesy of MUSA.

line of sight, well lit and preferably directly in front of objects. Each label will have a clear objective focused on encouraging exploration and conversation, for example to attract readers' interest and draw them in, or to anticipate and answer their questions. The label should address the reader directly and be written in a friendly, conversational tone and in language that is easy to understand. Whole books have been written on labels (e.g. Serrell 1996). I cannot add anything useful in the space available here beyond emphasising their absolute and fundamental importance.

- *Open Access* stores can add a further dimension. Glasgow Museums Resource Centre and the Darwin Centre at the Natural History Museum in London are the largest examples in the world of museum stores designed from the outset for public access to content and to staff, yet they are very different from each other. However, this approach is potentially even more relevant to small museums providing opportunities to engage closely with local users. The Museum of the University of St Andrews developed a new open access store at the same time as carrying out a full redisplay. Regular tours are offered to groups of between six and eight people, creating a remarkably intimate atmosphere. The store also organises open events for the annual Museums Night and Scottish Festival of Museums, including torchlight tours and storytelling for families. A case study can be found in Museum of the University of St Andrews (undated).

Self-referencing and the triggering of memories

Chapter 4, among other things, introduced the importance of the 'content hook' and of using Tilden's six principles of interpretation, particularly principle 1: 'Any interpretation that does not somehow relate what is being displayed or described to something within the personality or experience of the visitor will be sterile' (Tilden 1977: 9). Self-referencing relates the collections to users' own lives, experiences, interests and knowledge. It makes new information and ideas relevant and interesting by connecting them – in effect, personalising them – with users' own experiences. Supporting the concept of self-referencing, Paris and Mercer (2002: 407) emphasise the importance of personal relevance: 'Museum visitors discover bits and pieces of their own lives in the objects they encounter . . . the information becomes meaningful through reference to representations of who they are and who they want to become.' The conversations stimulated by such an encounter can frequently continue after the visit.

Stimulating conversation and memories through object handling

We are what we remember. Nothing is so uniquely one's own as one's memories.

Burnham (2000: 655)

The memories and meanings stimulated by objects arise not only as a result of visual access to museum collections but also from other forms of access. The importance of smell in provoking memory has long been understood. Touch is our most intimate sense, but it is only in recent years that touch has begun to return as an important element in the museum experience. Much of this has been driven by legal requirements to enhance access for the visually impaired. Museum responses have included tactile galleries with original objects and replicas, three-dimensional models where the original objects are over-sized or which give an overview of a building, relief sculptures of artworks and contemporary art that is made to be touched, guided and self-guided touch tours (with the latter supported by Braille and audio), and handling sessions, often in alternative spaces. There are many examples of good practice, but the reality remains that most museums and art galleries provide very inadequate access. People with visual impairments need significantly more opportunities to experience museum collections and the meanings they hold. Only a culture shift at managerial level can achieve this – but it should be a central ambition for the engaged museum.

This is not only an issue for the visually impaired. The opportunity to handle objects can make a huge difference to the experiences of all museum users. Recent research reflects the increasing understanding of the impact that touching objects can have on bringing memories to mind (e.g. see Gallace and Spence 2008). Most of our life experiences are multisensory – and children in particular respond to, and remember best, rich multisensory environments (Spock 2010: 123). In this context, it is important to note that the dominance of the visual in museums only dates from the nineteenth century. Collections gathered from the Grand Tour in the eighteenth century and the contents of earlier cabinets of curiosities were meant to be handled and smelled as a means of stimulating enlightened conversation among their aristocratic users (Zimmer et al. 2008: 151). A wonderful description by an eighteenth century visitor to the British Museum gives a vivid idea of the impact of an opportunity to handle collections:

> With what sensations one handles a Carthaginian helmet excavated near Capua, household utensils from Herculaneum … There are mirrors too, belonging to Roman matrons … with one of these mirrors in my hand I looked amongst the urns … Nor could I restrain my desire to touch the ashes of an urn on which a female figure was being mourned. I felt it gently with great feeling.
>
> Sophie de la Roche, quoted in Candlin (2008: 11)

I doubt that many conservators would be happy with this level of handling opportunities! However, the quote makes vividly clear how the subjective experience of touching objects can add dramatically to visual impact and lead to richer memories (Lehmann and Murray 2005). We must also think of the memories of touch brought back, for example, in exploring period houses in living history museums: 'of touching handles on doors, latches on windows, cutlery in drawers, plates in dark cupboards, and of dusting artefacts on mantelpieces and polishing furniture' (Rowlands 2008: 187). All such memories trigger conversations.

Touch is also essential for those who seek to protect, promote and be inspired by traditional art and craft forms. With original makers and users long deceased, only the historic objects retain evidence of the craft traditions that produced them. Often such evidence only reveals itself through a detailed physical study by contemporary craftspeople. Frequently these objects only survive in museums – particularly in tropical climates, where the organic materials commonly used to make them can decay rapidly.

Object handling has also become increasingly important in a specialised area of memory and conversation triggering – the opportunity to handle, explore and experience objects has become part of good practice in reminiscence work, helping people to recall, retrieve and recollect remembered experiences from their lives. Reminiscence work advocates a multisensory and inclusive approach. It is commonly a group activity with personal, social, educational and creative dimensions. It often involves the oldest age groups, and those with dementia, and frequently takes place in their care settings. Participants who share memories are respected and supported throughout the process. 'It is good practice to include objects that are recognizable from all stages of the target age-group's life, so that participants are not restricted as to what times of their lives they will be stimulated to recall' (Arigho 2008: 208). Many museums are involved in this work, creating 'reminiscence boxes' as the basis for activities led by their own staff or loaned to outside groups. People can respond to the objects in their own ways:

> The objects enabled different levels of interaction so that individuals could get involved at the level they felt most comfortable with: they could just handle and think, they could talk to their neighbour or perhaps to a friend or family member after the sessions, they could say something factual about something they recognized or just state they remembered it ... they could ask a question or allow the object to prompt the sharing of a memory.
>
> Phillips (2008: 202)

Smell, taste and sound as memory triggers

Smell, taste and sound often evoke memories and arouse emotions. It is said that we can identify as many as 10,000 different smells. And while we have only four recognised tastes – sweet, sour, salt and bitter – smell adds immeasurably to these. In Marcel Proust's *Remembrance of Things Past*, Charles Swann is transported back to his childhood when the smell of a biscuit dipped in tea triggers memories from his past. The voice of a loved one, children's laughter in a school, the sound of church bells, air raid sirens or textile machines, or the smell of a hospital ward, all instantly return us to past states. Favourite pop songs from our youth never leave us.

Smell and sound act as immediate triggers of memory and conversation in living history museums. City history museums from Dresden to Chicago are incorporating area sound maps while Chicago also has a smell map. Interpretation at the Museum of Musical Instruments of the University of Leipzig incorporates recordings made of some of its most important instruments, while others are played live in the galleries. It also contains a sound laboratory where instruments can be tested.

Industrial museums with working machines provide both sound and smell. Some natural history museums incorporate the sounds of the fauna displayed. Overall, however, the place granted to sound, smell and taste is still marginal in traditional museums and there are few published case studies of experimental use. How much richer could the museum experience and the conversations arising from it be if the senses were given their proper place?

Sound is, of course, a natural medium for online provision. The London Sound Survey has completed a sound grid series recorded at evenly spaced points across the city (www.soundsurvey.org.uk/index.php/survey/soundmaps). The sounds of New York City can be found at www.nysoundmap.org. What does Britain sound like? The British Library is currently creating the first nationwide sound map (http://sounds.

Figure 6.2 **Experimenting in the Sound Lab of the Museum of Musical Instruments, Leipzig**
Visitors can play replicas of historical instruments like the harpsichord or clavichord. They can see the inside workings of an organ and glass piano, and can experiment with instruments from around the world. Courtesy of Museum für Musikinstrumente der Universität Leipzig im GRASSI, photographer: Marion Wenzel.

bl.uk/uksoundmap/index.aspx) using the Audioboo app for both iPhone and Android smartphones. Not surprisingly there is also an online museum for contemporary sound art (http://soundmuseum.fm/Home).

Providing relevant activities in the gallery

The importance of regular activities and an events progamme was discussed in Chapter 4. For me, the opportunity to handle and discuss objects directly related to those in adjacent displays will always remain a primary need. However, I also recognise the many other ways individuals and groups of visitors can be encouraged to look more closely, to consider more deeply, to make connections and explore meanings. The challenge is to experiment, evaluate and improve over time. If 'dwell points' are built into galleries to support structured educational use they (when not being used by schools) can also provide natural locations for an activity programme. By having a table at the dwell point, with cupboards underneath, handling collections directly related to the adjacent cased exhibits can be stored and brought out for regular use. By minimising the effort involved in setting up such activities, a timed programme can be run at weekends, in school holidays, etc., including object handling, gallery tours, art trolleys, and many other possibilities. None of this is new thinking – it simply needs to be applied *systematically* and made available to adults as well as children.

The use of gallery enablers and docents

Social interaction, between visitors and between visitors and museum enablers/docents or curators, is a critical but hugely underestimated component in engaging visitors directly with collections, encouraging conversation and leading to visitor learning (see Cunningham 2004). Enablers and docents are also key to the operation of an activities programme, including object handling.

Figure 6.3 **A knowledgeable volunteer assists a visitor's research**
At the Imperial War Museum North, volunteers help visitors explore more deeply using online material – here, looking for information on a relative who fought in the Second World War.

The original function of the docent was to act as a knowledgeable companion for the visitor, directing his or her attention and supporting their understanding. It was directly related to museums' perceptions of themselves as educational institutions. Today, the docent as educator and gallery enabler remains a mainstay of the USA museum system:

> Docents are at the very center of the museum–visitor interface. They are responsible for sharing the fundamental intent of the curatorial staff, a staff that remains largely invisible and anonymous to visitors. It rests with them to prompt visitors to see the careful design decisions that are made, and to support an understanding and appreciation of the specific objects or the concepts that are being shared . . .
>
> The docents participate in training, practice their roles, and gradually gain experience that moves them from being peripheral participants to occupying a central position in the daily activity of the museum.
>
> Abu-Shumays and Leinhardt (2002: 47–8)

Some docents are paid, many are volunteers. There is no equivalent of the docent in the UK, although there is a long tradition of volunteering, mostly working with collections rather than audiences. The closest equivalent in the UK is probably in the developing role of the volunteer room steward in the National Trust – reflecting the Trust's 'vision for learning' strategy. What most visitors meet in UK museums will be attendant staff whose primary function remains security. This issue was discussed above in Chapter 3, but is returned to here specifically because of the essential need for enablers in galleries to support direct visitor engagement with collections.

Living history and museum theatre

Historical characters that greet and converse with visitors are at the heart of the living history museum, with a primary purpose of encouraging people to engage in conversation about the past – and often its relationship with the present. Museum professionals argue that living history sites provide a highly effective free choice learning experience, as there are no labels, barriers or pre-determined routes. 'Visitors are free to ask any question that occurs to them. Interpreters can assess the appropriate level of response at the moment questions are asked and fit the answer accordingly' (Rosenthal and Blankman-Hetrick 2002: 307). Well-trained, experienced interpreters will use their responses to stimulate further questions or to widen out the conversation, prompting the entire group to join in.

But living history need not only take place at specially created open air sites. It, and its cousin museum theatre, can also play an important role in stimulating conversations around collections within traditional museum galleries by means of monologues, short plays, first person interpretation (in character) or third person interaction (dressing and demonstrating skills from a time period, and putting in context). This field has grown considerably in the past two decades but its practice remains as diverse as the many sites in which it now takes place. Research by the Centre for Applied Theatre Research at the University of Manchester carried out from 2005 to 2008 was able to examine its immediate and longer term learning impacts among school

Figure 6.4 **The impact of museum theatre**
A promenade museum theatre performance of *This Accursed Thing*, on the abolition of the slave trade, at Manchester Museum, leads to sustained discussion. Courtesy of the Performance, Learning and Heritage Archive, Manchester University; actor Andrew Ashmore.

groups, families and older learners at four study sites: the National Maritime Museum, London, Llancaiach Fawr Manor, South Wales, the Herbert Art Gallery and Museum, Coventry, and The Manchester Museum (Jackson and Kidd 2008a).

Many of the results from this research reveal that performance in the galleries is effective in helping audiences engage more effectively with the meanings of the collections on display, as Box 6.4 outlines (overleaf).

Some of the richest comments in response to these performances – what the researchers called 'metacommentaries' – were about the *making* of the event: audiences commented on the design of the performance, the gallery spaces, the appropriateness of the acting styles, the effectiveness for other audience members, possible alternatives and how the events meshed with the museum's wider goals. Such responses directly reflect 'the active and multi-layered engagement of which audiences are clearly capable' (Jackson and Kidd 2008b: 53–4). This supports the 'learning talk' categories devised by Allen (2002) and discussed at the end of this chapter.

Museum theatre need not only be about the past. It can also, for example, engage audiences with artworks. The Gallery Shows at Tel Aviv Museum of Art use storytelling, music, pantomime, masks and visual media to engage children. They are given roles

---

Box 6.4 The impact of museum theatre in engaging audiences with collections

- Performance emerged as an important tool in unlocking the *'unheard' stories* linked with events in the past or with museum collections and historic buildings.
- The *'eventness'* – the *sense of occasion and immediacy* of performance – has a powerful impact on audiences. The realness, the closeness to and interaction with the actors, and the sense of going on a journey . . .
- Relating to a particular *character* brings the history alive and helps audiences to connect very personally to it . . .
- Many clearly enjoyed the experience of being 'inside' a performance rather than a passive observer – for many, the *interactivity was integral to their enjoyment.*
- The opportunities for two-way *dialogue* between audience and actor, or between two characters occupying opposing viewpoints, for *facilitated reflection and discussion* with out-of-role actor-interpreters following a performance, and for other conversations provoked by the experience, greatly added to visitors' engagement and understanding.
- A reinforcing factor was the use of *artefacts* as part of the performance, particularly if they could be handled by audience members. Making links with the surrounding site and collections is critical – and performance often gave respondents a strong sense of ownership over the site and the material.
- Respondents show they want the factual truth, and are sceptical of the 'fake', but see the performances they experienced as *'real'* in terms of emotional response. Actual, authentic *artefacts* (as opposed to 'stage props') emerge as crucial elements in the process of engaging with the past, especially where they are used creatively and as part of a process of questioning and dialogue.
- Enjoyment and surprise – the *'wow-factor'* – of a performance frequently inspires further desire in visitors to engage both with the subject and with the site.

based on Jackson and Kidd (2008a: 10–12)

---

and costumes, called on for advice and opinions and enlisted to search for 'missing' paintings.

In one of the current shows, *The Woman Who Lives in the Picture*, based on the *Princess of Babylon* by Kees Van Dongen and the *Portrait of Friedericke Maria Beer* by Gustav Klimt, the Princess of Babylon has lost her portrait. She enlists the help of the children, conversing with Friedericke Maria Beer in front of her picture. With the assistance of the children, the two women compare clothes and customs in ancient Babylon and early twentieth century Vienna. They consider the different styles of the artists and the relationships between figure and painter. Finally, the children help the princess to find her picture (pers. comm. Yael Borovich 2011).

Figure 6.5 **The woman who lives in the picture**
The Princess of Babylon and Friedericke Maria Beer enlist the help of children during a Gallery Show at Tel Aviv Museum of Art. Courtesy of Yael Borovich.

Stimulating conversation through handheld technologies

Since their invention in the early 1950s, handheld audio guides have become a mainstay of museum interpretation. They have been heavily criticised as anti-social (you listen alone, separated from the social group you came with) and the master of the visit rather than the tool of the user (you only view exhibits covered by the guide and only discover what the guide wants you to know). Clearly, like all interpretive media, they cannot meet the needs of everyone. However they have remarkable potential as today's mobile handheld technology offers visitors access to vast resources of information from which they can search and select items of interest. They also allow museums to cater for people with different learning styles.

As with interpretive planning for exhibition development or for online content, the starting point should be the user. Increasingly with modern technology, particularly for the smartphones, the user can choose their own content. But, whatever the technology, the challenge remains the same – to ensure that the content we develop provides a range of ways in which to support the user in interacting with the exhibits. Thinking of this in terms of conversations, it could include, for example:

- conversation led by the museum
- conversation stimulated by an artist, giving a personal tour of his or her work, or of others' works
- conversation stimulated by local community responses
- conversation between the user and museum as the user develops his or her own 'unauthorised' content.

Voting

The art of voting creates a notion of shared responsibility and pride in the final outcome ... There is recognition that everyone's opinion is valid and equal. As the only response required is to indicate a preference, there is no pressure to feel that any expertise is required and so there is a low threshold for taking part. This type of activity can involve a large audience.

Mackay (2010: 25)

One of the simplest ways of generating user feedback is through voting. In Top 40, at Worcester Art Gallery, UK, 40 artworks were initially chosen and displayed by curators. People could vote for their favourite piece using a ballot box in the gallery, and include their thoughts on the painting they were voting for (from art historical judgements to memories). The results were collated each week and presented in the gallery. The comments were exhibited alongside the artworks, leading to discussions between users. The curator, Phillipa Tinsley, believed people developed a sense of ownership for their favourite paintings and that the approach also encouraged repeat visits (Tinsley 2009).

The McCormick Freedom Museum in Chicago began as a physical site but now develops touring exhibitions, runs a 'Freedom Express Mobile Museum', provides 'discovery trunks' as loan boxes to schools, and maintains a series of online exhibits. The ambition is to 'engage visitors in dialogue about important issues we face collectively'. Visitors are introduced, both onsite and online, to issues challenging free speech in the USA and asked to vote on whether they agree or disagree with policy, court verdicts and popular opinion. They can then compare their responses to that of other visitors (McCormick Foundation undated).

Incorporating user-generated comments

Though conversations may be lively, they go home with the visitors leaving no trace.

Pollock (2007: 3)

There is a clear overlap here with Chapter 8, which explores the incorporation of multiple perspectives and support for civil engagement. McLean and Pollock's list of reasons why museums should include visitor responses (Box 6.5) reflects this overlap.

Box 6.5 Why use visitor response elements in exhibitions

- Validate visitors' experiences, knowledge and emotions
- Support visitors in personalising and integrating their exhibition experiences
- Redress a perceived imbalance in the content of an exhibition
- Enable the institution to engage with a wider audience
- Expose visitors and museum staff to diverse perspectives
- Open up possibilities for dialogue and exchange
- Extend participation beyond a programmatic event
- Reinforce visitors' intentions to take action
- Help people find others with common interests
- Provide a constructive way for a community to respond to a contentious or emotional issue
- Deepen museum staff's understanding of visitors' experiences
- Honour public creativity

McLean and Pollock (2007a: 20)

My focus at this point is on four types of user-generated comments that are part of museum users' conversations during their visit:

1 *Comments as the result of the museum's commitment to engagement with its users*: 'The very act of contributing changes the essential dynamic of the experience from a pre-determined production to one of exchange and reciprocity' (McLean 2007a: 11).

2 *Comments as a direct user response to content*: the very act of writing the comment will lead to reflection and conversation on what is to be written, which will influence the user directly.

3 *Comments that users want to share with others visiting the gallery*: an ongoing conversation over time.

4 *Comments as part of the conversation between users and the museum*: the act of contributing is a reciprocal one. On the one hand, the incorporation of visitor response elements recognises the value the museum places on the expertise and understanding users bring with them. On the other hand, the museum and its other users will benefit directly from the depth of visitors' responses.

There are major differences between the sorts of comments users make in comments books in a public area of the museum and the deep, thought-through responses obtained when comment devices are located within exhibitions and focus on specific content. It is these that can generate additional discussion, particularly when users can read or listen to the comments left by others. And it is up to the museum to create the location for responses and build an environment that encourages reflection and a desire to contribute:

We selected our artefacts to elicit a wide range of memories. We set aside a memorial area, a distinctive design indicating that it was intended for commemoration. And,

> most important, we asked our visitors to participate. We encouraged them to write down their memories of the war, and we displayed their contributions prominently, so that other visitors could share them.
>
> Lubar (1997: 18)

Today, museums would say that in the name of access, users should have the opportunity to comment in the form they feel most comfortable with, including provision of video booths. I retain a preference for writing, both because of the reflection involved in constructing a written response and because of the ease with which other users can share it.

I would add that a language also needs to be created across the museum, so visitors know what is being done with their input – whether it is forwarded to another institution, archived in the museum, or simply there for others to respond to and thrown out at the end of the day or month. For example, unlike most museum services, the London Transport Museum retains user-generated content alongside existing collections and documentation. The impact has added substantially to the number of images held. It has also led to several hundred cataloguing queries that challenge or correct existing museum information (Mackay 2010: 30).

Online conversations about collections

In 1985 Michael Ames appealed for the 'democratisation of the museum'. The tight control by staff of access to collections had given museums a reputation for elitism. Since then, the issue of access has moved dramatically up the ladder of priorities, resulting in museum initiatives from 'visible storage' (for example at the Museum of Science and Industry, Manchester, or Brooklyn Museum, Brooklyn) to the recent rise of digital access to collections and to the information held on them. This has been supported by changes in professional attitudes. The public right to access is now enshrined in the codes of ethics of most national museums associations. Museums have also appreciated both that digitisation makes greater use of previously underused assets (collections that are not on display) and that public expertise can add to knowledge and understanding of material held in their collections.

The remarkable expansion of online museum provision and the development of social media in the last decade means that conversations about collections can develop without a museum visit and continue after one. Many museums and archives hold collections acquired from former colonies at a time when Western culture was held to be superior. Many of the objects and images have very little documentation attached to them. I discuss in Chapter 8 the 'revisiting collections' initiatives through which museums are engaging with local communities to draw out new relevancies and additional meanings. The internet has become a global means of doing the same thing. In February 2011, for example, the UK National Archives uploaded on to Flickr several thousand pictures taken in Africa between 1860 and 1960 by staff from the former Colonial Office, inviting visitors to tag and comment on them in an attempt to add to our understanding of them (www.flickr.com/photos/nationalarchives/collections/7215762582738771). This approach has other uses also: for example, the Jewish Museum in Prague asked the public to identify members of the Jewish community from wartime photographs (Jelinek undated, www.jewishmuseum.cz, referenced in Mackay 2010). A better-known example is the USA Holocaust Memorial Museum's Remember Me project (http://rememberme.ushmm.org/), where the museum put up online the images of 1,100 children displaced during the Nazi era. The museum hopes the public will help to both identify and piece together the children's wartime and post-war experiences.

But the potential for online conversations goes beyond enhancing collections' documentation or providing access for what might be called 'citizen researchers'. Goal 3 (Learning) of the Smithsonian's Web and New Media Strategy (Smithsonian Institution 2009) focuses on 'facilitating a dialogue in a global community of learners', with programme goals that include online provision becoming 'an important catalyst for engagement and enquiry, particularly for younger and more "Web 2.0" kinds of audiences ... built on a foundation of broad and unrestricted access to information, social sharing, creativity, play, and participatory learning'.

Perhaps the most talked about example of museums using new media to develop conversations around collections has been the adoption of folksonomy, or 'social tagging'. Typically this is web-based, and the tags become immediately available for others to see. For museum collections, it allows ordinary users to assign their own keywords to describe an object or image, in contrast to museum standard descriptions. The best known case study remains the Steve Project (www.steve.museum), a collaboration particularly between the Smithsonian National Museum of American Art, the Metropolitan Museum of Art and the Guggenheim Museum:

> Steve is a collaboration of museum professionals and others who believe that social tagging may provide profound new ways to describe and access cultural heritage collections and encourage visitor engagement with collection objects. Our activities include researching social tagging and museum collections; developing open source software tools for tagging collections and managing tags; and engaging in discussion and outreach with members of the community who are interested in implementing social tagging for their own collections.
>
> Steve project, website introduction

There are clear positives to tagging. It gives the public direct influence on one of the inner workings of a museum, its documentation process, thereby democratising terminology by allowing the public to inform practice. Steve research found 86 per cent of tags used in response to the works of art included in the project were not found in museum documentation (Trant 2009). In the process, tagging enhances a sense of ownership and loyalty among users. There are also problems, not least in the lack of consistency and issues around bias. The Steve Project is now seeking to counter issues like these, particularly by ranking contributions by the level of knowledge they contain – users will be able to see if the comments are by experts, enthusiasts or the general public (Mackay 2010: 19–20). The approach to tagging at the Brooklyn Museum was discussed in Chapter 2. Tagging is at such an early stage that it is important also to explore its use in environments other than museums. Tonkin et al. (2008) provide an overview of wider research worldwide.

On-site voting was discussed above. Online voting is another means of engaging younger audiences particularly. The Click exhibition, again at Brooklyn Museum, is an example of this and is also discussed in Chapter 2.

Conversations about the work of the museum

Democratising the museum can go beyond providing enhanced access to collections. It can also help develop a greater understanding among users about what museums are for and what they do. One of the first areas to open up in this way was the work of conservators. The Conservation Centre, National Museums Liverpool, actually won the European Museum of the Year Award in 1998, eventually closing to the public in December 2010. Conservation-in-public programmes have become popular features in museums, including Manchester Art Gallery. Visitor access to those carrying out conservation and research lies at the heart of the Darwin Centre at the Natural History Museum in London. Behind-the-scenes tours are regular features at National Trust sites, particularly for events like 'putting the house to bed' as conservators prepare the Trust's historic houses for the winter period when they are closed to the public.

Opportunities to 'meet the expert' have been a feature of museums since their inception. In the last decade, however, online provision through blogs, Facebook and Twitter has transformed user access to 'behind-the-scenes', with regular opportunities to 'meet' staff and gain an in-depth understanding of what they do through following their activities and enthusiasms over time. These 'conversations' are surely vital to transforming museum visitors into users, bringing with them a depth of understanding about the role of museums in society and helping to engender loyalty and enthusiastic support.

Evaluating visitor engagement with objects

Research into the quality of the visitor's direct engagement with collections is still relatively in its infancy. It combines the observation of external evidence of visitor engagement through tracking and timing – see, for example, Serrell (1998) – with qualitative study of the less observable internal responses, through comment cards, visit diaries, qualitative interviews and real-time study of visitor conversations – see, for example, Abu-Shumays and Leinhardt (2002), Allen (2002), Falk and Dierking (2000), Hilke (1988) and Silverman (1995). Two of these articles are included in Leinhardt et al. (2002) *Learning Conversations in Museums*, a remarkable book which has transformed my own understanding of how visitors respond to objects.

In researching conversation, Fienberg and Leinhardt defined four levels of engagement among adults:

1. People may engage in a simple, unidimensional response to the content in the form of a phrase that identifies an object or a list of features, but seldom extends further. We call this Listing.
2. The conversation may include analysing underlying features of an object, a process or an abstract concept. We call this Analysis.
3. The conversation may integrate multiple ideas across knowledge sources (e.g. from outside the museum or from other exhibit stations within the museum) in order to support an idea. We call this Synthesis.

4. Some combination of analytic and synthetic discourse may be brought to bear on the task of helping one or another member of the group (including oneself) understand how or why something exists as it does, works the way it does, or happened the way it happened. We call this Explanation.

Fienberg and Leinhardt (2002: 170)

The authors recognised, of course, that users arrive with their own agendas, will view content through their own personal experiences and engage in these levels of activity informally.

Allen coded museum conversation (learning talk) around five main categories:

1   *Perceptual talk* ... all kinds of talk that had to do with visitors drawing attention to something ...
2   *Conceptual talk* ... cognitive interpretations of whatever was being attended to in the exhibit [a reflection on one's own current or previous knowledge] ...
3   *Connecting talk* ... any kind of talk that made explicit connections between something in the exhibition and some other knowledge or experience beyond it ...
4   *Strategic talk* ... explicit discussion of how to use exhibits ...
5   *Affective talk* ... all expressions of feeling, including pleasure, displeasure and surprise or intrigue ...

Allen (2002: 275–6)

Allen's evaluation of the Frogs exhibition at the Exploratorium in San Francisco showed that some form of learning talk took place at 83 per cent of the locations where groups stopped. At only 3 per cent of exhibit stops visitors discussed something that did not contribute to exhibit-related learning (Allen 2002: 293). These highly positive results bring us back once more to the concept of engaging *with* our users. While the objects themselves act as catalysts for conversation (Stainton 2002: 219), rather than just delivering didactic content, it is fundamentally important that museums continue to experiment with other forms of mediation designed to engender informal conversation and discovery that lead to explanation. But they must also do this sequentially, so our users move at their own choice from one conversation to the next.

7   Stimulating family conversations in the museum

INTRODUCTION

> The very first learning group a person belongs to is her family and this group is so important that anthropologists, sociologists and social psychologists refer to the family as an educational institution, similar to a museum or school but without the bricks and mortar.
>
> Dierking (2010a)

Families – by which I mean a 'multi-generational visiting group who are related to each other by blood, residence or close personal association' (Borun 2008: 6) – are already a core audience for museums, making up more than half of non-school visitors. Most museums recognise the clear benefits in reaching out to family groups, as outlined in Box 7.1.

Box 7.1 The benefits to a museum in reaching out to families

- Grow your audience.
- Enhance user engagement, enjoyment and satisfaction.
- Turn one-off visitors into regular users.
- Meet the needs of a unique learning group.
- Build future adult museum visitors through 'arts socialisation' as children.
- Engage with disadvantaged communities through their children.
- Help to develop the community you serve.

This chapter focuses on ways the engaging museum can and should further develop its support for family engagement and learning. It reflects a developing recognition worldwide of the critical role parents play in their children's education, and that child development suffers when parents are not actively involved. We can no longer allow the role of child educator to be the sole responsibility of schools ('even children spend 91 per cent of their waking hours outside of school', Dierking 2010b). As was discussed in Chapter 5 when exploring 'complementary learning', if we can recognise that child learning takes place in multiple contexts, not just in school, and that parents are at its heart, parental involvement becomes key:

Seen through this lens, parent involvement suddenly becomes not just a school problem, but a community problem that is the responsibility of each organization in the community that claims an educational mission. And that includes museums.

Luke and McCreedy (2010: 9), their italics

There are few resources available to help build the capabilities of parents to support their children's learning, and museums and other arts organisations have the potential to make an important contribution. Unlike the formal environments of schools, museums – if they get their welcome right – can be unthreatening, non-hierarchical environments in which families can engage, enjoy themselves and learn together. Museums already make a strong case for being dynamic centres for free-choice family learning:

- They offer opportunities for younger children to explore, discover, make their own choices on what to do, and make sense of the world and their place in it.
- They enable older children to engage actively and in more depth while developing their skills for social interaction and collaboration.
- They provide families with opportunities to interact and enjoy learning together.
- They support everyone to become learners for life.

However, museums and other cultural institutions can play even more fundamental roles in the learning lives of families if they are willing to meet families at least halfway, becoming resources *with* them rather than *for* and *to* them. In this way, they can also build better win–win relationships among families, museums and communities, enhancing the public value of all three. (This major idea is explored in depth in Dierking 2011.) The engaging museum of the future needs to build on successful current mainstream approaches to family provision through its *commitment to support parents as their children's educators*, providing not only opportunities for families to engage together but also in the process helping to develop parents' skills and confidence.

These opportunities go beyond the physical museum to include extended resources that families can use in the home and community. It also means looking beyond the museum to partner other community organisations and agencies. This is *not* an attempt to repeat the 'expert/novice' relationship of the formal education system, replacing the expert/teacher with the parent. Although many parents try to assume this role during museum visits, the ideal in a free choice learning environment is when parents and children learn together and the whole process is driven by joint exploration and interaction.

However, the family audience is not a passive one, there only to meet the museum's learning agenda. Rather, the family visit will be heavily influenced by agendas and motivations within the family group. In developing content and programming for families, museums must build from the family agenda, not from their own. At the heart of the family agenda will be a social experience – the pleasure of enjoying doing something together. Reach Advisors' 2010 national study of USA museum visitors, which achieved over 40,000 respondents, revealed different emphases within what is a mixed family agenda of fun, family time and learning (Reach Advisors, February–April 2011). Families will balance learning and play, varying the intensity and pace of their visit, with parents often stepping back or doing something else while children play. A well-paced family visit relies on the museum providing a combination of resources to explore on the move and places to stop to engage more deeply and/or play (Graham 2009: 12–13).

The family museum experience will also be affected by the very nature of family audiences. Because they come in groups, the group dynamic is an important issue. The ways in which family members engage with each other will depend on the number of adults and children in the group. *Scaffolding* is central to the family visit, with parents and older siblings supporting the younger ones by simplifying content, maintaining attention and motivation, highlighting key elements and minimising frustration, while still allowing the child to maintain some control (Gaskins 2008: 11). However the presence of a toddler can dominate, limiting interaction between parents and older children. Equally, family members will not want to do everything together. They need opportunities to engage independently, or at varying levels of togetherness (Graham 2009: 14).

If museums are not only to provide opportunities for family learning but also to seek actively to develop parental skills as educators, they need the willing support of the families. Museums may also wish to support and encourage the skills of families as free-choice learners As for all free-choice learners, family members will want to decide for themselves what to explore, how long they want to spend and how they wish to engage. So long as they continue to talk with each other while doing this, we can be confident that they are learning together:

> Memory studies have shown that children tend to remember activities and objects that they and their parents looked at or did together, but only if they also talked about those objects and activities together during the experience ... Problem solving studies have found that children spend more time on-task, and learn more about a topic, when they are with an adult than when they are alone ... Thus, when adults and children talk together to try to understand a topic, they are able to learn more effectively ...
>
> Sanford (2009: 11)

Fortunately, most families enjoy and are very experienced at exploring and talking together. Family members share the exploration of an exhibition, reporting back to the group on things that interest them, what McManus has described as 'forage, broadcast and comment' activity (McManus 1994: 91). Conversation already lies at the heart of the family museum experience. Falk and Dierking noted that:

> Families with children interact, converse and provide information to one another in recognizable patterned ways that are repeated throughout the visit. In fact, the entire visit can be characterised as one single, large-group conversation, even though families engage in numerous small conversations that are constantly beginning and ending.
>
> Falk and Dierking (2000: 93)

Our challenge is to keep the conversation flowing. We must also try to help parents develop their abilities as interpreters, supporting additional learning, while also expanding their own understanding.

PRINCIPLES FOR SUPPORTING FAMILY LEARNING IN A MUSEUM

There will be no single way of successfully achieving these challenges. Rather, museums must talk with families, experiment, evaluate and improve. It is possible, however, to provide a framework by establishing core principles, outlined in Box 7.2.

Box 7.2 **Ten principles for supporting family learning in a museum**

1 The family visit is a holistic experience – every element must be 'family friendly'.
2 The learning needs of families and children are fundamentally different to those of adult visitors.
3 Family-focused approaches must be embedded within galleries throughout the museum to support engagement and discovery.
4 Providing support materials and ideas will encourage families to explore together.
5 Museum interventions play a key role in keeping family conversations going.
6 Families that are not used to museum visiting need more support.
7 Do not be afraid to raise big issues.
8 Prototyping and formative evaluation are essential.
9 Help ensure the conversation carries on after the visit.
10 Many characteristics of family exhibits also work well with adults.

The remainder of this chapter seeks to put some flesh on the bones of these principles.

1 The family visit is a holistic experience – every element must be 'family friendly'

This principle builds from Chapter 3. The *whole experience* matters to families. Making families feel welcome and comfortable both online and throughout their visit, and anticipating their needs from the moment they step into the museum, is central to the overall success of a family museum experience. For this to happen, there must be a commitment to families that pervades the entire organisation, from director to cleaner. Start by training front-of-house staff to speak to all the family, not just the adults.

In the USA, the Family Learning Forum (http://familylearningforum.org) was established by the USS *Constitution* Museum in 2004 as a way for history museums to share ideas and experiences on enhancing the family visit, and to encourage museums to develop their family audiences. While focusing on how to enhance family learning in history museums, the museum recognised from the outset that family friendliness came first. The result was their ten steps to family friendliness for museum management to take as a basis for encouraging learning, listed in Box 7.3.

***Box 7.3* Ten steps to encourage family learning**

- Get acquainted with your family visitors: How many are coming in?
- Step into the shoes of your family visitor: How family friendly is your facility?
- Check out your exhibitions: Are there effective elements for family interaction?
- View your programme schedule: What types of events do you offer for families?
- Reread your institutional mission and goals: Are you ready to welcome families?
- Consider your commitment: Are you willing to be a family learning advocate?
- Observe your visitors: Find out what they already enjoy in your museum!
- Practice a family-friendly perspective: Transform a programme to attract families!
- Revisit your exhibition: Try a new technique to engage all family members!
- Reflect on your 'family friendliness': Strategize possibilities at your institution!

http://familylearningforum.org

In early 2003, the UK journalist Dea Birkett wrote in her 'Travelling with Kids' column in the *Guardian* newspaper about being thrown out of a major Aztecs exhibition at the Royal Academy of Arts in London because her 2-year-old son shouted 'Monster' at a statue of Eagle Man. Hundreds of parents responded to say they were fed up being treated like pariahs in UK museums and galleries. So the Kids in Museums campaign was born. The *Guardian* asked its readers for their nominations for the most family friendly museum in Britain, and then sent families to test them against a newly created Kids in Museums manifesto. The winner, Killhope North of England Lead Mining Museum, was announced in February 2004. This has since become a highly sought-after annual award, while the Kids in Museums Campaign has updated its manifesto annually to reflect the comments of museum visitors, as illustrated in Box 7.4, and holds an annual Great Museum Debate. The campaign became an independent charity in 2006 (www.kidsinmuseums.org.uk). More than 200 museums in the UK have now signed up as members.

The point of arrival is crucially important

The museum should start by welcoming families and making them feel secure and at ease. The attitudes of front-of-house staff will be central to this: they should have specific 'welcoming' training. Providing information at the beginning of a visit, a welcoming brochure or even an A-board at the entrance outlining family activities available that day can be a real help. Offering families a choice of resources, such as trail leaflets and activity backpacks, can help them select how they want to explore.

The availability of good basic facilities will transform a family visit

Create a clear 'brand' for activities so that resources have a similar look and feel. This encourages participation from families as they will recognise the identity of the resource as something for them and seek out the next activity.

Blackwell (2009: 14)

Box 7.4 **Kids in Museums manifesto 2011**

Be welcoming. Cleaners, curators, front of house staff and those in the café should all be involved in making families feel welcome. Consider different families' needs, with automatic doors, wheelchair-user friendly activities and Braille descriptions.

Have flexible family tickets. Don't dictate the size of a family. Families come in all shapes and sizes.

Give a hand to parents to help their children enjoy the museum. Sometimes it isn't the kids who are shy. Parents need your support too.

Don't say ssshhhush! Museums are places for debate and new ideas.

Answer kids' questions – not just those asked by adults. Address them directly when you do so. You don't have to be experts on everything, just enthusiastic and open.

'Don't touch' is never enough. Say why. Use positive remarks like, 'Isn't that a great painting! Let's look at it together from further back.' Teach respect by explaining why some things shouldn't be touched. Direct to something nearby which can be.

Reach out to homes and communities. Not everyone can come to you. Sometimes, you need to go to them first.

Use your website to encourage families to visit and give clear information. Be honest about what you can't provide, so visitors come prepared. No one can do everything.

Don't assume what kids want. They can appreciate fine art as well as finger painting. Involve kids, not just adults, in deciding what you offer.

Don't forget toddlers and teenagers. Older and younger children are often left out. Every age brings fresh ideas and insights.

Be height aware. Display objects, art and labels low enough for a child to see.

Watch your language! Use your imagination with signs, symbols and words understood by all ages.

Be interactive and hands on, not only with computer screens and fancy gadgets. Dressing up and getting messy are as important as buttons to push.

Produce guides, trails and activities for all the family together, not just the kids. Encourage families to chat.

Have different sorts of spaces – big open spaces for children to let off steam. Picnic areas for families to bring their own food. Small quiet spaces where children and families can reflect. Provide somewhere to sit down.

Keep an eye on your toilets, and make sure they're always pleasant places, with baby changing facilities and room for pushchairs. It's the one place every family will visit.

Provide healthy, good-value food, high chairs and unlimited tap water. Your café should work to the same family friendly values as the rest of the museum.

Provide a place to leave coats, bags and pushchairs. It makes it far easier for families to move around.

Sell items in your shop that aren't too expensive, and not just junk, but things kids will treasure.

Give a friendly goodbye. Ask families to describe the best bit of their visit, either in words or pictures. Respect these responses and act on them. Invite them back.

www.kidsinmuseums.org.uk

Lots of seating is a must – for adults and children. Seating for adults near child activity areas is particularly welcome. Comfort is equally important – soft areas encourage quiet play, while seats for curling up in lead naturally to storytelling. The shop is an important part of the visit for children and must include an exciting and affordable range of small items, targeted at their age range and pocket money.

Spaces designed for children must embrace the principles of Universal Design

Universal Design, making physical access an integral part of exhibition design from the outset, is discussed in Chapter 4 and should underpin every museum development. In practice, these guidelines enhance access for every visitor, and are an essential framework for ensuring that all children, those developing typically as well as those using assistive devices, can make full use of the museum environment. While the first principle (Equitable Use) is the ultimate goal of ensuring full access for everyone, the second principle (Flexibility in Use) is the easiest to illustrate in terms of relevance to all families. Here we are looking not only at different washroom options for children of different ages but also at different exhibit, table and chair heights; there should be different types of seating to meet differing needs, different sizes of handles, a variety of tools and props, and so forth. Intuitive design, easily understandable signage, and variety of content (including quiet areas, multisensory experiences, being able to learn from mistakes) make engagement possible at the cost of minimum fatigue. They support children to engage at their current developmental stage. All are essential (Kanics and Scrivner-Mediates 2008). Wide passageways not only allow children in wheelchairs to pass each other but also cater for children in groups. Staff training is, of course, a vital element:

> Staff members need to be trained to have a person-first focus, meaning that each child and visitor is seen as a person first, each with unique strengths and weaknesses, likes and dislikes. When a parent says, "My child has autism; tell me what play things are here for him," the answer should be, "Tell me what your child likes to do and then I can give you some ideas of the best place to start your visit with us."
> Kanics and Scrivner-Mediates (2008: 42)

Broken-down hands-on exhibits are highly frustrating

Children tend to hammer hands-on exhibits they like; these must therefore be capable of withstanding full frontal attack. Children get frustrated if the experience is disappointing, if there are large queues for popular hands-on exhibits, or if key exhibits are broken. Their boredom threshold is low.

The nature and quality of museum food offered to children in museums is a constant issue

I want to burn the ubiquitous cardboard box. It's usually covered in colourful cartoons of monkeys swinging in the jungle, and your child is invited to put five items inside, all of which taste rather like the cardboard container. Cheap crisps, curled sandwiches, processed cheese, crumbled crackers . . .

Birkett (undated)

Why is so much museum food, especially that targeted at children, so bad? Dea Birkett firmly believes that if you want 'to gain the heart and soul of a family, it is often easier if [you have] won over their stomachs first.' She highlights the wonderfully simple ideas of a small Belgian organisation Eetiket, dedicated to making the eating experiences of families more fun and more educational, especially in museums:

> The 22 Flemish museums that participate in EETiKET teach children about the food in their collection and serve special dishes in their restaurants. The dishes refer to what is to be seen in the museum itself. Hungry for a brainteaser soup in the toy museum and a Picasso sandwich in the museum of modern art?
>
> Birkett (undated)

Other examples Birkett explores include the Mitsitam Native Foods café at the National Museum of the American Indian in Washington, where traditional Native American food is cooked over timber fires and little 'food facts' are left on the tables each day. And, of course, meals stimulate conversation among family members – just what we want to encourage reflection on their visit. In the summer of 2008, a 'Big Lunch' initiative at the Eden Project in Cornwall, UK, included giant conversation starters hung from the ceiling in the cafe encouraging families to discuss where food came from.

A friendly departure also matters

This can include an invite to come back and news on forthcoming events. Feedback and evaluation form part of this and are vital to remaining family friendly.

A word about safety

In developing displays targeted at young children, there are some basic common sense practical issues to consider: using non-toxic materials, avoiding sharp edges, eliminating choking hazards, using hard and easily cleaned surfaces for messy areas. Doors, sockets and stairs need to be safe. It is important for young children to be able to move about freely and decide for themselves where to go and what to do. *However* – it is equally important for parents to be able to keep track of them. Having only one entrance/exit helps, as does an open floor plan. Exits should be young child proof. Safeguarding policies and procedures should be in place.

2 The learning needs of families and children are fundamentally different to those of adult visitors

> Interpretation addressed to children (say, up to the age of twelve) should not be a dilution of the presentation to adults, but should follow a fundamentally different approach.
>
> Tilden (1977: 9)

Family learning is a truly socio-cultural experience. Families are intergenerational groups that come in all shapes and sizes, and the group visit will frequently consist not just of parents and children but of grandparents and others too. A family visit will, therefore, involve not only different learning styles but also very different levels of experience, understanding, intellectual development and capabilities. The dynamics of the visit will also change, with children and adults leading at different times, driven by what grabs their attention. The reality is that no single kind of resource will meet all the needs of the wide variety of families visiting museums – but encouraging and enabling multi-sensory exploration, including exploratory play, will always be an essential element.

There is one increasingly important change in the family visit agenda. Whereas parents in the past were perhaps focused on the learning of their children, they now expect to engage with content also. Taylor and Houting examine contemporary adult motivations behind family visits:

> Nearly 75% of elementary school aged children have parents who are part of Generation X ... Gen X parents, born between 1961 and 1981, are more interested in spending leisure time with their children than were previous generations ... Whereas a baby boomer parent visited a museum *for* their child, a Gen X parent now wants to visit a museum *with* their child. This nuance is important; museums must now serve the needs of both parents and children. Gen X parents come to the museum expecting that they and their children will have a good time and will each learn something new.
>
> Taylor and Twiss Houting (2010: 241–2)

There are also major differences in the ways families seek to engage with museum content from the way those without children do, reflected in a Reach Advisors study using the example of history museums, outlined in Box 7.5.

Children bring with them many physical and sensory needs. Their social and communication skills are still developing. They have a remarkable capacity for excitement, vivid imaginations and an overwhelming desire to get involved. They are immensely curious when engaged, and like to learn through play and active exploration. They will show high levels of concentration and also return to the same activity time and time again. As a starting point, Rawson (2010) highlights the importance of the application of child developmental frameworks to the creation of exhibitions. These frameworks, in common use by paediatricians and educators, define the milestones in a child's social, linguistic, cognitive and physical development that reflect the vast differences between 3- and 12-year-olds. In museum use, they 'distil research on children's capabilities at various ages as they relate to specific exhibition content ... A developmental framework ensures an exhibition is shaped – not only by content and a point of view but also by a focussed understanding of kids' (Rawson 2010: 51). In particular,

---

Box 7.5 How visitors prefer to engage with history museum content

For those without children at home:

On our own (61% prefer)
By talking with staff (59%)
Viewing objects (50%)
Attending programmes/events (48%)

Parents who have children at home respond in a similar order, with one notable exception:

By talking with staff (60%)
On our own (58%)
Hands on activities (55%)
Attending programmes/events (43%)

Hands on activities, which scores a 26% preference for adults without children, is a preference for 55% of those with kids, while viewing objects drops off the list.

Reach Advisors (May 2010)

Rawson's chapter includes a case study of the creation and application of a developmental framework for the World Brooklyn exhibition at Brooklyn Children's Museum. A generalised developmental framework can be found at Gyllenhaal (2006).

3 Family-focused approaches must be embedded within galleries throughout the museum to support engagement and discovery

Many museums run family activities at weekends and during school holidays, but it is essential to have things that are always available, to ensure consistent opportunities for family engagement and to signal that families are always welcome, throughout the museum, not only in certain places at certain times.

Unsuccessful exhibits for children tend to be passive with little or no interaction, to require reading skills, to have confusing or unclear spaces, and to be not directly related to children's experiences – in other words, many typical museum displays. However, it is not difficult to create successful, child friendly exhibits; there is no need for a museum to start from scratch. Thanks to the success of the children's museum movement, there has been specific research on what type of exhibits work with young children. This work has had an increasingly important influence on the wider museum movement. Regnier (1997) identified several elements in successful designs for children's exhibits, including gross motor activities, multisensory activities, sand and water, real objects, role-playing with costumes and props, animals, places to hide, opportunities to emulate adult activities, assembly and disassembly, and experimentation that requires little formal instruction. For very young children (under c. 3 years of age), the most appropriate approach is almost certainly to create small, safe environments within galleries, alongside displays, containing toys and other material that children can play with:

Young children learn by doing. Every action – including pushing, pulling, mouth-ing, grabbing, throwing and balancing – gives them more information to make sense of a complicated world.

Young children are tuned in to myriad sensations at any given moment – the sur-prise at hearing a new sound, the fascination with a whirling ceiling fan, the endless experiments to see "what would happen if?"

A child's task is to figure out the nature of objects, materials and people, and how they all interact.

The challenge then is to create exhibits and experiences that match the develop-mental levels and needs of young visitors . . .

Oltman (2000: 15)

For children aged 3–7, museums can aim much higher than this. All children learn by doing and by imagining. It is the museum's task to provide opportunities for both. This is relevant both to structured educational use by 3- to 7-year-olds and for use during family visits. For children of all ages, tactile experiences are an essential. Natural objects, replicas and authentic handling objects should all be incorporated into displays. For some material, extra depth can be added by a staff member at a handling session pro-viding support for closer observation by supplying magnifying glasses for looking, for example, at minibeasts. Engagement in this way will stimulate family interaction.

Interactive exhibits have been a growing element in museum content since the late 1960s. Most early examples were developed substantially for use by children, with par-ents talking and explaining. For example, '81% of children's time in the [original version of the] *Launch Pad* at the Science Museum in London was spent interacting with family members and other visitors, with the adults playing the roles of interpreter, teacher and explainer' (Astor-Jack et al. 2007: 220). Today, there is much more interest in the development of exhibits where groups, especially families, can interact together – and designers must learn how to design for multi-age groups. The evidence suggests that, for families with children of over 7, the exhibits that most effectively support user engage-ment are those that encourage social interaction, discussion and involvement within and beyond the groups involved. When it comes to the design of exhibits that groups can explore together, we can look at the work of the Family Science Learning Research Project established by four museums in the Philadelphia area in 1998. The results were published as Borun et al. (1998) *Family Learning in Museums: The PISEC Perspective.* The authors established a list of seven characteristics of family friendly exhibits (p. 23):

1 Multi-sided – the family can cluster around the exhibit.
2 Multi-user – interaction allows for several sets of hands and bodies.
3 Accessible – the exhibit can be comfortably used by children and adults (for ex-ample, there are varying exhibit heights so that all of the group can use them – im-portant for those with disabilities as well as for children).
4 Multi-outcome – observation and interaction are sufficiently complex to foster group discussion.
5 Multi-modal – the activity appeals to different learning styles and levels of knowledge.
6 Readable – text is arranged in easily-understood segments.
7 Relevant – the exhibit provides cognitive links to visitors' existing knowledge and experience.

When exhibit components that embodied these characteristics were added to existing exhibitions in the four PISEC museums, family learning was measurably increased.

This framework does not just apply to science exhibits – the USS *Constitution* Museum used the PISEC framework to develop an interactive exhibition for families called A Sailor's Life for Me (http://familylearningforum.org). The framework is also not only relevant to exhibits targeted at families. The defined characteristics relate to any exhibit that people are encouraged to use together.

Based on research with four UK museums services in 2006–8, Blackwell (2009) highlighted five display elements that help to engage families, outlined in Box 7.6.

Box 7.6 Elements to incorporate within displays to engage family audiences

Looking through
Children and adults like looking at each other through display cases. This simple effect prompted people to communicate their pleasure and excitement, especially where the cases are low and families can move around all sides.

Looking in
Ideas which work well are peepholes, magnifying glasses, lifting flaps, clear domes and exhibits where visitors can poke their heads in. Providing things for visitors to peer through doesn't have to be expensive. The Potteries Museum, Stoke on Trent, put a small willow screen in their river display, with a hole cut out. Peeping through gave children a 'secret' view of a duck's nest and prompted lots of family communication.

Getting close
Children get really excited if they can touch things, especially animals, large objects and unusually shaped items. They also love different textures and things that provide an unexpected surprise (a sound going off or something popping out). Carers will respond by also touching and talking about the object. You can hide objects behind curtains or in 'feely holes' to add an element of expectation.

Making a noise
You can encourage carers to make the noises of animals or machines for their children to copy by providing the relevant toys, puppets, hats and so on. However, everyone finds excess noise disruptive. Musical instruments for example, whilst child friendly, can stifle communication. Too much noise will mean some groups move away from an activity or people begin to shout. Planning for quieter activities and using sound absorbent materials in more noisy areas can help keep the right balance.

Be aware of physical spaces
Intimate spaces, such as places to crawl inside for both an adult and child, encourage communication, as long as such spaces are welcoming. Routes which are atmospheric, such as a themed corridor leading to an exhibition, also encourage closeness between adult and child.

Blackwell (2009: 15–16)

Fantasy is an intimate, personal and imaginative thing. To the child there is a potential for fantasy within every experience. Interpretive displays that encourage fantasy can spark interest and involvement, even though the display itself may be quite static. Dressing up, as well as opportunities to listen to or tell or draw or read or write or re-enact stories, will all be successful with children. Places to read stories together can often be calming for families. Story reading will not be universally popular, however, as it is in competition with more physical activities. Parents will also often choose puppets as an activity and then have difficulty thinking about how to use them. Dressing up can also have limitations:

> Where children did dress up, it tended to lead to the child pretending independently. Interaction was limited to parental comments on how nice children looked, although this did provide positive affirmation and the photo opportunity it provided may have led to further interaction after the visit.
>
> Graham (2009: 10)

Denver Art Museum has 25 locations across its galleries containing almost 50 family activities. Given the need to convert family visitors into regular users and the obvious fact that children get older over time, the Denver approach of rotating activities over a two-year cycle makes a lot of sense: it is 'a cost-effective and efficient way to change offerings while keeping their quality high. It also allows the museum to invest in new backdrops that can be used again and again' (Denver Art Museum 2002a: Kids' Corner 7).

While a major replanning of the overall provision was possible at Denver Art Museum, people rarely have the opportunity to do this. As a complete contrast, Hardwick Hall is a sixteenth century mansion in Derbyshire, UK, managed by the National Trust. As it still contains most of its original furnishings, there is limited scope for change to the visitor experience. Yet, even here, it was possible in 2010 to develop 10 hands-on interactive activities and locate these in rooms along the visitor route. The activities included wooden floor jigsaws located adjacent to the relevant portraits in the Long Gallery, accompanied by a self-portrait drawing activity table; there was also provision of close-up details of parts of objects and furniture in the High Great Chamber, with families encouraged to locate the objects themselves. The result, for a total spend of £1,200 ($2,000), has been a much longer family stay, with parents and children all deeply engaged in the activities.

4 Providing support materials and ideas will encourage families to explore together

Developing support materials and ideas based around existing displays as well as new ones can comprehensively enhance the family visit and the quality of engagement and learning that takes place. The formats used must be easily understood but, done well, the activities created will enable children and adults to be equal co-learners. The materials can help children develop learning skills that will stay with them for life, while also developing the skills of the adults at facilitating their children's learning (Adams 2005: 10). This is important for all family groups, but it has a particular resonance for home-educating families. With an estimated 1.5 to 2.5 million home-educated students in the USA alone, this is a considerable potential audience of regular users for museums (Bachman and Dierking 2010).

Trails

Trails are cheap to create and popular with both adults and children. Imagination, lateral thinking and piloting are key to the process. For younger children, the challenge is to position objects that get children talking and then develop a series of multi-capability activities (such as finding, counting, comparing, drawing and touching) around them. In Brian's Mouse Trail at the Pitt Rivers Museum in Oxford, children must find 12 wooden mice hidden in cases around the museum, using clues and a map to help their search. When children have found all the mice they write a letter to the museum mouse and are given a 'mouse collector' sticker. For older children, pictures of objects to find, drawings to complete and carry-round challenges – such as finding a 'home' for toy farm animals, solving riddles or scavenger hunts – can add a new dimension. Riddles can be particularly effective in drawing a child's (and parent's) attention to the details in paintings and objects, as in the case of this rhyme as riddle about a suit of Samurai armour at the Denver Art Museum:

> I may be bold, my armour is black.
> I carry a sword upon my back.
> I fight for Japan, day by night,
> In hopes of chasing enemies out of sight.
> I wear a mask on my face,
> With some string held in place.
> I am a warrior, big and bright.
> Who am I? You guessed right.
>
> Denver Art Museum (2002a: Holiday Weeks 3)

Activity backpacks

Backpacks cost time and money to develop and pilot, but children love to carry them and enjoy the self-paced activities – both the independence they bring and the opportunities to do things with their families. The Victoria & Albert Museum in London provides good advice in developing packs in V&A (undated). Piloting of activities is essential and I particularly like the advice not to make the pack too heavy for the child to carry! Good activities will seek to immerse young visitors into the experience, treating them not as passive observers but as participants. They will also encourage direct and immediate experiencing of objects. They should preferably support family use – providing a model for how parents and children can engage and hold conversations together around collections – and help pace visits by creating places to stop to complete tasks.

Jo Graham builds from the idea of the backpack by recommending the use of 'exploring tools' to add imagination and additional activity:

> Torches, binoculars, magnifying glasses and cameras (pretend or real) were universally popular and resulted in visits where children determined the visit route, and what was examined and discussed ... A torch can allow a child to independently

explore and investigate or it can be the start of an intrepid family adventure. It can even be both things in the course of one family visit.

The exploring tools seemed to act as a non-verbal indication of children's interest for parents. Parents would notice what their child shone their torch onto, or see their child peering through their magnifying glass at something and talk with them about it. Parents frequently asked children what they could see through the binoculars or commented on things they thought children could see.

Graham (2009: 7)

'Unpacking the box'

Blackwell's research showed that having activities in boxes to unpack together encouraged families to communicate and gave adults a clear role: 'Children really enjoy taking things out of boxes and bags, showing their carers what they have found and talking about them' (Blackwell 2009: 17).

Linking the contents of the box to the gallery it was in encouraged further exploration. At the Royal Albert Memorial Museum in Exeter, the gallery boxes were locked. I thought this would be off-putting, but the children enjoyed going to the very friendly museum attendants for the key, as it made the box special to them.

Tables and art trolleys

All the available observational evidence suggests that basic colouring sheets do not generate conversation or engagement between family members. However, planned drawing and making activities do. At The Pottery Museum, Stoke-on-Trent, children were asked to design their own cow-creamers and then compare them with ceramic ones on display (Blackwell 2009: 17).

Drawing is universally popular. Art trolleys in galleries the world over encourage children to engage directly with the paintings or objects in front of them:

> Parents often joined in drawing activities, usually doing their own drawing but sometimes working jointly with children. Drawing together, side by side, seemed a very natural way for parents to model learning behaviour for their children.

Graham (2009: 16)

Play to the child's relationship with technology

Today's children have a special relationship with technology, having grown up with personal computers, the internet and mobile phones. Even young children use this technology to stay in constant contact and share experiences with friends, as outlined in Box 7.7. They will expect to be able to use this technology in the museum, for example downloading content or taking photographs and sending them to friends. Wireless access to the internet is becoming increasingly important.

Figure 7.1 **Utterly engaged**
A young child is captivated by the ceramic cow creamers at The Potteries Museum, Stoke. Courtesy of Stoke Museums.

Box 7.7 **Children and new technology**

- Children are immersed in a world of media and gadgets.
- They expect to gather and share information on multiple devices in multiple places.
- They prefer to get the material they want on a smartphone if they have one.
- Their technology is increasingly mobile.
- They have grown up with interactive media and want to manipulate, remix and share content.
- They are multi-taskers.
- Their approach to learning and research is shaped by this techno-world – more self-directed and less dependent on top-down instruction, more reliant on feedback and response, more tied to group knowledge, more open to cross-disciplinary insights.

based on Rainie (2006), as referenced in OP&A (2007a: 9–10)

Figure 7.2 Re-creating our street

Families, surrounded by images of historic Mansfield, draw their own street. All the activity cost was the price of a few rolls of lining paper, yet families were absorbed for hours by the scale of it. Courtesy of Mansfield Museum.

Just one aspect of the potential for the use of new technology is reflected in a report by Frankly, Green + Webb (2010), reflecting the growing impact of smartphones and apps since their first appearance in 2008. By mid-2010 there had been 4 *billion* downloads from the Apple App Store, while it is estimated that by 2014 half the population of western Europe and the USA will be using smartphones. Obviously it will be a long time before museums can rely on users to bring smartphones with them to access essential content, but we are already at a point where museums are using them to target specific audiences, particularly young people and families.

One of their more surprising discoveries was the high percentage of mothers who were downloading apps to support their children's learning. The report suggested two potential ways of using the smartphone to enhance the shared family experience of museum visiting:

1 helping parents create the visit content by providing tips, tricks, games and background information
2 using existing app technology to encourage making (photography, audio, drawing) and sharing (email, posting online, device to device connection).

This is very different to the traditional audio tour, which is normally a much more passive, listening-only experience and tends to isolate users from each other. Families, of course, have their own techniques for audio tours, such as synchronising usage to listen at the same time.

Special activities and events ensure there is 'always something new'

To keep children and the adults who accompany them coming back, programs need to be fed, watered and weeded on an ongoing basis. By continuing to listen to family visitors and to adjust programs as childhood itself changes, the museum can ... create a broad family audience.

Denver Art Museum (2002b: 6)

Special events should be planned on an ongoing basis, not as one-offs. This is important in turning families from visitors into loyal users, as activities can provide a focus for a return visit. When looking for new ideas, it is well worth asking your existing family audience for guidance on the types of programming they would like to see. Craft sessions are winners and reveal how effectively even children under 5 years old can concentrate for sustained periods of time if engaged:

An under-fives craft session at the Geffrye Museum [in London] lasts one hour 15 mins. In that time children handled snow globes from the handling collection, drew round their hands, cut them out, decorated them with shiny materials, created a reindeer headband, helped colour a large scale backdrop with chalks, posed for their photo, cut round and stuck photos on to a backing. Children from 22 months to five years were fully engaged for the time it took them to complete the activities, which varied between individuals.

Graham (2008: 13)

Stimulating return visits does not just build the museum's visitor numbers. Crucially, the more often families visit, the more 'museum literate' they will become, developing the skills and confidence to use the museum to the full. Building a loyal user base through an events programme can be an expensive business, but there are many opportunities for partnerships. In Oxford, the University Museums have come together to deliver a range of collections-based activities and events across the city, opening up the museums and their collections to people from a range of communities, many of whom had not previously used them. There are now activities every Saturday and Sunday and on many weekdays in school holidays. The museums encourage families to shift activities around the different venues, so there might be something for families in the Pitt Rivers Museum in the morning and something at the Oxford University Museum of Natural History in the afternoon. They have now developed enough family activities to provide a three-year rolling programme, although when an activity is repeated it is generally revised and improved. A cross-museums website lists all activities as well as promoting other museums in the city (http://www.museums.ox.ac.uk/db/events).

Some museums and art galleries, from the Guggenheim in New York to the Gallery of Modern Art in Tel Aviv, have introduced annual family day events, successfully bringing in hundreds of families. Many others, like Denver Art Museum, target family events to school holiday weeks.

Otago Museum case study

Otago Museum in Dunedin, New Zealand, first opened its doors in the 1860s and has had close links with the University of Otago since the latter was created in 1869. As a result, the museum has always seen itself as a teaching and learning institution. It has outstanding collections of culture, natural history and science. The museum underwent major redevelopment in the 1990s, beginning with the Discovery World science centre in 1991. Its Tangata Whenua Gallery, with important displays of Maori artefacts, was created with the help and guidance of representatives of Ngai Tahu, the local iwi, or tribe, in Otago. The museum is heavily used by local people and is also a major visitor attraction. The museum has worked hard to ensure a close link between its onsite and online provision.

The redevelopment of the museum provided an opportunity to build in family learning across the galleries, with a focus on providing parents with the skills to teach their children both within the museum and at home. Discovery World, the interactive science centre, is designed to encourage parental involvement. Entry level texts are kept simple, with support material readily available. Activity backpacks contain material relevant throughout the museum and include extra information aimed at parents. Regularly updated question trails lead families around the museum; they encourage parents' input by the way questions are structured. An interactive trolley contains touchable objects and specimens which appeal to adults but also has an associated activity developed for children.

Activities and events are free of charge or subsidised whenever possible, and are offered at times when families are more likely to be able to participate together. 'Good Morning Science' offers pre-school children a supervised science programme while their caregiver is shown simple ways to teach science in the home. Education, sleepover and birthday party programmes require a 1:6 adult to child ratio for all age groups

Figure 7.3 **Activity backpacks made highly visible**
Backpacks displayed prominently at Otago Museum provide an important avenue for young visitors and families to explore the themes of current exhibitions. Courtesy of Otago Museum.

and include stimulating content for the adults aimed at encouraging and empowering parental participation in their children's learning. For working parents, the Otago Museum offers after-school clubs, weekend activities and school holiday programmes which provide a supervised and fun educational experience for children within the museum. Science outreach programmes target families that don't come into the museum and are held at locations where families congregate, like shopping malls and beaches.

5 Museum interventions play a key role in keeping family conversations going

Family learning in museums comes only partly from museum content. Most of it comes through the family interactions and conversations that take place around that content. Sanford (2009: 12) defined four characteristics in adult–child learning conversations:

- involves talk around content
- takes on an explanatory stance
- connects to prior experiences or ideas
- provokes curiosity through questioning.

Thus, for example, children will understand more after their visit if parents made personal connections to content (Crowley and Jacobs 2002). It is crucial, therefore, to stimulate and support conversation. We cannot always rely on families to achieve this on their own – the way that museums develop their content can have a major influence as a catalyst for discourse (Borun 2008: 9).

Ensuring parents feel they have a clear role

[W]e need to anticipate the dynamics in family audiences – primarily by giving adults explicit roles that still leave room for kids to follow their instincts, take control, and indulge their sense of curiosity.

Ringel (2005: 2)

If the adults in the family group feel 'stupid' in their lack of knowledge, or uncertain and uncomfortable in their role in the visit, they will fail to interact with their children and may even move them on. It is essential that the museum does its best to help the adults and to encourage them to relax. Key issues, some already discussed, include:

- good conceptual orientation – what is this all about?
- ease of access to information
- clear signage for family-focused activities
- trails and similar activities that provide a clear route to engagement.

Writing for a family audience

Families WILL read – and engage – with labels, if we write, design and place them so families can easily see them, read them and use them!

Rand (2010b)

The cliché is that 'adults read while children *do*'. The really good news, however, is that adults *will* read labels aloud to children. We just have to provide text in a format they will use. Think *relevance* and *readability*. Rand emphasises that key essentials include the use of short texts (no more than 50 words), active language and simple words that present no need for parents to think of alternatives. Texts should be focused on what families can see and do at that point; they should be about what families want to find out rather than on what the museum thinks they should know. As for all visitors, the content will come alive if you can make personal connections between them and the stories you are telling, and ensure there is a human perspective. Labels that visitors find interesting will be read aloud more:

Find out from families what they are interested in, how they want to learn about the topic, and what will make the topic compelling, memorable, personally relevant and enjoyable. Just ask, they will tell you.

USS *Constitution* Museum (2010a)

Beyond these points, there is no right answer – you must experiment, pilot with families, and constantly try to improve. In a living history environment, the USS *Constitution* Museum found that first person labels made a real difference, as described in Box 7.8.

Box 7.8 The impact of first person text on family users

By simply changing the voice from third to first person the same content suddenly came alive.

Text delivered in third person
Every morning sailors holystoned (scrubbed) the deck. They took off their shoes, rolled up their pants and then got on their knees and scrubbed with water and sand. Sailors disliked this chore especially when it was cold.

Text delivered in first person
One of the things I dislike the most about being a sailor is holystoning (scrubbing) the decks each morning day after day. The worst is when it's cold. We take off our shoes, roll up our pants and get on our hands and knees, add salt water and sand, then scrub … scrub … scrub.

The proof is in the numbers
The Museum tracked and timed family visitors through two exhibitions: our traditional Old Ironsides in War and Peace exhibition and our family-focused prototype exhibit, A Sailor's Life for Me?

War and Peace is a 3,000 square foot exhibit with many long text panels totaling nearly 4,500 words, sensational objects, and a few interactives. We found that family visitors spent an average of 7 minutes in the War and Peace exhibit.

A Sailor's Life for Me? is only 2,000 square feet and contains about 1,500 words of text. Families spent nearly 22 minutes in the smaller exhibition and just as important talked to each other significantly more than in the War and Peace exhibition.

USS *Constitution* Museum (2010b)

Lateral thinking about location of text can also make a big difference. In the same exhibition, the museum team placed relevant text on mess plates, on pieces of sail on the 'deck', and on the ceiling in the hammocks area. Some of these are given in Box 7.9 overleaf.

Box 7.9 **Texts from the hammocks area, USS *Constitution* Museum**

Do you get more than 4 hours of sleep at a time? Not if you are a sailor in 1812!

Can you nap in your hammock during the day? No, off-duty sailors have to curl up on the wooden deck.

Do you like to sleep on your stomach? A sailor's life may not be for you.

USS *Constitution* Museum (2010b)

Supporting parents as 'instant experts'

Imagine someone at your elbow, someone friendly,
who knew the inside story.
Who could answer your questions.
Point out things you might not notice.

And know when to stop talking and be quiet.

based on Rand (2010b)

Judy Rand wrote this text thinking of the role of the label as the stand-in for that ideal companion. Instead, I want to think of the parent as the ideal companion who is actually there – and think of the museum's role as providing the information in the form and place needed by the parent to be that companion. Audio guides are not the answer – they are unsuitable for young children and separate family members from each other, the opposite of what we should be trying to achieve.

There is a basic need to ensure easy access to key information that will allow parents both to develop an adequate understanding to answer children's questions and to help them to make connections to children's previous experiences. If they do not have that understanding, they will not support/scaffold their children's engagement. Ensuring easy access means big bold headlines that parents can easily locate and skim, few words, the use of other media like images and diagrams, and the location of the information exactly where parents need it. For more depth, museums should consider placing display-related material adjacent to seating so that parents can read it, perhaps while their children play. Providing additional content online, targeted at children as well as adults, can be a further support mechanism.

However, there is always a risk of introducing a strong boredom factor into the visit. When led by adults, there is a tendency for conversations to focus on describing and identifying objects, with the answers given by parents rather than actively requested by children (Ash 2002: 7; Crowley and Galco 2001: 407). We do not want to lose sight of this form of knowledge-building, but we should actively seek to experiment with other ways to support conversation.

Figure 7.4 **Playing the game**
In displaying a British Museum touring exhibition of historic games, New Walk Museum at Leicester created replica copies of the games and encouraged visitors to play. Many families became engrossed.

Intuitive but intriguing hands-on activities can prompt parents to facilitate and explain

The most effective activities are invariably self-explanatory. However a key exception is an activity that the parents know and understand but is unfamiliar to children while also exciting their curiosity. These will encourage parents to support their children:

> Hands-on activities that needed no instructions for adults, but where children were not immediately sure what to do, encouraged parents to facilitate. For example, brass rubbing, grinding with a pestle and mortar and using a kaleidoscope. These kinds of activities often prompted parents to explain to children how a quill is used, what binoculars do or the most effective way to use a pestle.
>
> Graham (2009: 9)

Family friendly questions can encourage exploration and discussion

In my view, the best questions are those that come from the children and parents themselves, prompted by their curiosity and interest. However, family friendly questions posed by the museum can be another important way of stimulating discussion. Ones directly related to objects are outlined in Box 7.10.

Box 7.10 Questions that support conversation among families

Attention-focusing questions. Have you seen *x*? What have you noticed about *x*? How does it feel/smell/look/sound/taste? What are they doing?

Measuring and counting questions. How many, how often, how long, how much?

Comparison questions. How are these the same or different? How do they go together?

Action questions. What happens if?

Problem-posing questions. Can you figure out how to?

Reasoning questions. Why do you think?

based on Rand (2010a: 271)

Based on interviews with 300 families and tracking of a further 500, the USS *Constitution* Museum found that the most successful questions were ones that put visitors back in the historic time period and linked them directly to the story, with the most popular text panel being questions on the theme of 'How do you compare to an average [1812] sailor?' (Kiihne 2008: 58).

Living history can trigger conversation especially if combined with activities

At Conner Prairie, Indiana, Rosenthal and Blankman-Hetrick devised a scale of responses to indicate the family's level of involvement with the interpreter, outlined in Box 7.11.

Box 7.11 Family responses to a living history interpreter

Utterance: a family member acknowledges the interpreter by a polite utterance – 'hmmm', 'uh huh' and so on.

One word response: a family member acknowledges the interpreter with one word, such as yes or no.

Adult and interpreter dialogue: an adult or both adults are involved in a reciprocal and reflexive dialogue with the interpreter. Children are not participants.

Child and interpreter dialogue: Children in the family respond to and interact with the interpreter. There is little interaction with parents or other adults in the family.

Reciprocal and reflexive dialogue between all members: All family members are engaged in dialogue with the interpreter and express comments, reflections and questions.

Rosenthal and Blankman-Hetrick (2002: 315)

Their research highlighted the centrality of the role of the interpreter in stimulating exploration and conversation, and thus supporting learning: 'learning indicators occurred only occasionally during intra-family conversation without stimulus from an interpreter. Even though parents made repeated efforts to prompt their children to connect to what they were seeing, they usually had limited success' (Rosenthal and Blankman-Hetrick 2002: 316). It was the interpreters who provided the main impetus for active engagement.

At the USS *Constitution* Museum, the living history is supported by activities, from fetching water in a bucket, sweeping the floor or stirring soup to churning butter and playing historic board games. Here, the activities trigger engagement, conversations and future memories.

Seating has an active role

Seating can separate or unite a family; it can put parents/carers at the heart of the action or on the sidelines.

Cave (2010: 116)

Seating is not just a comfort issue. Its location, as the quote above from Vicky Cave emphasises, can decide whether parents and children engage together or not. It also creates remarkable opportunities for family conversation. Blackwell makes a particularly strong case for seating:

Providing cushions, carpet squares, mats or appropriate seating next to the displays encourages families to stay longer, look more closely and talk together. In a relaxing space, children are far more likely to initiate activities and carers are more likely to respond. Put well-lit, comfy seating in the centre of an activity, directly next to the related display.

Blackwell (2009: 14)

Family observation at the USS *Constitution* Museum also found that encouraging families to sit facing each other while engaging with exhibits stimulated conversation (Kiihne 2008: 59).

6 Families that are not used to museum visiting need more support

In England almost one half of all adults (17 million) have poor numeracy skills, and about 5 million have poor reading and writing skills (DfES 2007: 10). Many people in these circumstances lack the confidence to support their children. For example, ongoing research has revealed the vital importance of talking to babies and children in terms of their personal, social and emotional development – yet many parents and carers are unaware of this. Research across the UK has discovered high levels of language delay. One such example is in Stoke-on-Trent, where research in 2001 (Stoke Speaks Out undated) indicated that around 70 per cent of children entering nursery had a language delay. A UK government review in 2008 (Bercow 2008) argued strongly for an increased focus on support for the development of speaking, listening and communication skills in children.

What role could museums play in combating this? In 2009, Jonathan Douglas, Director of the UK National Literacy Trust, wrote:

> It is impossible to overstate the potential of museums in this context. They are echo chambers of the community's memory. In museums the voices of past generations as well as the experience of today can be heard. They are centres of story and identity. They stimulate talk like no other community space. Where else is the potential for intergenerational reminiscing so rich and stimulating? Museums make people chat. They have a unique role in supporting parents, grandparents and carers in talking to their children.
>
> Blackwell (2009: 4)

Yet there are huge barriers to overcome if we are to succeed in attracting those who believe museums are 'not for the likes of us'. The positive starting point is that all parents want to support their children and help them learn. They will be more likely to use museums if they feel their children will benefit. The considerable success of museums in attracting school groups from disadvantaged areas can be an important means of reaching these families – if the children are enthused, they will try to persuade their families to bring them back, especially if museums give them marketing materials and/or vouchers to take home. However, museums must recognise that the needs of families from disadvantaged communities will not always be the same as the needs of those from more advantaged backgrounds.

The warmth of welcome, and in particular the importance of personal contact with staff at the entrance, is vital in encouraging families who would not have previously considered coming to a museum to visit. Parents will feel very uncertain about 'how to behave' and will need encouragement to feel at home and relax. There is considerable evidence that encouraging parents to take part in activities with their children can help to develop speaking and listening skills and to build the confidence of both the adults and the children (National Literacy Trust 2006). Activities that are not collections-based but work well as ice-breakers may be an essential starting point. Jo Graham points to success with parents of young children:

> Using familiar toys encouraged families to interact and helped them make connections with home. Tea sets and pretend food for example were universally popular and encouraged imaginary play. Parents modelled how to use the toys to encourage children who were reluctant to join in.
>
> Graham (2009: 9)

Inviting groups of families to come together can be highly effective. The primary aim initially must be to build relationships and confidence. One way to achieve this is through the provision of learning programmes running over an extended period. Between 2006 and 2008, four museum services in England – The Potteries Museum and Art Gallery in Stoke-on-Trent, Peterborough Museum and Art Gallery, Worcester Museum and Art Gallery and the New Art Gallery Walsall – took part in a partnership project to investigate how collections and their interpretation can be used to nurture communication between babies, young children and their parents. The inclusion of

Stoke Speaks Out, a multi-agency partnership focusing on the issues underlying children's language deficits, was crucial in ensuring that project members understood the issues surrounding family communication. With this support the museums set out to create warm, welcoming and safe environments that encouraged communication and close family interaction – including comfortable seating close to displays, trails, treasure baskets, costumes, musical instruments, puppets, puzzles and places to play.

Parents and toddlers from the Stoke Speaks Out campaign were involved in the planning:

> By involving our parent and toddler groups it has empowered parents to have influence over their community environments which has given them in turn confidence and a feeling of being listened to – all good for their self-esteem.
>
> Stoke Speaks Out manager, quoted in Blackwell (2009: 10)

The museums involved saw considerable increases in visitor numbers, in dwell time and in return visits, as well as inspiring front-of-house staff who, like the parents, were involved from the planning stage.

7 Do not be afraid to raise big issues

Children's museums have been tackling difficult issues with their young audiences for decades. We can point, for example, to the development of Kids Bridge, an exhibition on multicultural themes, developed at Boston Children's Museum in 1989, at a time when the city was in the national spotlight as a racist city (Jones-Rizzi 2008: 22).

In the Power of Children exhibition at the Children's Museum of Indianapolis, children meet the stories of Anne Frank, Ruby Bridges and Ryan White, which are used to show how every individual can make a difference. Anne Frank was a Jewish girl who had to go into hiding during the Second World War to escape the Nazis and whose diary is now famous across the world. In 1960, Ruby Bridges, then 4 years old, was the first African-American child to attend an all-white school in the southern USA, on the first day of school integration in New Orleans. Ryan White (1971–90) was an American teenager who became a poster child for HIV/AIDS after being expelled from school because of his infection. He was a haemophiliac who caught the disease from contaminated blood.

The exhibition culminates at the 'Tree of Promise'. At computer keyboards in the gallery, children can make a promise that will change the world that will 'float up' into the tree, and can send that promise home or on to others via email:

> Families can then elect to join the Tree of Promise social network, an online space where they can share, expand and manage their promises. If at-home users complete their promises they can return to the museum, where the tree "remembers" and congratulates them on their success. In this way, the "Tree of Promise" takes a quick participatory in-museum experience – writing down a promise – and provides a supportive platform on which users can cultivate and substantiate that action.
>
> Simon (2007)

The same strong message 'that each person, child or adult, can make a difference in the world around us, and that change doesn't come mysteriously from on high but rather from our own, often collective efforts' (Bernstein and Gittleman 2010: 55) promoted in the Noah's Ark gallery at Skirball Cultural Center in Los Angeles, culminating in the Center's Build a Better World initiative.

The issue of mainstream museums tackling contentious questions will be discussed in Chapter 8.

8 Prototyping and formative evaluation are essential

Serving a family audience begins with knowing who that audience is, and understanding agendas, motivations and expectations. It moves on to testing, evaluating and seeking to improve every aspect of the family visitor experience. In particular, we need to know much more about how to design museum experiences that stimulate carers' interactions with their children more effectively.

Families are remarkably willing to assist in this task. Tracking, observation and careful listening, supported by interviews, can give a detailed understanding of how they engage with content and interact together. From this we can learn how best to support adult carers in developing the skills and confidence to scaffold their children's learning and interact with them around content. Boston Children's Museum, for example, is currently engaged in a research study looking at adult interactions with pre-school children, looking at the variety of roles the adult care-giver may play:

> The Adult-Child Interaction Inventory (ACII) was designed by Boston Children's Museum as a result of a three-year research study to answer the following questions:
>
> 1. What verbal and non-verbal interactions are families using to support pre-school children's STEM [science, technology, engineering, maths] learning?
> 2. What are the specific types of design strategies that support effective verbal and nonverbal interactions that can result in stronger STEM learning for pre-school children?
>
> Boston Children's Museum (2010: 1)

At the USS *Constitution* Museum, also in Boston, tracking and observation were supported by detailed evaluations of individual exhibits, illustrated by the extended quote below:

> Our fresh summer researchers tested the first interactive with family visitors. Families did not like it. The recruiting station is a simple two-sided table-top interactive with questions on one side and a related image on the other. We wanted families to take turns asking each other recruiting questions ... We hoped to encourage conversation about joining the ship's crew in 1812. The interactive met the PISEC criteria: it was multi-sided, multi-outcome, contained no pieces of text longer than 50 words, and had fun content. The problem? For starters, families did not know what to do ...

In just a few days, a procedure emerged. Our two researchers asked 10 or so families to try the interactive and recorded their feedback. We made changes on paper and taped them to the interactive. The next day we repeated the process. In less than two weeks the team significantly changed family satisfaction.

Kiihne (2008: 56)

Staff at the USS *Constitution* Museum came to see family visitors as partners in the development of the exhibition. Other approaches to the evaluation and refinement of individual exhibits can be seen, for example, in the work of Denver Art Museum (Denver Art Museum 2002 a and b).

9 Help ensure the conversations carry on after the visit

There has been limited research into the long term impact of the museum experience on family learning. Most of the research looks at relatively short timeframes (Anderson et al. 2007: 199). What is generally revealed is that cognitive and affective changes decline over time unless reinforced by subsequent experiences or by the impact becoming more personally relevant. While the ideal for the museum is to convert families into regular users, the minimum required is to make every attempt to encourage families to continue talking about their experience afterwards.

Conversations that began in the museum frequently continue on the journey home and afterwards:

Families can actively rehearse their museum visit by discussing their experiences with others ... or engaging in complementary activities like reading books on a topic they encountered within an exhibition ... In general, talking about and interacting with objects that reference a prior event like a museum visit, positively impacts what individuals remember about the event itself, and improves subsequent learning ... By linking ideas from a previous museum experience to conversations in everyday settings, families can also build upon their shared content understanding ... In contrast, if families do not engage in these reinforcing experiences, their memory of the original museum visit will decline.

Sanford (2009: 18–19)

Personal relevance can be hugely important and can trigger memories in the participants with dramatic impacts:

My mum – in her 70s – took my nine-year-old twins to the Imperial War Museum. They wandered around the 1940s house and she pointed out familiar objects from her childhood – the wireless, the tin of powdered milk, the quilted bedspread and china hot water bottle. She rarely speaks about her childhood. The following weekend, she came round with her identity card from the war. She hadn't taken it out for over 40 years. But a museum visit encouraged her to talk to her grandchildren about her youth, and entranced them. This conversation wouldn't have happened otherwise.

Birkett (2011)

However, having things to take away is a guaranteed way to encourage further conversation about the visit – completed trails, drawings done, objects from 'make and take' activities, stickers to collect, photographs taken. At Discover in Stratford, London, children receive a 'Story Book Bag' in which to build a personalised memento. This can combine items they collect around the site, such as tickets and maps, with their drawings and story-writing (Cave 2010: 111). The museum website also has an essential role to play, not just in allowing family members to follow up content but also enabling them to upload images and contribute their own content. Children can create their own gallery visit diary to share with friends and others.

We already have the technology for museums to email back to participants additional information on the material they accessed on-site. Hopefully the conversations are only just beginning.

10 Many characteristics of family exhibits also work well with adults

Many of the techniques discussed in this chapter are equally applicable to adults and will stimulate conversation and deeper engagement. The key is to not design exhibits and other elements to look as if they are targeted at children only.

DISCUSSION: CREATING A SPECIFIC GALLERY FOR CHILDREN AND FAMILIES

> Overwhelmingly, parents stressed that they needed a place in the museum where they could let their guard down, let their kids run free and play, and not worry about them touching things. Jungle gyms weren't the answer. Clearly and directly, parents said they wanted to feel like they were visiting the art museum.
>
> Denver Art Museum (2002b: Family Center 5)

More than any other audience segment, children will experience museum displays as part of a group, almost invariably including adults. But is this best done by creating a gallery targeted specifically at children and/or families or by incorporating relevant material throughout the museum? And, if we think of the family as an organic learning institution, will its need to interact together be best met in isolation or as part of a wider experience across the museum?

There is heated debate over whether families are best served by separate galleries or by integrating family content across the museum. Family galleries provide a 'place of their own' that is intentionally designed as such. Equally, creating a children's, or family, gallery is a clear physical commitment. It is lasting proof that your museum wants families to relax, enjoy themselves and engage with content in a child and family friendly way. Many art and history museums have created such galleries to counter the argument that they are passive and boring compared with sporting activities, zoos and science interactive centres. Family galleries are also a recognition that many children 'learn some tasks more easily via hands-on experiences' (Blake 2005: 1) and that younger children (say, under 5) may need to have an environment that specifically allows them to engage using all their senses. From the perspective of the museum

Figure 7.5 **Family Centre, Tel Aviv Museum of Art**
The centre is used heavily by families, but the museum also incorporates family focused activities throughout its galleries, including special events in the evenings on 'Enchanted Tuesdays'. Courtesy of Yael Borovich.

learning team, a child/family gallery may allow them to do things they cannot do elsewhere, experimenting with different interpretive techniques. Noise levels can also be higher, without disturbing other users. Such a gallery also provides an instantly recognisable advertisement for families who might be thinking of coming to the museum for the first time, providing a good introduction to the museum or just a change of pace (Denver Art Museum 2002b: Family Center 6).

The counter-argument would be that it is not enough just to build an area that is specifically targeted at children and/or families; it is as important to ensure that there are things for children and families to enjoy doing throughout the museum. We should want families to engage with the 'real thing' and to experience, appreciate and enjoy the full range of collections that the museum has to offer. Spreading family content across the site gives families an opportunity to engage with a wider range of material, and is more likely to encourage family interaction than in galleries specifically targeted at children. Having family content across the museum is a clear statement that families are welcome everywhere. In contrast, not encouraging and supporting family usage across the site could be interpreted as saying the rest of the museum really is passive and boring.

Like all aspects of interpretive planning, if museums create separate galleries targeted at children or families, they should be clear on why, and on what outcomes they are seeking. Are these galleries best as an introduction to new family visitors? Does the change of pace they permit provide an essential element in the whole visit – a key location, for example, where children can let off steam without risk of damaging priceless objects or disturbing other visitors? Can these galleries be used to introduce and build the skills required for engaging with collections as a family, including conversation? Can families then be encouraged to take those skills out into the galleries, perhaps using support materials?

In a perfect world, with plenty of available space and funds, museums should perhaps seek to do both. There is plenty of evidence of this being achieved successfully. Kids' Island at the Australian Museum, Sydney, was created in 1999 after extensive research through focus groups and interviews. These found that parents/carers wanted:

- plenty of space, including outdoor areas for play, exploration, fresh air and eating,
- activities where you actively participate through sensory experiences, especially touch, and where you can 'get up close',
- experiences that are content-rich, not superficial, and based on the organisation's strength,
- to start with, and then build on, familiar concepts and ideas,
- activities that are fun,
- a mixture of physical and quiet activities,
- activities that are specifically catered to the age/developmental needs of children,
- activities where parents can choose join in or just sit, watch and relax,
- facilities close by (e.g. toilet, nappy change and feeding areas),
- a safe environment where children can't escape, and
- an Australian focus on animals and culture, including Indigenous culture.

Kelly (2002: 7)

However, the voices of the young children themselves are rarely heard in the planning and evaluation of museum spaces developed for them. When the Australian Museum came to redevelop Kids' Island in 2005–6 audience research included 'opportunities for children to consider their understandings and impressions of that space, data about how they perceive and interact in the space and how they would change the space' (Kelly et al. 2006). Research participants were 40 children aged 0–5 who were regular visitors to the Australian Museum, and their families. Researchers used observation, interviews, structured activities, multisensory approaches and feedback sessions. Together these revealed children's competence with technology in the museum, the social nature of their learning and interacting, the attraction of 'real' as well as 'play' objects (particularly seeing animals and objects up close, as well as objects of different sizes), their sense of humour, and their ability to make connections between the museum and their homes or other settings.

While most children's galleries tend to target younger children, the Denver Art Museum Just for Fun Center, opened in 1999, is actually aimed at 6- to 12-year-olds, although it accommodates younger and older siblings and adults. Targeting different ages, styles and interests, 'its activities revolve around four types of play—challenge play where there is a definite outcome or winner, small world play where a child can create or imagine a world, dress up, and art making' (Denver Art Museum 2002b: 3). The centre was developed following meetings with their visitor panel. Importantly, those using it are encouraged to go back into the galleries also.

Case study: Mansfield Museum: UK kid-friendly museum of the year 2011

Whatever else you do, you want the children to feel that museums are to be enjoyed.

Liz Weston, Curator, Mansfield Museum

Mansfield is a small town in north Nottinghamshire which has suffered severe economic hardship since the collapse of its traditional industries of coal-mining, textiles, brewing and shoemaking. But it is a small town with a big heart. Its swimming club has produced an Olympic Gold Medal winner (Rebecca Adlington). Its ladies' choir (Cantamus) has a deserved international reputation. And now its museum has shown us all what can be achieved with vision, drive and imagination, despite few staff and a meagre budget. It has a part-time curator, a full-time museum development officer and a full-time education officer, together with the equivalent of 3.5 full-time gallery assistants.

Mansfield Museum first opened its doors in 1904, and for a century it remained a typical, small local museum with adult focused displays that rarely changed. But in 2004, while celebrating its centenary, the curator and her colleagues made a momentous decision to rebrand as a child friendly museum. They submitted a successful bid for grant aid to re-display the museum frontage, create a new children's gallery (XplorActive) and associated interactive website, and to fund the museum's first education officer. The museum has never looked back.

The children's gallery was only one element in the transformation. Although there was (and still is) no budget to replace the other displays, staff introduced brighter colour schemes and developed child-focused trails for other galleries and around the museum. The trails are changed regularly to keep families returning. Little details were also added – for example, in the very traditional ceramics gallery you will find a corner set up as a tea party with a child-sized table, chairs and plastic tea service. There are book corners throughout the museum. The shop stock was also changed to ensure there was something for all the children to buy.

Temporary exhibitions with associated events are central to their success. There are two exhibition spaces, one larger than the other. With an annual budget of just £4,000 ($6,500) the museum manages to mount about 20 shows a year. Some are hired in, others provided by local societies and the like, and others – especially the 'summer blockbuster' – produced in-house. Each year the local youth club produces a graffiti exhibition, sprayed directly onto the gallery walls, which brings teenagers and their music into the museum.

The museum always produces child friendly add-ons to accompany the externally produced displays. The exhibitions are also accompanied by events and activities. In the February school holiday in 2011, the museum held a 'Dinosaurs' picnic' attended by more than 500 people, each with a picnic and plastic dinosaur. Many activities are

Figure 7.6 'Cool Choirs'
Primary school children dressed in the 'latest' 1970s fashion sing their hearts out at Mansfield Museum.
Courtesy of Mansfield Museum.

crafts based, and enthusiastically led by the gallery assistants, who make and design pilot materials and then support children and families to make their own. Events in the news are not missed – for the wedding of Prince William and Catherine Middleton, children were encouraged to design wedding souvenirs and the wedding dress!

The education officer appointed proved so inspirational that the district council, despite its very tight budget, took over responsibility for funding the post. There are now booked primary school groups on virtually every day of the school year, all focusing on the national curriculum. Children of all abilities take part in the activities, and a very high percentage, including many from economically deprived backgrounds, return with their families. But the links with local schools go well beyond this. There are regular opportunities for schools to display their work, while events such as 'Cool Choirs' are a roaring success. All such activities bring in the children's families, including grandparents.

The museum now uses social media as a key part of building relationships with its users. You will find Mansfield Museum on Twitter, Facebook and YouTube, as well as having its own website. This freedom of online expression is rarely allowed in a local authority environment in the UK – councillors, other officers in the authority and the editor of the local newspaper now all follow the museum on Twitter. It is also using QR codes as part of its gallery interpretation.

What makes the museum so successful? Its local authority is highly supportive and has positively backed the museum's move in its chosen direction. Its staff have focus, enthusiasm, commitment *and* excellent time management skills – the certainty of purpose and direction shines through. They have reached out to form partnerships wherever possible, but recognise that most of these still rely on personal contact. Partnership working is also becoming more difficult in this era of cuts as community posts in other departments and agencies are left unfilled. All the staff – from curator to gallery assistants – engage positively with the children and families. And local families have responded in kind. A high percentage are regular users.

8   From engaging communities to civil engagement

INTRODUCTION

> It is clearly more challenging in hard times for arts organizations to take the long view and continue to devote time and effort to building new audiences, but that work and the resulting lessons are also more vital than ever to the long-term health of arts organizations and the entire arts sector.
>
> Wallace Foundation (2009: 2)

There are three main ways in which museums can develop their audiences:

1. by encouraging existing audiences to come more often and to make greater use of all the museum has to offer, including online provision, transforming them from visitors into users
2. by attracting more members of the audience segments which already use the museum
3. by reaching out to new audiences who have not previously considered visiting a museum.

All three are important to the future of museums and will influence the nature of the services provided. However, each requires a different strategic approach. While most of the book has focused on the first two, this chapter looks at the third and most difficult – *diversifying* the user base by reaching out to engage with new communities – and the impact this continues to have on museums. It is this process that is normally referred to as *audience development*:

> Audience development is about breaking down the barriers which hinder access to museums and 'building bridges' with different groups to ensure their specific needs are met. It is a process by which a museum seeks to create access to, and encourage greater use of, its collections and services . . .
>
> Dodd and Sandell (1998: 6)

The chapter begins with a brief examination of the impact on museums of reaching out to marginalised communities over the last 30 years. It then looks at how museums today are responding to what have become core issues, namely inclusion, representation and multiple perspectives. Finally it explores how some museums have sought to set the agenda, becoming centres for dialogue, civil engagement and the building of community. Underpinning all of this is the realisation that, for most museums, the diversification of the audience base is no longer a positive aspiration but a necessity. Future survival depends on ever-closer engagement with their audiences, existing and new.

In the Introduction I discussed the financial crisis facing publicly funded museums; the resulting temptations were to regroup around 'core' functions of collection, conservation and documentation, and to concentrate on growing the traditional audiences further. But I also spoke of the rapid demographic change taking place, particularly in our cities, and the increasing demands for recognition and representation by previously marginalised communities. In Chapter 1, I showed that overreliance on traditional audiences was not a long term option. As well as new communities, the next generations are coming through who are more demanding and have different expectations. Museums that continue to be geared to the needs of the Baby Boomers will be left behind.

What I did not speak of were the positives in reaching out to new audiences – the challenges, the disparate perspectives, the questioning, the demands for new ways of doing things and the inspiration that will banish complacency and drive museums to a new dynamism – the essential underpinning to what would be called 'great art' in a performing arts environment. This chapter sets out to redress that balance.

REACHING OUT TO NEW AUDIENCES

Reaching out to new audiences is not new

There is nothing new to the concept of museums seeking to diversify their audience base. We can look at the work of Theodore Low who published his *The Museum as a Social Instrument* on behalf of the American Association of Museums in 1942, and to John Cotton Dana, founder of the Newark (New Jersey) Museum in 1909. The USA also led the world in the development of Community and Neighborhood Museums, which were established in poor areas of New York, Washington, Chicago and other cities by the 1970s. Anacostia, the influential museum in a black district of Washington DC, was set up in 1967 with the help and financial backing of the Smithsonian Institution in a small disused cinema, under the direction of a 30-year-old black youth worker, John Kinard:

> What he envisaged was something which had not existed previously, a museum which grew naturally from the life of the district, a museum with a creative flow of ideas, exhibits and people between itself and the outside world.
>
> de Varine (1993)

In the 1970s and 1980s, more conventional museums such as the Philadelphia Museum of Art and New York City Museum began what became known as 'outreach' activities, staging festivals and exhibitions in poor neighbourhoods. They both used their collections and explored themes such as drugs, violence and sexually transmitted diseases. Alexander wrote on the success of the Philadelphia outreach programme begun in 1970:

> It has observed well the basic principles of community-oriented programmes: to respect the wishes and ideas of the groups, to help them whenever feasible, provided assistance is asked, and to keep the museum in the background.
>
> Alexander (1979: 224)

By 1972, the American Association of Museums had already produced a major report on these new museums and potential new audiences (AAM 1972). Alexander's description of the criticisms that gave rise to this new movement bears a striking resemblance to comments still being made today:

> . . . the criticism that they [museums] appealed only to the educated few and collected objects valued by wealthy leaders, that the immigrants, blacks, and other deprived minorities as well as the poor had been ignored, their cultural contributions and needs forgotten . . .
>
> Alexander (1979: 14)

This same drive towards community engagement can also be seen in resolutions by ICOM's General Assembly in the late 1960s and early 1970s which focused on the contributions museums could make to the cultural, social and economic life of their communities. It underpinned the Round Table on the Development and the Role of Museums in the Contemporary World held in Chile in 1972, with its long-lasting impact on museums across Latin America, particularly through the concept of the Integrated Museum (Silverman 2010: 12). In Europe, community engagement is best seen in the deep community involvement at the heart of the ecomuseum movement, whose defining project – the ecomuseum of Le Creusot-Montceau-les-Mines – was created in France between 1971 and 1974 (Davis 2008).

While community museums and outreach programmes are now a relatively common feature of the museum world in the USA, they could still not be defined as part of the mainstream. Equally, in western Europe, while the rise of social history and industrial museums since the 1960s was based on a groundswell of support within communities, and while the concepts of ecomuseums, community museums and outreach have been present since the 1970s (see, for example, Merriman 1991), they were rarely seen as a priority by more traditional museum services. It is only from the late 1970s that we begin to see the rise of a political agenda that committed all museums to playing a role in tackling social issues within society.

The social inclusion agenda

In Europe since the 1990s, those within the museums profession who believe in the positive contributions museums can make to the lives of the individuals and communities they serve have focused on the museum response to the social inclusion agenda:

> Social exclusion is something that can happen to anyone. But some people are significantly more at risk than others. Research has found that people with certain backgrounds and experiences are disproportionately likely to suffer social exclusion. The key risk factors include: low income; family conflict; being in care; school problems; being an ex-prisoner; being from an ethnic minority; living in a deprived neighbourhood in urban and rural areas; mental health problems, age and disability.
>
> Cabinet Office (2001: 11).

The emphasis when analysing social exclusion is on connectedness. Rather than focusing on one factor, most often poverty, it is important to understand the range of factors involved, the linkages between them and the complexity of the issue. An initiative to solve one aspect may not be enough; there must be an inter-agency response. Initial priorities for the UK Social Exclusion Unit were combating truancy at school, reducing the number of people sleeping rough and developing strategies for the renewal of deprived neighbourhoods. It was this latter issue that brought museums into the picture. In 2001, the government asked a committee from the museum sector to define how UK regional museums could best support learning, access and social inclusion. Their report, *Renaissance in the Regions* (MLA 2001), led for the first time to central government money going directly into regional museums – currently about £35 million a year, closely linked to audience development, social inclusion and learning. Thanks to funding through Renaissance in the Regions, UK museums have been able to develop both their work with local communities and their own expertise. Longevity and sustainability have become core ambitions; leading institutions, such as Tyne & Wear Museums and National Museums Liverpool, have transformed their missions and organisational structures to become community focused.

UK central government funding brought with it a need for museums to *prove* their effectiveness as learning and socially inclusive environments by establishing ways to measure the outcomes for those involved. This led to the development of the Inspiring Learning for All initiative (www.inspiringlearningforall.gov.uk), which in turn produced learning impact assessment criteria (GLOs – discussed in Chapter 5) and then criteria for assessing generic social outcomes (GSOs). GSOs were first piloted in the UK in Newcastle and Bristol (AEA Consulting 2005), revealing the scale of the social impact museum projects could have on individuals, as shown in Figure 8.1.

Figure 8.1 **Overall social impact of projects, Tyne & Wear Museums (based on AEA Consulting 2005: 60)**

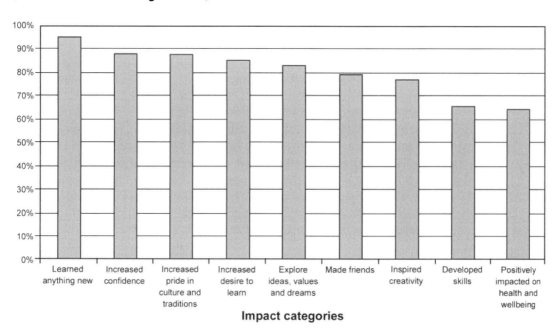

This is, however, not just a UK development. In the USA, museums which have received grants for community learning projects from the Institute of Museum and Library Services must use an equivalent model of outcome-based evaluation. This is specifically intended to measure and document 'achievements or changes in skill, knowledge, attitude, behaviour, condition, or life status for program participants' (IMLS 2007). Similar research in Canada, by the Working Group on Museums and Sustainable Communities, points to changes not only within individuals but also within communities, with resulting effects on museums (Worts 2006).

Others, while recognising impacts on individuals, have been much less convinced of the power of museums to transform wider society. Research funded by the UK Economic and Social Research Council reflects this, suggesting the role of museums within the bigger picture of social inclusion strategies is, at best, not proven:

> The ability of museums and galleries to socially engineer society … cannot at present be demonstrated. A policy encouraging museums and galleries to focus on such indices of inclusion appears misguided. But so far, our research indicates that initiatives do have an impact. This might be related to the way people develop a sense of who they are. The profession and the various elements of government appear to misunderstand the importance of this. It could be a first step to inclusion for many people.
>
> Newman (2001: 36)

The impact on governance and values

For museums to engage with their communities successfully and sustainably, the experience of the last 30 years has shown that there must be a clear and explicit commitment by the governing body and senior management. In the 1990s and early noughties, the focus for traditional museums reaching out to develop new audiences was on increasing previously under-represented audiences' public access to and experience of the arts and heritage. In too many cases, community outreach was there to meet the institution's agenda, whether political or financial. Most outreach projects have been both short term and peripheral to the core activities of the museum – using marginal funding and marginal staff to work with communities who already felt marginalised. In the UK, a ground-breaking study by Bernadette Lynch showed that:

> Communities remain, or at least perceive themselves to be, fundamentally separated from processes within these organisations: rather than engaging at every level of their work, they are relegated to mere consumption of museums' and galleries' 'products'. Despite presenting numerous examples of ground-breaking, innovative practice, the funding invested in public engagement and participation in the UK's museums and galleries has not significantly succeeded in shifting the work from the margins to the core of many of these organisations.
>
> Lynch (2011: 5)

This is not to deny a place for project work within museums. The opportunity for individuals and groups to engage with museum collections and staff in a sustained manner over a period of time should be fundamental to the service museums provide.

However, sustained engagement with communities cannot be achieved through marginal activities. Instead, it requires the transformation of the museum at its core, in all its operation, and in its whole attitude to those audiences:

> This can only be achieved if the museum is able to evolve into an institution which is less self-referential, more rooted in the life of the surrounding community, and more open to exploring collaborative modes of operation, to sharing strategies and objectives, to including new voices, skills and narratives.
>
> Bodo (2010: 84)

Despite the criticisms that can be made, museum services and individual staff members have built considerable expertise over the last 30 years. Both museums and their community partners have gained a better mutual understanding, and a greater appreciation of the opportunities and benefits linked to collaborative working. Organisations such as The Network (www.seapn.org.uk) have enabled participants to share information and ideas. Overall, enough experience has been gained to make it possible for organisations to begin to develop concepts around best practice, including:

- a commitment from the top of the organisation
- clear vision and goals
- good planning and evaluation
- clear principles and standards
- staff and community training and development needs identified and met
- issues and tensions understood and addressed.

based on Renaissance North-West (2005)

Beyond these, as staff have developed their community engagement skills, come the voices of experience:

- community work is complex and must be long term
- one size does not fit all
- do not raise expectations that cannot be met
- you must enjoy the process of working with partners
- you must share ownership and acknowledge the skills your community partners bring
- you must be flexible – the end result may be very different to what you set out to do.

What comes out of most case studies is that engaging communities cannot be a marginal activity for museums, but it must be at their heart. Museums focused on the development of new audiences will share a number of characteristics. They will know their audiences and will support ongoing user and community-based research. Audience development and work will be driven by a committed governing body and staff. It will be at the core of what the museum does – reflected in the mission statement, the strategic objectives, business planning and staff structure. There will be a clear vision, a long term plan and core funding to support it. The entire organisation will be involved, not just the 'audience development and access team'. There will be an underpinning passion and commitment to the process of working *with* individuals and communities in partnerships based not only on working together but on sharing authority. '*Consult and involve*' will be a core maxim. All of this, in turn, requires both ongoing evaluation and a commitment to staff and community training to support the development of relevant new expertise: in building relationships and working sensitively with communities; in sharing expertise; in developing new, collaborative approaches; in representing multiple perspectives; and in mediating between community memories. As such, it is crucial for museums to continue to learn from each other and share experience across the sector. Finally, over time, the museum workforce will come to reflect its audiences.

A key element will be the recognition and combating of barriers to community participation and engagement. As discussed in Chapters 2 and 3, external image and the creation of a visitor-friendly environment are crucial. Museum staff must go out to meet local communities, in community venues. Working through trusted and familiar channels, and using existing social networks, can increase the willingness of local people to become involved. Partnerships with other agencies will regularly be far more successful than the museum trying to go it alone, so long as objectives are shared and everyone is clear about their commitments, expectations, responsibilities, etc. Reaching out to schools in areas where families traditionally do not use the museum can be a key way to engage new audiences, with up to a third of children regularly returning to the museum with families and friends. Interest will also depend on a sense of inclusion, representation and communities feeling that their voices are part of the museum content. Opportunities to contribute to content are a vital tool.

The greatest barrier, however, as discussed in Chapter 1, remains lack of interest. Overcoming the 'interest' barrier will depend on museums ensuring the relevance of their content and programming to communities. The Canadian Working Group on Museums and Sustainable Communities created a 'critical assessment framework' as a discussion document on how museums addressed meeting the cultural needs of their communities through their programming:

The team should ask itself how well the programme will:

- address vital and relevant needs/issues within the community
- generate information and connection at the personal, community, provincial/ territorial, national and global levels
- engage a diverse public
- provide an outlet for the voices of diverse groups
- encourage social interactions and debate
- act as a catalyst for action
- stimulate intergenerational interactions
- link existing community groups to one another
- initiate or enhance long term collaborative relationships
- create partnerships that empower community groups
- enhance the credibility of all involved
- result in products/processes that have tangible impacts in the community
- generate information applicable to museum and community decision-making.
  Worts (2006: 45)

Reaching out to communities today: the Open Museum, Glasgow

People think they are not interested in things for all sorts of reasons – class, religion, education, upbringing, culture, financial aspiration (they are all related) – and many of these prevent people developing interests that could enrich their lives, even change their lives.

Spalding (2010: 120)

The good news is that 'museums are in the interest-generation business' (Spalding 2010: 120). As such, the responsibility lies with the museum to reach out constantly towards new audiences, to engage them in what we do. Part of this relies on museums working *with* communities, rather than believing they are producing a service *for* communities which is then delivered *to* them. Such commitments will require the development of new provision to meet community needs, is likely to involve changing the ethos behind the presentation of museum collections, and will certainly require organisational change. A change in staff structure and a change in the nature of jobs will be necessary to deliver on, for example, newly established inclusivity objectives.

The Open Museum in Glasgow is a remarkable example of what this means in practice. The Open Museum began as a pilot project in 1990, during the razzamatazz of Glasgow's year as European City of Culture. It has now been operating continuously for over 20 years and is still pushing boundaries. The premise behind it seemed simple:

> we . . . felt there was a need to offer a museum service to people who for one reason or another seldom, if at all, came to museums, by providing displays in more accessible venues – libraries, community centres, hospitals, prisons, old people's homes. But rather than just creating touring exhibitions, we wanted to share the curatorial experience, to work in partnership with local people to create displays.
>
> O'Neill (2002: 2)

From the outset partnerships included education and social services departments as well as community groups. It also benefited from the museum service's previous experience of partnership working at the Springburn Museum in an area of high unemployment; started in 1986, the project sought to tell the story of the area through community objects. Communities were expected to play an active role in partnership with the museum service – they would come into the museum to select what they wanted, then take that material back into their communities and display it. Themes for exhibitions have included everything from community histories and fashion inspired by museum collections to hard-hitting studies on gay rights and homelessness. Gallus Glasgow was a 'map' of an alternative Glasgow, based on the memories of long term prisoners at HMP Glenochil. At any one time, there are 20 Open Museum displays touring community venues. Evaluation has been built in to the Open Museum's work since the outset, with Dodd et al. (2002) providing core evidence of the impact it has had on the individuals and communities it has worked with. Edwards (2010: 123) has also noted that 'people in care demonstrated faster recovery . . . participants in the Pollok Kist demonstrated significant increase in personal capacity and confidence'. The evaluations have recorded failures as well as successes, which is crucial both to understanding how to move forward and to sharing expertise and experiences nationally.

The Open Museum was also expected to have an impact across the Glasgow museum service. By c. 2000, all curatorial staff were expected to be involved in at least one Open Museum project. It was presumed that objects would be loaned from the service's collections, unless there was a very good reason not to: 'Central to the Open Museum philosophy was that the loaned objects would be registered museum objects – the objects owned by the citizens of the city' (Dodd et al. 2002: 9). To support this approach, the museum offered training to groups in how to look after the collections. In 2003, the Open Museum team moved into the newly created Glasgow Museums Resource Centre which, alongside the Natural History Museum's Darwin Centre, in London, is the most accessible museum store in the world.

The Open Museum has recently published *Out There* (Glasgow Museums 2010) to celebrate its first 20 years and explore some of its key projects. The team held a conference under the same title in 2010 to bring together museum practitioners from across the world with others from outside the museum sector. What linked their work was a desire to support communities to create positive social change. Three main themes were evident: these projects responded to the needs of a particular locality, they supported groups and individuals in building their own capabilities, and they shared decision making with people. One result of the conference was the production of a manifesto, a living document seen as the basis for a continuing ideas exchange, outlined in Box 8.1.

REPRESENTATION, INCLUSION AND MULTIPLE PERSPECTIVES

The history of the West Midlands in the twentieth century . . . is a history of the emergence of multicultural, multilingual and multifaith communities, of Black, Muslim, Sikh, Jewish, Irish, refugee and travelling peoples. The stories that make up this history remain largely hidden . . . stories of common experiences, shared struggles and aspirations.

Davies (2007b: 5)

One result of community engagement work has been a widespread recognition within the museum profession that museum collections and the stories they tell should reflect the pluralist nature of modern society. A core criticism of Western museums as instruments of those in power is that the versions of other cultures and of the past they have given form to are based on the selective collection, preservation and presentation of evidence of past human society which prioritises an elite. Objects relating to wealthier classes have a far higher likelihood of survival in society as a whole. They also dominate museum collections, due to past collecting policies which reflected the priorities and tastes of the ruling bodies within a community. In the process of collecting this material, museums both create knowledge and manipulate it, and through interpretation and transmission they define its relative importance or authority. Meanwhile, through the silences in a museum's collections and narratives, 'in what it allows to go unnoticed, unrecognized and unacknowledged' (Mezaros 2008: 243), the contribution of the bulk of the community the museum serves is ignored. Museums thus legitimate a particular construct, an 'official' past, focused on the activities and cultural tastes of the

Box 8.1 Out There manifesto

We will aim to keep these thoughts in mind to guide us in our working:

Sharing authority
We will be brave in our work and share control with the groups and individuals who participate in our programmes. We will see participants as contributors rather than passive beneficiaries of our work.
We will consider our projects in their entirety before we commit to participants and external partners; to ensure that people are empowered and involved in the decision-making process and that projects can be made sustainable when desired.

Building capabilities
We recognise the importance of work and skills building to people's confidence, motivation and mental well-being. We aim to reflect the importance of industriousness and purpose in future projects.
We aim to support capability building in all projects and to work with external partners who can offer pathways to continue active participation and the further development of capabilities after a project has ended.

Micro geographies of hope
We will invite people to comment on, share and create the interpretation for our collections and acknowledge that there are multiple narratives. Where conflict arises we will provide a space for dialogue.
We will be open to learn from the stories, experiences and skills of colleagues, participants and those who challenge what we do.
We will treat our museums as living, changing organisations which reflect the future as well as preserving the past. We will be responsive to our locality.

Conflict
We will be brave in addressing issues that affect people's lives and will provide opportunities for dialogue to encourage understanding and mutual respect.

Joy
We are passionate about the collections that we work with and have witnessed the power of objects as catalysts for creativity, understanding and exploration. We will continue to facilitate connections between people, objects and places and celebrate the potential for heritage to build relationships, demonstrate and encourage innovation and foster a sense of identity and worth.

Taking it forward
We aim to inform and influence the wider museum and gallery sector and encourage social engagement by publishing about our work, building links with external partners and continuing connections with contemporaries in the UK and internationally.
We see engagement as a core function of museums and galleries and recognise that facilitating learning in groups and individuals is a specialism.
We will be open to sharing our skills and knowledge with other museum and gallery professionals who may wish to develop relationships with communities.
We aim to learn from inspiring practitioners outside the museum and gallery sector and utilise transferable approaches.

We wish to continue the ideas exchange and will utilise the Out There blog (http://openmuseumoutthere.wordpress.com) as a forum to support socially engaged practice. This will be a place where people can share their work and challenges openly amongst a supportive network of critical friends. [It includes copies of the conference presentations].

Open Museum, Glasgow (2010)

elite. As such, museums could perhaps be described more accurately as places of selective memory rather than collective memory (Davison 2005: 186).

Can museums change from this representation of a single 'official' past to help communities to reclaim their pasts? To do so they must go further in representing the communities they serve and in acknowledging the contributions those communities have made to wider society. Museums are at a crossroads in deciding to what extent they wish to place themselves at the heart of their communities – if communities will permit this – rather than remaining in the safe intellectual environment they have occupied for the last century. For museums to take any further steps towards their communities will involve them breaking away from an assumption about 'the ignorance of the masses which in turn requires the assistance, good will and guidance of the more educated elite' (Perkin 2010: 109). This kind of attitude has all too frequently resulted in a top-down approach, with museums determining what communities needed, how programmes should develop and what should be accomplished. Can museums instead work *with* their communities? Can community engagement by museums change the role museums see for themselves to that of cultural mediator, including and representing the memories of previously marginalised groups (Misztal 2003: 20)? Can museums thereby empower communities to research and represent their own unique identities? Judy Ling Wong makes clear that the interpretation of cultural diversity is both a celebration of identity and a rooting of all in an 'inclusive heritage', a 'common history':

> The mono-cultural dominance of the official histories of many countries means that citizens whose cultures are neglected cannot begin to mould their presence and make their contribution towards an inclusive heritage. It is time for them to make their legitimate claim and situate themselves within the socio-cultural history and heritage of their countries in order to advance from the position of the normal social strength of being rooted in a common history and heritage into the future.
>
> Wong (2002: 5)

A similarly strong case about the lack of representation of disabled people in museums is made by Annie Delin:

> Within museums, disabled people might not find a single image of a person like themselves – no affirmation that in the past people like themselves lived, worked, created great art, wore clothes, were loved or esteemed ... The heroic stories about admirals and poets, artists and craftspeople often neglect to point out when the illustrious were also unusual in the way they walked or spoke.
>
> Delin (2002: 85)

This attitude among communities that a museum 'doesn't relate to me' will only fully disappear when those communities are not only welcomed into the museum but also become an inclusive part of it – in the collections, in the histories presented, in the programming, in the development of multiple perspectives within exhibitions, and in the staff. And representation means not only the presence of relevant objects but a public recognition of the contributions communities have made to society at large. It also means overcoming the power imbalance that results from the perception of a position of authority that museums hold and replacing it with true partnerships based on a collaboration among equals that values the contributions, knowledge and perspectives of local people (Perkin 2010: 110 and 112).

Moving towards more inclusive collections

Museums that are seeking to represent all the communities they serve must change their collecting policies to reflect this, and must develop proactive approaches both to contemporary collecting and to the re-evaluation of existing collections.

Because of the way objects have been collected in the past, presenting other cultures or history in a museum is also partly about the history of the museum itself. Thus we can note that a sea change in the way museums sought to collect and present the past began in the 1960s at the same time as the rise of the 'new social history', although there is some relevant earlier work. New social and industrial history museums opened the gates to pluralism and multiple perspectives, based on the principle that the present is the result of the life contributions of *all* who have made up society in the past, not just of the elites. The development of these new museum fields led in turn to a surge in the collection of the 'everyday', particularly in the 1960s and 1970s (see, for example, Kavanagh 1990, 2000).

But this period also saw a critique of the primacy of the object, reflecting both the lack of representativeness in most museum collections, and a growth of curatorial understanding of the importance of other sources of evidence when seeking to reflect previously silent voices (Fleming 1998: 134). Thus, alongside the development of new social and industrial history object collections came an extension of the museum remit to include archives, photographs, film and, particularly, oral histories, representing both individual and community memories that were a direct connection between a *lived* past and the present. Through this material, a new window was opened into the life experiences and contributions of working men and women.

Starting from the representation by museums of a white working class, the development of a multi-perspectives approach has become increasingly important as Western society has become more culturally diverse. It has been central to the audience development work museums have been doing with communities over the last 20 years. Again, new collections have been developed, mostly through outreach programmes in which museums have worked in partnership with minority communities within their localities and which have combined oral histories with collecting. These have often resulted in exhibitions and website development at the museums. Moving Here, for example, has so far involved over 30 UK museums and archives and 45 communities (www.movinghere.org.uk) in developing an online catalogue of over 200,000 items relating to the history of migration to the UK as well as a range of virtual exhibits.

Stevens (2009) provides an overview of the representation of migration in the UK heritage sector. Museums have also developed proactive policies on revisiting existing collections to draw out new relevancies (for cultural diversity, see for example Bott et al. 2005; Collections Management Network 2010; Denniston 2003. For disability see Dodd et al. 2004).

This representation of multiple perspectives has also begun to feed back into an

Figure 8.2 **Recording personal experiences**
Members of the Asian community in Leicester record their memories for the Moving Here project.
Courtesy of City of Leicester Museums.

ongoing redefinition of collective memory. In the past, a dominant group could define the collective memory for a community or nation, with minority groups welcomed in if they accepted that version or otherwise cast out if they did not. Today, instead, there is a growing recognition that differing points of view can be incorporated within the collective, rather than collective memory speaking with a single authorised voice – in fact individual and group memories become essential parts of the collective, made part of the wider community's memory by the very act of being shared (Crane 1997: 1,376). Representation and inclusion within the collective are also essential elements in the construction of both individual and community identity, for all of us – we are looking for reflections of our sense of belonging over time and space, of our place in the human story. Where museums have become involved in collecting and transmitting community memory, for example in the ecomuseum movement, they have also become part of the construction and mediation of community identity.

Ensuring display and programme content is inclusive

> At that time [1993] . . . nowhere in the Museum of London's displays was there evidence of the medieval Jewish community (and its subsequent expulsion and return), the continuous black presence since the sixteenth century, the establishment of Asian communities since the seventeenth century and the significant populations of Chinese, Italian and German origin in the nineteenth century. The cultural heritage of traveller communities . . . is also invariably absent . . .
>
> Stevens (2009: 6)

Stating the obvious, museums must ensure that display content is inclusive, and is representative of local communities. This will involve:

- researching diverse cultural aspects of sites and collections
- integrating diverse aspects of history and heritage into displays and ensuring representative interpretation
- involving diverse cultural and community groups in developing displays, resources and interpretation
- partnering and sharing authority with groups and communities to research and celebrate memory
- developing imaginative events and activities to highlight the diverse nature of heritage.

(based on Wong 2002: 7)

The use of a wide spectrum of sources, incorporating objects, pictures and moving electronic images, written texts, smells, sounds, voices and music, is a key starting point. It both ensures a multisensory approach and provokes a lively and critical historical dialogue about the past. The museum also loses some of its 'authoritative' position as an expert on objects because there is a wider range of sources available (based on Nakou 2005: 10). The use of oral histories and video testimonies, developed by working with local communities, will provide powerful insights through people talking about their lived experiences. This is one way the museum represents those previously silent or 'spoken for'. They present the opportunity for multiple perspectives and can provide plural, alternative and perhaps even contradictory versions of the past and the present.

Partnering community groups will encourage ownership of exhibitions and events, ensure changing content in the museum and add to the provision of multiple perspectives. The long term success of such partnerships – not only for content development but also for the museum's ongoing relationship with its communities – relies on sharing authority and recognising how important it is to reach consensus in all decision making (Conaty and Carter 2005). Such partnerships can take a number of forms, for example:

- Direct community participation in content development and the incorporation of community exhibits into permanent displays and online provision can be an important means of ensuring inclusive content. The Glenbow Museum in Calgary,

Canada, for example, gave over authority for the development of a new permanent exhibition to the Blackfoot-speaking people (Conaty and Carter 2005).

- Developing a temporary exhibitions programme. Temporary displays are more suitable for some kinds of subject matter. They can also provide an opportunity to experiment before incorporating material in permanent content. Temporary exhibitions can also act as a focus for community-led research, while the public display of their work is source of pride and confidence for participants.
- The production and incorporation of support materials, from community- and school-produced exhibit labels to layered content and downloadable multiperspectival gallery tours, will add depth and encourage others to respond to content.
- As noted below, community volunteers acting as gallery guides can bring content alive.

A key way of including many voices and multiple perspectives in the museum will be through the people in the galleries – both staff and volunteers from local communities. The participants in the associated programme of activities – from museum theatre and storytelling, object handling and gallery tours to the organisation of debates – also need to reflect the diversity of the local community. It is essential that spaces are designed in for them, staff roles carefully defined before appointment and a wide range of volunteers sought to ensure different voices are heard. Actively seeking community involvement and offering training will be an ongoing task.

Again based on working with local communities, the development of oral and written testimonies, short films, soundscapes and images on what life is like in a locality now can capture a multitude of connecting narratives and contribute to a wider understanding of a locality's complex culture and history. Elements could include:

- linkages, for example with community media, to incorporate up-to-the-minute stories
- opportunities for users to add content in the museum and online
- the incorporation of school projects
- the recording of people's own experiences/life stories as part of the museum's role as a 'storehouse of memories', through video booths or online. Since 2003, Storycorps in the USA (http://storycorps.org) has collected and archived more than 30,000 interviews. The approach taken could form the basis for a local museum initiative.

The development of user-generated content was discussed in Chapter 6. It is also essential to the representation of multiple perspectives. The museum must build-in opportunities for users to reflect and review the experiences of their visit and potentially augment their understanding (linking to layering of content). Users must have the chance to voice their theories and opinions. Providing opportunities to respond directly to content – for example through comment cards, recorded content or online, and ensuring that other users can read and respond to those comments in turn – makes the museum a centre for dialogue. Opportunities for such user-generated content must be designed in from the outset. Crucially, contributors should clearly understand the importance the museum places on their views and experiences. Simon's book *The Participatory Museum* (2010) gives inspiring examples.

Working in partnership with communities

In working with communities, the museum must look beyond what *it* wants to do so that it can identify contemporary relevance within the community at large and those areas where its expertise can make a difference. This requires a 'wholehearted externalisation of purpose' (Koster and Baumann 2005: 86). As part of this, a museum committed to reflecting multiple perspectives through partnership with its communities must break the stranglehold of its physical site and restricted opening hours and look outwards, beyond its walls, housed collections, 'safe' history and traditional audiences. This principle of a museum without walls should influence every aspect of the museum's activities. Phil Nowlen (2009), Director of the Getty Leadership Institution, spoke of this when he challenged museums to 'move beyond their comfortable street addresses ... the better to advance society's culture, capacity for compassion, sense of community and strength of democracy'. He spoke of museums as being places *from which* services flow rather than just places *to which* people go.

The Center for Cultural Understanding and Change at the Field Museum in Chicago has developed a programme of activities and exhibitions that respond to common concerns across its region. It has been defined through over 100 conversations held with communities and organisations in 2007. Its website, in outlining current projects and programmes, shows how effectively its mission works in practice:

> The Center for Cultural Understanding and Change (CCUC) at the Field Museum uses problem-solving anthropological research to identify and catalyse strengths and assets of communities in Chicago and beyond. In doing so, CCUC helps communities identify new solutions to critical challenges such as education, housing, health care, environmental conservation and leadership development. Through research, programs and access to collections, CCUC reveals the power of cultural difference to transform social life and promote social change.
>
> www.fieldmuseum.org/ccuc/

A current (2011) example of the work of the Field Museum is that it has been commissioned by the City of Chicago to engage diverse communities in the implementation of the Chicago Climate Action Plan. The museum is conducting rapid ethnographic studies in communities throughout Chicago to identify community concerns and assets that can serve as springboards for climate action. It is also translating the findings into community engagement programmes. Working with Chicago Wilderness, for example, it has launched an Energy Action Network which directly engages 21 community organisations, targeted at integrating environmental sustainability into their core agendas for improving quality of life. This is the opposite of a museum seeking a neutral role. It has confronted this issue even though many Americans are still climate-change deniers (Janes, pers. comm. 2011). Full details on this and other projects can be found at the museum's website.

History museums are increasingly seeking to encourage local communities to investigate their own pasts and share their experiences and to enthuse museum visitors to go out and actively explore the locality. They are using local voices (live or audio) to reach below the surface patina. Oral and written testimonies, short films, soundscapes and images contribute to a wider understanding of a locality's complex culture and history, and can include the recording of personal experiences/life stories as part of the museum's role as a repository of community memory. This is not new. When Boston Children's Museum developed its 5,000 square foot Kids Bridge exhibition in 1989, espousing multicultural themes, it included an interactive video *The Great Boston Treasure Hunt*, which

> invited viewers to virtually explore four Boston area neighbourhoods with young video guides. On the "treasure hunt" the viewers "met" the guides' families and friends, and visited their homes and schools in search of culturally specific objects. The interactive treasure hunt aspect of the video provided visitors with a medium to explore and enjoy cultural diversity.
>
> Jones-Rizzi (2008: 23)

In a contemporary equivalent targeted at adults, at Grand Rapids in Michigan, the museum and local communities organise an annual 'grand race' through neighbourhoods that participants had never visited before, again using the idea of a treasure hunt:

> "The Grand Race" utilizes the real evidences of ethnicity in the community—neighbourhood streets and butcher shops, churches and forgotten landmarks, factories and wall murals—to improve racial sensitivity and increase cultural awareness. It breaks down fear of the unknown by inviting groups of people into storefronts and community gardens that they would never visit on their own. There they are greeted by cultural ambassadors who are waiting to answer their questions and make them feel welcome.
>
> Carron (2010)

The potential for online partnerships can be seen readily in local history museums, where the museum's most important exhibit should be the locality it serves: 'The bigger museum, the main stage, is here on the streets, enclosed in the repeated stories of grandmothers and grandfathers' (Archibald 2004: 8).

You can see this, for example, in the collaboration between Missouri History Society and the communities of St Louis in exploring the cultural landscapes of the city (www.historyhappenedhere.org) and in the Levine Museum of the New South project, Changing Places (http://changingplacesproject.org).

Issues with the representation of multiple perspectives

Museums must recognise, however, that there are problems associated with developing a multiperspectival approach, few of them yet resolved. The need to change collection policies and to extract new meanings from existing collections has already been discussed. I focus on four other aspects here. These revolve around a central issue: working in partnership with communities means recognising that there will be differing points of view. Museums need to accept that individuals and communities may question who has the authority to interpret history and culture to the public and who has the right to shape museum interpretations.

Selective perspectives

In seeking to incorporate the lived experiences of the previously marginalised, there will always be a risk that museums will reflect perspectives in their content that they feel comfortable with – often due to a tendency to keep working with those community groups they have come to know. Alternatively, museums can give too much space to those groups which have the strongest sense of past neglect or persecution and have pushed hardest to have their stories told. Both of these approaches effectively invite in some previously marginalised groups to become part of the 'authorised version' of the past – while others will remain silent and ignored. However, I do not wish to sound over-critical here. It can take many years to build up a close relationship with a community, and focusing on that community may well be the correct course of action. The Glenbow Museum in Calgary, for example, has focused on the Blackfoot because the museum is located in their homeland.

Equally, communities developing their own museums can focus on a narrow perspective in seeking to reflect their cultures. A core criticism of museums created by Native American communities is that they tend to reflect a conservative focus on religion, ceremony and tradition and downplay other aspects of contemporary culture. This concern has been levelled, for example, at the National Museum of the American Indian since its founding in 1989: 'the museum risks reproducing old anthropological notions of "traditional" or "primitive" cultures as unchanging, static and ahistorical' (Henning 2006: 119).

Sharing authority

Curators must recognise that they need to share authority for museum content. The work of the Glenbow Museum with the Blackfoot, introduced earlier in this chapter, is a classic example of this being done well (Conaty and Carter 2005). However, sharing authority involves confronting a primary fear of all professionals, not just museum curators, of their expertise not being recognised and of losing control. Lynch and Alberti (2010) provide an example from the Manchester Museum where museum staff, although well intentioned, still failed to establish a genuine collaboration.

Ciolfi et al. (2008: 355–6) point out that it is more common for visitor contributions to be elicited in science exhibits than in more traditional museums because 'museums tend to assume the role of authority when it comes to providing information about their holdings ... the narrative that is presented to visitors is not really open to challenges or external contributions'. If a museum is committed to reflecting multiple perspectives, this must change. This is best achieved in mutually beneficial partnerships, seen for example in the involvement of Leicester museums in the Moving Here project mentioned earlier in this chapter. For communities, they know their voices have been listened to and their life experiences included. For Leicester Museums, projects like this are vital. The city is the most diverse in the UK outside London and will be the first with a majority minority population. In projects like Moving Here, individual and community users of the museum bring their ideas, feelings and personal experiences with them, while museums provide context for the life stories generated and act as a 'mediator of many voices'.

Yet a true sharing of authority with users and communities must go beyond this to offer individuals and communities direct involvement in the *production* of knowledge.

This raises a further issue in that a shared authority must always be underpinned by the understanding that with such authority comes trust – the trust of museum users in the content provided. In history museums, for example, there is always potential for direct conflict between academic history and community memory – what a community *feels and believes* happened can be more important to them than what actually did happen. While the memories of a community may not present a picture which is in all cases balanced or accurate, it is the storytelling and the engagement in the emotion of the memory which creates the richest resource, and in a community setting this rich forum for memory sharing should be encouraged. By owning the content, the community can take pride in the recording of its heritage and identity. The issue is how to transfer such content into the museum while maintaining an overall balance and ensuring the museum's expertise has not been compromised.

This is not an either/or situation. The ambition should not be to find a new route to a single authoritative view. A key point of representing multiple perspectives is to stimulate thought, dialogue and understanding, not necessarily to reach consensus. In this situation, the representation of multiple perspectives requires an acknowledgment of authorship – including the museum's own contribution. Museums must not believe they alone occupy the high ground here. They have been guilty in the past of presenting as authoritative what have actually been very selective and elitist accounts of the past and of other cultures.

The establishment of agreed ground rules is key to partnership and the sharing of authority. The underpinning principle must remain that we are not talking of museums ceding absolute responsibility for content to communities. We *are* trying to provide a platform that recognises that there is more than one authorised point of view. The museum can retain authority over the platform to the extent it deems necessary. It can decide the types of interaction available to users, set the rules of behaviour, and choose which user-generated content to use (Simon 2010: 120–6). However, the focus must be on collaboration rather than top-down control.

Community politics

In seeking to develop a multiperspectival approach, museums will invariably have to work with different groups and individuals, and therefore have to negotiate their way around different issues, goals, interests and agendas; staff must have the training and experience to do this. Issues can include perceived neglect or lack of support in the past, uneven funding, disagreements between groups and the lack of wider recognition of group efforts within the community as a whole. Yet plotting a route through these without disregarding or alienating particular groups is essential to the long term benefit of both the museum and the groups involved.

In Bendigo, Australia, the first task of the manager appointed to coordinate a new community-driven project was to meet and learn about the scope and diversity of all the local groups. The manager had to understand the issues from their perspective, and then work to balance their interests against those of the funding providers and supporting organisations:

> The establishment of the Bendigo Heritage Representative Group and the implementation of joint projects such as exhibitions and public programmes slowly

began to overcome long-established barriers between groups and allow them to learn from and about each other. An increased shared understanding of the needs of all heritage groups, combined with the success of joint projects ... encouraged even the most politically minded to consider the collective needs of heritage rather than focus on individual group perspectives.

Perkin (2010: 118)

Representing multiple perspectives will not necessarily lead to harmony

Quite simply multiple, conflicting points of view exist and clash. Differing versions of the past constantly compete for control of the present within and between communities. For many previously marginalised groups, shared 'memories of past injustices are a critical source of empowerment' (Misztal 2003: 18). This is both a problem and a challenge. There is a need to develop approaches to display that engage people with the points of view of others and encourage reflection and understanding. This can be a particular issue when communities create their own museums. It raises questions such as who owns the past, or what is the differing bias that museums decide to present. And how are we, in these circumstances, to encourage people to reflect on the experiences of others?

Danilov (2009) listed 622 museums, galleries, historic sites and other facilities founded and operated by ethnic groups in the USA, and 478 others that he called 'ethnically related'; together they told the stories of 55 ethnic groups. These included 302 Native American museums, cultural centres, galleries and historic and prehistoric sites, most founded by American Indian tribes and located on reservations; there were 189 African-American museums and historic sites. There were also 112 Jewish museums, galleries, collection exhibit areas and historic sites. The oldest operating ethnic museum in the USA is the Hampton University Museum, an African-American museum founded in 1868 in Hampton, Virginia (Danilov 2009: 4). The largest is the 308,000 square foot Mashantucket Pequot Museum and Research Center, opened in Mashantucket, Connecticut, in 1998 at a cost of $193.4 million (Danilov 2009: 8), although many are small and run by volunteers. Danilov describes a slow but steady creation of ethnic museums before accelerated development following the Second World War, with greater expansion from the 1960s. The story continues today: Danilov recorded eight new ethnic museums created between 2000 and 2006, with at least a further dozen at planning stage when he went to press.

All of this is a reflection of the USA: it 'may be a melting pot, but it is still a nation of people of many nationalities who treasure their origins and cultures' (Danilov 2009: 28). However, the development of ethnic museums in the USA since at least the 1960s has been much more than this. The social and intellectual upheavals of the 1960s saw marginalised communities across the Western world demand equal status. The clamour for recognition both of their contribution to wider society and of the value of differing perspectives on the past, led to a huge expansion in the number of communities seeking to create their own museums to tell their stories. Thus, Kreamer (2002: 376) notes that the vast majority of African-American museums and cultural institutions were founded during the Black Consciousness era of the latter part of the twentieth century with a mandate for positive education, to develop as vehicles for social change and to reflect the diversity and complexity of the African-American experience through representing a multiplicity of voices.

For Native Americans, North American museums were seen as actively degrading their culture by depriving them of artefacts that possessed religious and ceremonial significance. It was again during the upheavals of the 1960s that museums, like other sectors, came under intense scrutiny as part of the revival and growing confidence of the Native American communities. Repatriation was a core element in the rise of museums created by those communities: 'A stronger cultural base, it was thought, would provide Native people with a stronger sense of self, a stronger sense of place, and a stronger sense of destiny' (Hill 2007: 314). In the USA, since 1990, the Native American Graves Protection and Repatriation Act has required museums who receive federal funding to negotiate repatriation of this material to Native American communities. And the process and act of repatriation can be a positive experience for the museum as well as the community, in building long term relationships, as can be seen in the impact of the return of sacred bundles by the Glenbow Museum in Canada to the Blackfoot people (Conaty 2008).

Holo (2009) speaks strongly in favour of community-created museums:

> They fulfilled an emerging need in the United States, a need not expressed anywhere else in the world [at the time], and they did so with intensity and urgency. It was a need determined by cultural insiders, representatives of living and evolving communities, for there to be museums that were demonstrably relevant – on terms set by communities themselves ... [to] the particular ethnicity or culture that the museum is celebrating as the center of its own universe.
>
> Holo (2009: 41)

She defines the characteristics of these museums as clearly American but through an 'other' prism. They have a coherent narrative framed from the inside but transmissible to both insider and outsider audiences – a narrative that covers both the community's achievements and its struggles and challenges in white Anglo-Saxon America. They also have an ambition to spread a greater understanding of the community to the outside world, keeping their histories alive for posterity. She references four successful examples in the Skirball Cultural Center and Museum of the American Jewish Experience, the Japanese American National Museum, the California African American Museum and the Arab American Museum (Holo 2009: 42–3), the first three in Los Angeles and the last in Dearborn. She concludes by suggesting these museums have served two significant societal purposes:

> The first is that they have come to be agents of stability – conceived as such by groups who feel themselves misunderstood or mischaracterized in American life as a way to retain and tell their stories ... And, second, they can be agents of positive change in that they promote tolerance and understanding to outsiders by insisting on the notion of a shared humanity.
>
> Holo (2009: 44)

Guzmán and Tortolero promote the same argument in their discussion of the National Museum of Mexican Art (NMMA) in Chicago, highlighting its ability to reach diverse and ethnic audiences that big institutions did not. They also emphasise that at institutions like NMMA members of the community are active participants who help to guide the museum's programming: 'The NMMA is able to serve its community because it IS the community' (Guzmán and Tortolero 2010: 91).

Of course, museums created by their communities are not unique to the USA. For example, the issue of repatriation of sacred objects and the reburial of human remains is also important in Australia. Kelly and Gordon's account (2002) of 'keeping places' or cultural centres examined their establishment and management by Indigenous people in their local areas to house repatriated objects, host exhibitions, conduct education and research, and provide employment and a meeting place. They have become important to the reconciliation process, to the maintenance and preservation of cultural heritage and to promoting Indigenous culture to the broader Australian community and overseas visitors: 'it's educating the local non-Indigenous community of our ways [and because of that] we are getting a lot more respect from them now' (interviewee, quoted by Kelly and Gordon 2002: 166). There is also a direct relationship with the rise of community museums in South America and of the ecomuseum movement, with its emphasis in community and the distinctiveness of place, which emerged in Europe and has since spread worldwide (Davis 2008).

But separateness can also re-enforce barriers between communities. From the late 1960s, Northern Ireland witnessed 30 years of violence centred on whether the province should remain part of the United Kingdom or become part of the Republic of Ireland. Underpinning this was the relationship between mainly Protestant Unionists and mainly Roman Catholic Republicans. Over 3,500 died. For most of the period, the contested city of Derry/Londonderry was at the heart of these 'Troubles'. It even has two names: Derry (from the Irish *Doire*) for the Republicans, Londonderry for the Unionists.

Figures 8.3 and 8.4 How objects can become symbols of memory
A mural on the side of a house in Bogside, Derry/Londonderry depicts a white handkerchief being waved as civilians carry a wounded marcher through army lines on 'Bloody Sunday'. That handkerchief has now become an iconic object in the Museum of Free Derry.

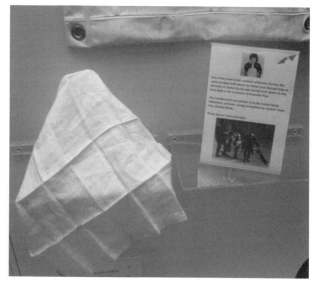

Today, three museums in the city explore this political division. The Tower Museum, operated by City of Derry Museums Service, examines the background and tragedy of the Troubles through the perspectives of both communities – and has been highly praised for doing so. The Museum of Free Derry, operated by the Bloody Sunday Trust, sets out the 'subjective but honest' (www.museumoffreederry.org) lived experiences of the Republican community, focusing on the events of 30 January 1972, when a march by protesters ended in a clash with security forces that left 13 civilians dead (ruled unjustifiable by a public enquiry in 2010). As a result, the story told in the museum is a partial one, narrated in a 'highly volatile political context' (Crooke 2008: 423). The local Unionist community also has its own museum, in the Apprentice Boys Hall.

Yet, even here, all is not lost. The city's museum service has been able to persuade the two sides to sit down together and plan visitor tours that take in both venues. Much as I would prefer a shared location and the encouragement of dialogue, this is at least a start.

THE MUSEUM AS A CATALYST FOR DIALOGUE AND CIVIL ENGAGEMENT

As discussed above, many museums have sought to engage with, and represent, the full range of communities in their regions. However, a study of European museum approaches in 2007 highlighted their tendency to follow three main policy models:

- Showcasing difference: a "knowledge-oriented" multiculturalism intended as an educational strategy to inform the [indigenous] public about "other" cultures [and communities] which have traditionally been misrepresented or made invisible in our museums;
- Integrating "new citizens" within mainstream culture, by helping them to learn more about a country's history, language, values and traditions;
- Promoting cultural self-awareness in migrant communities (especially refugees and asylum seekers) through "culturally specific" programming.

Bodo (2009: 22)

These models continue to have an important part to play in promoting the richness of diversity, representing the contributions that all communities have made to wider society, helping communities retain an awareness of their cultural background and creating the conditions for encounters between communities. However, they are not enough on their own. Alongside them we need museums to take on the role of 'third places', non-threatening surroundings away from normal social spaces at home and work, in which the process of dialogue can develop (Bodo 2009: 23). The challenge for the remainder of this chapter is to explore themes and examples where museums have sought to act as 'third places', and through this strengthen communities and support civil engagement.

As contemporary societies become increasingly culturally diverse, dialogue between different communities and cultures has an essential role in promoting understanding and fostering a shared identity. Linked to this, strengthening democratic citizenship and participation is key to promoting the rights and responsibilities of previously marginalised communities so that they may participate actively in wider society. Governments worldwide agree they must strengthen the participatory processes that support the building of *community capacity* to respond to social, environmental and economic issues. Through this, they hope to foster community engagement within civil society:

> Community capacity is the sum of two important concepts – human and social capacity. Human capacity is the skills, knowledge and abilities of individuals. Social capacity is the nature and strength of relationships and level of trust that exists between individuals. These two elements can be mutually reinforcing. For example, individual skills can be applied much more effectively in an environment where there is trust and cooperation. Similarly, a close-knit community can respond more quickly to change if there is a range of individual skills and leadership abilities available to sustain development.
>
> International Association for Public Participation (2009)

Community engagement work, with the goals of shifting towards more participatory forms of governance and building the capacity of communities to implement projects, is now relatively common in the fields of public health, the environment and town planning. However, much of this continues to be institution-led (see for example the 'Public Participation Spectrum' and 'State of the Practice' Reports on the International Association for Public Participation website at www.IAP2.org). In fact, Cuthill and Fein's research (2005) found it difficult in practice to achieve participation and collaboration in local government projects in Australia.

Can museums go beyond top-down content development, even when supposedly working with their communities, to develop partnerships that promote dialogue, build community capacity and support civil engagement? The idea of museums partnering communities in planning for the future is not new; in North America it goes back to the work of John Cotton Dana in the early twentieth century. However, only in the last decade have we seen the active promotion of museums' capacity to empower communities to engage with, consider different perspectives on, and then respond to the great and the local issues of the day. In the USA, a national 'Museums and Community Initiative' promoted from 1998 by the American Association of Museums (following a pilot scheme in Philadelphia) led to the publication of *Mastering Civic Engagement* (AAM 2002). This outlined core principles for museums of greater civic engagement, democracy and community building, and challenged USA museums to build and strengthen their community bonds. We see it also in the Animating Democracy initiative of Americans for the Arts, which applied across the cultural spectrum, not just to museums (www.artsusa.org/animatingdemocracy). However, in both the USA and Western Europe, the response by museums to the civil engagement agenda has been, at best, piecemeal.

Janes believes it is 'the responsibility of civil society organizations to purposefully craft missions that enable participation in public life' (Janes 2009: 21). As one of the first contemporary writers on the potential of museums as agents for civil engagement (Janes 1997: 254–8), he called on museums to create an environment and a sense of community that will enable and support citizen participation. In principle, through representation and the fostering of understanding, museums can ensure community voices are heard, help to create a culture of tolerance and stimulate participation in wider society. As such, they have real potential to play a role in how we go beyond being socially divided and culturally separate societies to become 'societies where a plurality of cultures cooperates in dialogue and shared responsibility' (Figel 2008).

If there is full commitment from the museum's governing body and leadership, we can look specifically at the nature of museums and define core principles, outlined in Box 8.2, which underpin why they are particularly appropriate for the role of building community capacity.

***Box 8.2* Principles underpinning the capacity of museums to build community capacity**

1   Museums as memory institutions can collect, conserve, document and represent the cultures and life experiences of all those who live within their localities, helping to create an inclusive civil environment. Representing diverse communities and multiple perspectives is key to making people feel part of civil society, the starting point for building community capacity.
2   Museums as social institutions can reach out to welcome, support and represent the many voices within the communities they serve – in partnerships of equals.
3   Museums as learning institutions can help to develop informed individuals and communities, developing the skills, knowledge and abilities – both individual and collaborative – that build human capacity.
4   Museums as democratic institutions can actively promote civil dialogue, reflective participation and tolerance in civil society.
5   Museums as responsive institutions can work to change their organisation and culture to engage more effectively with their communities.
6   Museums as volunteering institutions provide direct opportunities for civil engagement.

based on Black (2010)

The roles of the engaged museum as memory institution, social institution and learning institution are discussed elsewhere in this book. In the remainder of this chapter, I want to focus on the engaged museum as a democratic institution, building community capacity by promoting dialogue and participation.

Building community capacity through dialogue

In debate, representatives of two or more opposed points of view slog it out until one is declared the winner. By contrast, in dialogue, parties with differing viewpoints work towards common understanding through an open and respectful exchange of views:

Dialogue is inclusive of multiple and possibly conflicting perspectives rather than promoting a single point of view. It:

- allows assumptions to be brought out into the open and encourages participants to suspend judgment in order to foster understanding
- seeks to create equality among participants
- aims for a greater understanding of others' viewpoints through empathy.

Korza et al. (2005: 47–8)

The dialogue I am concerned with here is within and between the different communities and cultures that make up contemporary society, and between those communities and civil authorities.

Museums, as 'third places', are remarkable in their ability to attract people who are radically different to each other. Such institutions that facilitate social, cultural and generational mixing are the bedrock for a civil society. We can build on these qualities, reaching out to wider audiences and, through an engaging approach to display and programming, encourage conversation between visitors. Conversation in turn can lead to wider dialogue. Dialogue can also be planned for through design and programming. Thus museums have the potential to become venues where people can challenge themselves and each other – an ideal location to act as a catalyst for unleashing comment, conversation, ideas, emotion and reflection both from local people and from users further afield, particularly about issues of contemporary relevance to a locality.

This ability to act as a centre for dialogue within and between communities is at the heart of the museum's capacity to play an active role within contemporary society. It can, for example, reduce tension between community memories; it can promote understanding between communities by developing approaches to display and programming that engage users with the lived experiences of others, and so encourage reflection and understanding. However, there is no guarantee that the approach will work, or that previously marginalised individuals and communities will be willing, for example, to consider a view of the past that does not support their sense of conflict with the mainstream and with each other (Connerton 1989: 19).

Having a general ambition to act as a centre for dialogue around museum content and programming is not enough. To successfully promote and support civil dialogue, museums must be clear on the goals they set out to achieve and have these stated explicitly in their mission statement, as has been done for example by the Field Museum in Chicago. It is only with a clear understanding of objectives that they can plan content and forge the effective partnerships to make them possible. Some common goals are outlined in Box 8.3.

Box 8.3 Common civil dialogue goals

- Increase visibility for, or awareness of, the issue.
- Deepen understanding of the complex dimensions of the issue.
- Increase tolerance and respect among people who hold different beliefs or values.
- Increase participants' sense of individual or collective efficacy for action on the issue.
- Help people recognize their own roles in, and responsibility for, community norms and values.
- Engage civic leaders in a mutually responsive environment.
- Broaden participation in dialogue about the issue, including people who are concerned about the issue but don't typically become engaged.
- Enable people to see connections between personal experiences and civic issues.

Korza et al. (2005: 85–6)

I have attempted below to provide a range of examples that respond to these general goals.

Increase visibility of contentious issues: the rise of issues-based display

The hot topic exhibition inevitably asks as many questions as it answers: it satisfies an audience by transforming the museum into a meaning-rich site of plural reflexivity, which also refuses to patronise with easy truths . . . they possess the ability to speak both to our heads and our hearts; deepening thought around important issues so that visitors are offered the opportunity to leave the space of the exhibition with expanded perspectives, changed minds and open eyes.

Williams (2010: 32–3)

What topics – historic and/or contemporary – do different stakeholders associated with museums consider too controversial to display? A list provided by Ferguson (2010) includes terrorism, asylum seekers, religion, racism, sex and drugs. She suggests one reason these subjects are not displayed is because they contradict 'things that people value about museums – their roles in providing certainty, representing identity, producing "good" citizens and spreading the accepted values of "civilised society"' (Ferguson 2010: 35–6). I am sure this is true, with museums also concerned that their audiences come for a gentle leisure experience, not to be confronted with difficult questions. There are particular concerns about children being exposed to 'adult' issues. Cameron's research (2003, 2005) is important here:

> Should they act as provocateurs, leaders of public opinion and offer transformative spaces to challenge and change views? Or are museums to be safe civic places for the exploration of a range of views? Can museums take on a social activism role, to assist in the resolution of issues on a personal or political level or should they be places for non-challenging social experiences? Alternatively can museums be all of these things at once?
>
> Cameron (2003: 4)

Cameron also highlights the dilemma in balancing the perceived objective basis of knowledge in museums with the subjective interpretations that challenging topics necessarily entail; museums have difficulties in navigating between 'facts'/opinion, authority/expertise, advocacy/neutrality, censorship/exposure (Cameron 2010: 3). Yet, to avoid this sort of content would suggest that silence represents institutional policy. Should mainstream museums be dealing with difficult contemporary issues or should this be left, within the arts, to theatre and contemporary artists?

Researchers from the Exhibitions as Contested Sites international research project (Kelly, start date 2002) questioned visitors to museums in Australia and Canada on their views of whether museums should be 'places to explore important issues'. Over 90 per cent agreed or strongly agreed that they should (Kelly and Russo 2010: 287). Cameron (2005: 228) explores public attitudes to the presentation of contentious issues in museums in Australia, noting that 'bringing important, challenging and controversial points of view in a democratic, free-thinking society was seen as a key role for museums by many'. However, the ability of museums to explore contentious issues and to promote understanding between communities relies both on public trust in them as institutions and on their capacity to create an atmosphere of reflection and dialogue. They will be judged on their choices of display approaches and other means of engagement.

One approach is the inclusion of a 'dialogue space' within individual exhibitions, such as in the Sweatshops in America exhibition at the National Museum of American History in 1998, where different points of view could be represented and engaged with before users contributed their responses:

- Displays included statements and artefacts from a range of individual viewpoints;
- These were supported with scrapbooks of newspaper articles, flipbooks, etc., presenting different perspectives, so that users can develop informed opinions;
- Discussion could be encouraged by users posting or recording their comments.

National Museum of American History (undated)

Cooks wrote of this in relation to a travelling exhibition (What About AIDS?) that she helped to organise:

> Our experience dealing with strong feelings around this exhibit made us realise that we needed a place where visitors could safely express their views ... We also covered a wall with visitors' positive and negative comments to let people know this was an exhibit that welcomed many different points of view.
>
> Cooks (1999: 19)

In Glasgow, the Gallery of Modern Art has become well known for biennial projects involving artists working with local communities, leading to temporary exhibitions that tackle contentious issues relating to social justice.

The exhibition Sanctuary, which was the first of a series (2002–3), looked at the lives of 10,000 asylum seekers who were housed in the Glasgow suburb of Sighthill, one of the most deprived places in Europe. The gallery's visitor research revealed strong public outrage at the issues raised, reflected in Box 8.4.

Box 8.4 Visitor responses to the Sanctuary exhibition

'Shock, anger, horror, despair, hope, inspiration and admiration.'

'It has been very upsetting, but powerful and needed.'

'We all live in comfort, oblivious to these things, and it is good to see somewhere not afraid to talk about them.'

'This has brought me a new viewpoint.'

Glasgow Museums (2007: 12)

Figure 8.5 Rebelland
Image from the exhibition Blind Faith which explored sectarianism in Glasgow, reproduced courtesy of the artist Anthony Schrag. More information on this project can be found at www.anthonyschrag.com/Doing-Stuff-Together/Legacy.html

The relevance of the Glasgow programme lies not only in its content but also in the decision to evaluate in detail and to communicate the results. They have revealed the importance of the medium of contemporary art itself: 'to go beyond the sound-bite, digging deeper to focus on the human issues of today, "earthing" ideas and realities that can make us consider them afresh or, perhaps, crucially, even for the first time …' Hollows (2010: 92).

They have also uncovered essential practicalities, not least the emotional demands these kinds of programme place on all those involved, including the artists. They have also affirmed the positive impacts on the institution, including the opportunities to work with a wider range of artists, the development of staff expertise and external funding for the purchase of contemporary works.

In 2007 the New Jersey Historical Association mounted an exhibition examining the events around riots in Newark in 1967, when 26 people were killed. There were riots in the same period in 127 other USA cities, and riots again in 1968 following the murder of Martin Luther King. Unrest continued sporadically into the early 1970s. Newark, along with several other USA cities, was stigmatised by the media as riot-torn.

After 10 years of increasing involvement with local communities, the Historical Society took up the challenge of trying to depict what happened and place it in context. There was no formal record of events – in fact, there was profound disagreement. For example, the police and people in the establishment thought the unrest was planned, while black leaders and others believed it was spontaneous. So the Society devised a project to build dialogue and understanding. They involved both school children and the Facing History organisation (www.facinghistory.org), which has more than 30 years' experience of using workshops to nurture understanding and democracy. The Society was fortunate to be able to uncover powerful memories that were made available for recording. The end result – an exhibition entitled What's Going On? – placed the unrest within 1960s culture and the struggle for renewal and rebirth since that time. It also incorporated a response booth so visitors could leave their comments and reflections. It did not suggest there was only one truth, but the capacity of all involved – 40 years after the event – to share perspectives represented an important healing process and showed the importance of civil engagement. The Society continues to offer guided walking tours of the area hardest hit by the riots.

The use of interactive technology to encourage reflection and discussion, and to elicit responses from visitors, is only just being recognised. See, for example, the 'Room of Opinion' in the Re-tracing the Past exhibition at the Hunt Museum, Limerick (Ciolfi et al. 2008). Better known is the Free2Choose exhibit at the Anne Frank House in Amsterdam, which invites participants to reflect and then vote on a variety of human rights issues in a way that allows users to compare their own votes with those of others taking part at the same time and with 'all visitors' (Simon 2008). In a wider context, outreach projects and the museum website play an important role in taking such 'museum conversations' beyond the museum.

Deepen understanding of complex issues

While the encouragement of reflection and resulting contributions should be a core objective, sustained and meaningful dialogue is unlikely to happen between groups of visitors moving through exhibition galleries. To nurture active user involvement and in-depth discussion of issues, we need to look beyond provision in individual galleries to create spaces, or 'dialogue centres', where this can happen. It is perhaps surprising that few museums have taken this approach. A key example, the purpose-built Dana Centre at the Science Museum in London, has an adults-only programme committed to the debate of key contemporary issues in science (www.danacentre.org.uk). It continues these debates, and seeks suggestions for potential subject matter through its website, Facebook and Twitter. The state of the art Wosk Dialogue Centre, not part of a museum, can be seen at the Simon Fraser University in Vancouver, Canada. While no museum could hope to replicate this, it provides an exemplar to learn from.

Korza et al. (2005) provide a number of examples of programming for dialogue in USA museums. McRainey (2008) discusses programming at the Chicago History Museum as a means of supporting civil dialogue. The whole approach to programming at the museum was replanned in the lead-up to the major refurbishment completed in 2006, moving 'the interpretive focus in programme design away from an exhibition-centred approach to one that is creating new connections between adults, history and the city' (McRainey 2008: 33). The programming includes 'panel presentations, forums for debate, seminar discussions and tours' that together 'offer participants multiple points for exploration and diverse perspectives for meaning-making' (p. 39). It is the forums that most obviously reflect the new role the museum has taken in supporting civil engagement. These were carefully planned, following audience studies, to include 'diverse perspectives for new insights into topics; primary voices of individuals who have first-hand knowledge; and dialogue among panellists as well as between panellists and participants' (p. 38). There is no opportunity for the museum to rest on its laurels:

> With the recurring monthly schedule, the structure challenges staff to demonstrate their nimbleness and flexibility in program design in timely responses to stories that headline local papers and issues discussed in community centres.
>
> McRainey (2008: 40)

Increase tolerance and respect

> A vital aspect of [cultural learning's] civic potential is to foster understanding between cultures, and to reflect the diversity that exists through race, ethnicity, faith, disability, sexuality, class, and economic situation.
>
> Culture and Learning Consortium (2009: 18)

A remarkable range of museums across the world have committed themselves to focusing on positive ways of working with their communities to address political, religious and cultural divisions through increased understanding and a shared humanity, often in the most difficult of circumstances. Since its foundation in 1932 a mission of the Tel Aviv Museum of Art has been to build bridges between art and society. 'The Art Road to Peace' is a long-running project that brings together Jewish and Arab children in week-long workshops and activities. It is a major commitment by the museum to employing art as a mediation tool between Israeli societies in conflict, working to promote tolerance and understanding through collaborative art projects.

In Northern Ireland, museums have a specific commitment under the government's A Shared Future initiative to promote peace and reconciliation following over 30 years of inter-community conflict:

> a shared society defined by a culture of tolerance: a normal, civic society, in which all individuals are considered equals, where differences are resolved through dialogue in the public sphere and where all individuals are treated impartially. A society where there is equality, respect for diversity and recognition of our interdependence.
>
> Office of the First Minister and Deputy First Minister (2005: 3)

Under this initiative the 37 publicly funded museums in Northern Ireland are expected to promote a society which is at ease with individual diversity through a culture of tolerance and to:

- encourage understanding of the complexity of our history . . .;
- support cultural projects which highlight the complexity and overlapping nature of identities and their wider global connections;
- develop cultural capital through the principles of creativity learning and diversity.

Office of the First Minister and Deputy First Minister (2005: 31)

Figure 8.6 **Celebrating the Art Road to Peace**
The final event of an Art Road to Peace project brings together Jewish and Arab children in an art-based performance at Tel Aviv Museum of Art. Courtesy of Yael Borovich.

Fifteen museums in Northern Ireland are currently involved in reconciliation projects.

The city of Coventry, England, has had a commitment to peace and reconciliation since its devastation during the Second World War. When the city's Herbert Art Gallery and Museum was redisplayed in 2007 and 2008, a Peace and Reconciliation gallery was a key element. It explores complex themes around peace and conflict through the Coventry experience of the Second World War, but it continues to the present day through the new communities who have settled in the city as a result of conflict in their homelands. The Imperial War Museum in London and museums in Dresden and Warsaw are linked to the gallery and have helped develop the displays, bringing film, oral histories and object loans. In addition to the gallery, the museum runs an extensive programme of activities, particularly with schools (see Chapter 5).

Since 1986, the National Museum of Denmark in Copenhagen has worked with children who come to the country as refugees or immigrants. It has also sought to give Danish school children a glimpse of the countries from which the nation's new inhabitants have come, as well as the traditions and customs they have brought with them. But the museum also raises contentious issues. Recent themes for dialogue, underpinned by material in the permanent displays, have included arranged marriages and the concept of family honour – linked to news of so-called 'honour killings':

> The key/method is to use other cultures or historical material as a sort of mirror that can make the young people reflect on their own life and on the traditions and practices in their own society ... We have learned much about how young people with different backgrounds think and reflect on matters. And the important part is precisely that they get to reflect on things, and that we in the museums can take part in getting some thoughts going.
>
> Boritz (pers. comm. 2009)

Increase participants' sense of individual or collective efficacy for action

The Chicago Field Museum, discussed above, is a first class example of this.

The Freedom Centre, on Constitution Hill, Johannesburg, South Africa, was built on the site of the city's notorious Old Fort prison. In its time, this prison held the leaders of every major South African liberation group, from Gandhi to Nelson Mandela – although most of those held were ordinary people arrested under the apartheid Pass Laws. In 1995 South African judges selected the prison as the site for the new Constitutional Court. Combining the old prison and new court juxtaposes past abuse and hope for the future. The mission for the Freedom Centre includes encouraging civic responsibility and popular participation in the process of democracy. It uses the struggles of people in the past to reveal the difference committed people can make. Its public participation programme, We the People, has begun a nationwide process of inviting ex-prisoners and warders back to the site to take part in workshops and record their experiences. The museum has developed a programme of dialogues for democracy based on the *lekgotla*, a Sotho/Tswana word meaning non-hierarchical dialogues conducted at public gatherings to decide matters of group or social importance. These are used also to help people draw connections between the past and the present.

The 'We the People Wall' is a growing record of the thoughts and impressions of everyone from ex-prisoners to recent visitors on the experience of Constitution Hill today. Hand-written messages are etched on to copper 'bricks' and added to the wall, with one of the first bricks laid by Nelson Mandela.

Help people recognise their own responsibility for community norms and values

In the USA, the Greater Philadelphia Cultural Alliance seeks to increase dramatically cultural participation in the region by 2020. It underpins its activities by research using a Cultural Engagement Index (CEI) with core objectives of stimulating innovation, tracking engagement over time, informing policy and reinforcing culture as a valued component of the region's quality of life (Greater Philadelphia Cultural Alliance 2009). Preliminary findings suggest that:

- Cultural role models are a linchpin in the cultural system. Those who can cite both in-family and out-of-family cultural role models engage at twice the level of those with neither.
- The presence of children in the household appears to increase, not decrease, cultural engagement.

- Personal practice correlates with higher levels of engagement.
- Cultural engagement levels for African-Americans and Hispanics were consistently higher than those for whites.
- Higher civic engagement is directly correlated with higher cultural engagement – investments in culture are also investments in civic engagement and quality of life.

A new survey in 2011, again using CEI, suggests there has been an 11 per cent increase in cultural participation since the initiative was launched (www.philaculture.org).

Engage civic leaders

In 2004, the Levine Museum of the New South accompanied its Civil Rights exhibition COURAGE: The Carolina Story that Changed America with a civil dialogue component, 'Conversations on COURAGE' (Deuel et al. 2007). There was a real concern that the current civic and corporate leadership in Charlotte knew little of the historical background so, rather than reaching out to disadvantaged groups, the specific aim here was 'to use history to help engage current leaders in contemporary issues of race, education and social justice.' The ambition was to bring in corporate leaders and their lieutenants to visit the exhibition in teams and then spend an hour in a facilitator-led discussion, making the shared experience into a long term reference point. The 'Conversations' proved highly successful, with 111 teams taking part, from the police chief and his staff to the Bank of America. This proved to be the first of a series of successful projects, with civil dialogue now a standard part of the museum operation, and a new phrase to sum up the museum mission: 'Using History to Build Community'.

Include people who don't typically become engaged

We shall never forget but we cannot stay for ever on the battlefield.
> Quote from an archaeologist in Bosnia and Herzegovina, *Cultural Heritage without Borders* (2010: back cover)

Museum curators can be among the most reluctant to become involved, yet we need them to play an active role, rather than stay neutral, if museums are truly to be centres for the promotion of understanding and civil engagement.

The conflicts in the western Balkans in the 1990s are infamous for civilian slaughter on a scale not seen in Europe since the Second World War. Although direct conflict has now ended, the disputes underpinning it continue. Many countries, for example, have not recognised the Republic of Kosovo. Tension and political instability is a constant issue. In this context, attempts within local communities to promote understanding and reconciliation require both commitment and courage. Museum curators have chosen to become engaged in this work through the creation of the Western Balkan Regional Museum Network. The Network was initiated in 2006 with the support of Cultural Heritage without Borders, as part of its overall response to the destruction of cultural property in the region. The ambition was to focus on the heritage that the region held in common rather than on differences:

> There is a huge amount of shared heritage that can reveal a very different view of the region; one of rich diversity, human achievement, ancient civilizations and contemporary artistic excellence. Museums can ... present this face to the world and become places of creativity, conflict resolution and dialogue.
>
> Cultural Heritage without Borders (2010: 3)

The Network involves 11 museums of varying sizes, from national institutions to small period houses, located in six Balkan countries. They set out not only to actively strengthen the role of museums as democratic and creative meeting places but also to support each other professionally and personally through working together, sharing resources and taking part in regular workshops and study visits. Key challenges have included supporting museum directors to become creative leaders and creating a network of female managers to discuss and share problems and solutions.

On 11 March 2011, all 11 museums simultaneously opened an exhibition called '1 + 1, Life and Love' to promote a more positive image of a shared heritage that had been artificially divided and problematised through conflict. Work in developing the exhibitions also involved creating interdisciplinary project teams: educators, technicians and marketing staff worked alongside curators, meaning that curators in what were previously very hierarchical institutions had to learn to work in new ways. The exhibition opening was followed by a 'peace bus', with a diverse group of curators, educators, technicians and even an independent film crew from Belgrade travelling together to visit many of the museums.

Like the Field Museum in Chicago, discussed above, here we have museums not hiding behind a need to be a neutral space but instead helping to set the agenda. As the Network moves towards becoming an autonomous organisation based entirely in the region, it deserves the recognition and support of the entire international museum community.

Make connections between personal experiences and civic issues

Being the American-born child of an immigrant father . . . was, for me, a defining experience. My dad would frequently respond to something I said or did by asking "Are you an American?"

Liz Sevchenko, quoted in Abram (2005: 25)

Sevchenko works for the Lower East Side Tenement Museum, mission driven since its creation in 1988 around the question 'What can history do to improve the world?' Telling the powerful stories of succeeding generations of immigrants who lived at 97 Orchard Street, it uses the past and present personal experiences of immigrants to:

- showcase and interpret the cultural and artistic expressions of immigrants/migrants, past and present
- raise awareness of the contemporary implications and/or counterparts of the history the museum interprets and offer visitors the means to evaluate these issues on their own

- stimulate dialogue among people of diverse backgrounds focusing on immigration and related enduring social issues ... and suggest opportunities for audiences to become involved in addressing these issues
- encourage and assist immigrants/migrants of all ages to participate fully in political, civic and social life ...

Abram (2005: 28)

In 1999, the museum was a founder member of the International Coalition of Sites of Conscience, a worldwide network of historic sites dedicated to remembering past struggles for justice and human rights, and addressing their contemporary legacies (www.sitesofconscience.org). The coalition currently consists of 17 sites, witness in the past to both individual struggles and mass atrocity. They are committed to drawing connections between their histories and their contemporary implications through stimulating dialogue on pressing social issues and promoting humanitarian and democratic values. Its most recent member (2010) is the Memoria Abierta in Buenos Aires, Argentina, site of a centre for state terror, kidnapping and torture particularly between 1976 and 1983.

The need for continuing evaluation

The examples given above are presented without any formal critique. However, if we are to take seriously the capacity of museums to reflect multiple perspectives and to promote dialogue and civil engagement – and if our claims that we can do so are to be taken seriously – we must come up with effective ways of evaluating their performance. Such evaluation is crucial, and depends vitally on museums acknowledging failure as well as success. It must explore the issues that evaluation raises for the whole institution, not just for individual exhibitions or projects. It must focus on the effectiveness of visitor engagement, the contributions visitors make and the meanings they construct. Sharing experience and expertise is core to moving us all forward. We need this work:

- to evaluate both the process of developing content for prolonged engagement, including the stimulation of user conversation and contributions, and the effectiveness or otherwise of the end product (ongoing as the product will keep changing). We also need to share the results with the museum community;
- to examine the practical and institutional issues around reflecting multiple perspectives;
- to highlight the need for ongoing training for staff and volunteers;
- for museums to build on their experience of developing successful, long term partnerships with communities *and* learn from the experience of others;
- to support communities in applying best practice advice;
- to establish how museums can best make a positive difference as agents for civil engagement and any impacts that result from this role.

A range of articles provide a useful starting point for the debate on evaluation that we need to have. For example, Douglas Worts has spent more than a decade exploring the opportunities open to museums that seek to serve the cultural needs of individuals and communities, and how museums measure their successes and failures in this field. His article 'Measuring museum meaning: a critical assessment framework' (Worts 2006) discusses the development of evaluative approaches and performance indicators, such as the extent to which the museum addresses vital community needs and acts as a catalyst for action. Economou (2004) outlines the range of evaluation approaches she developed at Kelvingrove Museum and Art Gallery, Glasgow, creating a strategy which she suggests 'addressed evaluation holistically, and planned extensively and in-depth how it could be used as a useful tool to support the key activities throughout the organisation' (Economou 2004: 31). McLean and Cooke (2003: 161), in their interviews of visitors to the then newly opened Museum of Scotland, were able to show that 'Rather than reading a one-dimensional static narrative of a nation, the visitors constructed multifarious readings that reflected both their individual identities and their collective identities in an imagined community.'

CONCLUDING THOUGHTS

This chapter is built around the inspiring examples of a minority of museums. Most museums remain unconscious and unmindful of the issues it discusses. Yet, if you want your museum to be truly relevant to contemporary society, to help people grow as individuals and communities, and to support social cohesion, then the ideals underpinning the chapter must be enshrined in your mission statement and drive a sense of collective purpose across your institution. 'Without a clear mission, endorsed by the museum's governing body and leadership, there is no collective purpose and the work will not happen' (Janes, pers. comm. 2011). Drawing on Peter Block's work (2002) on organisational values, Janes and Conaty (2005) suggest that four core values must be present: idealism, intimacy, depth and interconnectedness, as outlined in Box 8.5.

Box 8.5 The four values needed for community-focused museums

Idealism	Thinking about the way things could be, rather than simply accepting the way things are
Intimacy	The quality of contact that is made … there is no substitute for human relationships and all the time, energy and consideration they require
Depth	Depth is about being thorough and complete, even when this requires a tremendous investment in time and resources … building relationships with particular groups of people all in an effort to try to understand what is important
Interconnectedness	A growing societal awareness of the interconnectedness of things

based on Janes and Conaty (2005: 8–10)

Enshrining these values in a collective mission can only be to the benefit of museums and the communities they serve:

- Museums that place communities at their hearts will benefit from new audiences, and an enhanced position as part of their community.
- Both they and their users will be stimulated by the diversity of contributions.
- The previously silent voices of local communities will be replaced by their own narratives.
- Museum values of trust and tolerance, dialogue and interdependence can support different communities in gaining a greater understanding of each other.
- Together their voices have the potential to influence the future of their localities for the better.

Such a mission statement can be seen, for example, at Tyne & Wear Museums:

- We make a positive difference to people's lives
- We inspire and challenge people to explore their world and open up new horizons
- We are a powerful learning resource for people of all ages, needs and backgrounds
- We act as an agent of economic regeneration and help build and develop communities and the aspirations of individuals
- We are fully accountable to our stakeholders and users
- Our resources should be accessible to everyone.

Tyne & Wear Archives and Museums (undated)

It is not all one way – communities too must gain an understanding of wider museum goals and of what museums can and cannot do. They must also begin to accept museums as non-threatening 'third places' rather than the tools of an elite. This will take much time and involve reaching out to those who have in the past seen museums as 'not for us'.

To develop and *sustain* museum participation over the longer term among previously under-represented groups within society requires an active, prolonged commitment from top-level management downwards; there must be a planned exercise in defining target audiences, establishing their needs and expectations, and then meeting them. It also requires an equal commitment to direct involvement with the communities concerned because the museum must establish an active presence in the community.

Endpiece: the future of the museum exhibition

A concern I reluctantly have been entertaining these days [is] that museum exhibitions might be an obsolete medium, out on the dying limb of an evolutionary tree, and unless they significantly adapt to their rapidly changing environments in the coming years, they could be headed toward extinction.

McLean (2007b: 117)

McLean's sad tale of neglect in dreadful visits to three museums in Toronto, followed by experiencing the vibrancy of the fleshpots of the city (OK – a video arcade, a jazz club and a Chinatown restaurant) will resonate with all of us. There is a direct relationship between rarely changing museum content and a take it or leave it attitude to users. Much of this is down to the continuing dominance of the so-called permanent exhibition.

Since museums were first established, the permanent exhibition has been viewed as the primary means of granting public access to the collections held. While enabling close and sustained access to the 'real thing' is the permanent exhibition's greatest strength, it has been shown to have other benefits also. From an operational management point of view, the permanent exhibition is an efficient way of providing public access. In the past, once the exhibition had been installed, the curatorial team was freed to carry out other tasks. The exhibition itself can cater for irregular levels of audience usage. Collections are protected from theft and/or damage by efficient security measures including casing, and through control of the gallery environment and lighting. Revenue costs can be predicted. And, if no additional capital funding becomes available at the proposed end date, the life of the exhibition can be extended. Crucially, the museum controls exhibition content – both the objects and the information that accompanies them.

From the point of view of the user, traditional audiences are accustomed to the exhibition format as a communication medium, and museums have been able to use visitor studies to some extent to evaluate visit outcomes. Museum exhibitions lend themselves naturally to unpressurised, free-choice visitor learning (Falk and Dierking 2002). People come when they want and decide for themselves when to leave. While in the exhibition, users can normally move through the spaces involved at their own pace and often in an order they choose – they select for themselves what they want to view and the amount of time they want to spend – based, as discussed in Chapter 1, on their own agendas, motivations and expectations. As the exhibition will remain in place for an extended period of time, people can return time and again to re-experience it, if they so desire. Exhibitions can also satisfy the need for a social experience – unless on a structured educational visit, users select for themselves who to share the visit with. In practice, their experience of the exhibition will vary depending on whom they are accompanied by. They also experience the exhibition with many other people they do not know but who share their interest in visiting.

Of course, not all exhibitions are the same. A 2002 report by the Smithsonian Institution defines four general approaches, as outlined in Box 9.1.

Box 9.1 Four approaches to the ways exhibitions function

1 *Exhibition as artefact display*	e.g. Art Galleries Selection and arrangement of objects the primary focus. Messages conveyed through the objects – from 'the art can speak for itself' to groups of objects to represent a greater whole.
2 *Exhibition as communicator of ideas*	e.g. History Museums The heart of the exhibition is the set of messages, narratives, or facts that the exhibition-makers wish to deliver.
3 *Exhibition as visitor activity*	e.g. Science Centers Emphasis on interactivity: the activity-exhibition puts visitor behaviour and interaction at the centre.
4 *Exhibition as environment*	e.g. immersive Natural History Museums or Period Rooms The visitor gets a sense of the environment and explores the possibilities that the setting evokes and permits.

based on OP&A (2002)

Many exhibitions are hybrids of these models. However, in general, museums have tended to favour one concept model over the others. This in turn influences what we could call the 'traditional' characteristics of the exhibitions – as defined by the museum – explored in Box 9.2.

Box 9.2 'Traditional' characteristics of different exhibition types

Exhibition type	Central focus	Major activity	Major media	Primary experience type
1 *Artefact*	Artefacts	Looking	Artefacts	Settings
2 *Ideas*	Ideas/stories	Reading, listening, doing	Full range of design media	Cognitive
3 *Activity*	Activities	Touching	Interactives	Social
4 *Environment*	Settings	Exploring, sensing	Immersive spaces	Introspective

based on OP&A (2002: 9)

Figure 9.1 **Exhibition as artefact display: New Green Vault, Dresden Castle**
Reopened in 2006, the 3,000 remarkable objects in the historic Green Vault, founded c. 1560, represent Europe's richest treasure chamber museum, displayed in an appropriate historical layout. The 1,000 most important items are housed in new galleries, named the New Green Vault, with a display approach that focuses on individual objects. Internally lit cases were rejected in favour of bespoke lighting from above. The glass is non-reflective and super white quality, ensuring no distortion of the light spectrum. The result is close and sustained access to the objects and a flexible display space, but limited support information. Courtesy of Green Vault, Staatliche Kunstammlungen, Dresden.

Where the display's primary objective is to focus on an artefact, and particularly when the emphasis is on aesthetic appeal, design approaches have on the whole enhanced direct engagement with collections. The ambition to widen audiences for such content, and enhance the experience for all, has led to the development of reasonably subtle interpretive approaches that provide visitor access to supporting information on multiple levels while not competing with the objects or art works. Examples of this approach are the British Gallery at the Victoria & Albert Museum, London, winner of the European Museum of the Year Award in 2003, and the Wedgwood Museum in Stoke, winner of the £100,000 Art Prize in 2009.

The real problem lies in permanent exhibitions which focus on the communication of ideas, not least in history galleries. While museums have continued to focus on the delivery of content, and largely maintained a linear narrative approach based on chronology, they have recognised that they must meet the needs of a multiplicity of audiences with different motivations, levels of understanding and learning styles. They have sought to do this by having increasingly complex expectations of exhibition design, with the balance in display content often moving away from collections and towards the media used. This has had a number of unfortunate consequences:

- Exhibitions have become increasingly expensive and time-consuming to mount and to maintain.
- The emphasis on the exhibition narrative and on the design media used to tell the story has frequently reduced collections to the role of illustration or 'window dressing'.
- Exhibitions, even when poor in terms of user engagement, have lingered on well beyond their 'sell by' date because they are too expensive to replace.
- As exhibitions have become more complex, more expensive and more focused on the design media used, the power of design companies has grown, often at the expense of the museum's original exhibition objectives.
- While new media have brought with them some dynamism and action in the galleries, with hands-on elements to encourage active involvement by users, the role of the audience has remained passive in terms of receipt of information.
- Once opened, the exhibitions are abandoned by the team involved as they rush on to the next new thing. What starts off as new and fresh for museum users within a few years becomes 'nothing new to see, no need to go back'. We witness a combination of neglect by the museum and abandonment by audiences as they too rush on to the next new thing.

In these circumstances, McLean is right to worry that the museum exhibition will shortly become an obsolete medium. But it does not have to be this way. I believe strongly in the potential of the long term exhibition, but as a living, growing, developing creature, not a neglected, over-priced corpse. If museums can break away from the mind-set of the ultra-expensive exhibitions we have created over the last 20 years and apply the experimentation and innovation we display in many of our temporary exhibitions, we can give the concept of the user-driven exhibition a future. The simple principle here is to start small, experiment, involve our users in that experimentation, and then go forward.

I hope this whole book, and particularly the examples it contains, has revealed alternative approaches that will work. I have no intention of repeating book highlights here, but I do want to outline some core principles for the development of what I shall call long term exhibitions, leaving individual museums to fill in the details. So, here are some thoughts, by no means definitive:

1 Take time to engage with your users on the subjects they would like to see explored through exhibitions. Imagine developing content you know your audiences want to find out about. Imagine being able to rely on user expertise to help develop that content. Remember to always ask 'What will our users want to know about this?'
2 Allow considerable additional time for piloting and prototyping with users, as this

will result in a much improved end product. Follow the Wikipedia example – try things out quickly and cheaply, admit failure when appropriate, recognise success when it happens and build on it (Connor 2009: 10).

3 Allow much more space than Maximea suggests (see Chapter 3) for people and activities within the exhibition galleries, including space for reflection. This space can have many functions – seating, handling corner, dwell point for school pupils, etc.

4 Take a pluralistic approach to content from the outset, ensuring a platform for a multiplicity of perspectives and encouraging conversation/dialogue.

5 Drum into all involved that the exhibition is a 'live' project and will never be 'finished'. This does *not* mean people can miss their deadlines. It does mean you place real value on user contributions and will give them a central role in adding to and refreshing content on an ongoing basis after opening. This means taking a highly flexible approach to design!

6 Ensure multiple entry points and layering of content.

7 Ensure the creation of support materials and programmes of activities (*not* one-offs) as an integral part of the project from the start – from trails to study zones, to object-handling sessions, to whatever.

8 Develop a masterplan for the whole museum from the outset that tries to link on-site, online and mobile provision seamlessly. In particular, look for ways to bring social media on-site: 'if we focus exclusively on fostering discussion through online activity, we miss out on the social value this can bring to a gallery experience' (Antrobus 2010: 8).

9 Provide for an 'exhibition manager' role to oversee/co-ordinate the ongoing development of the exhibition after its opening through collaboration with and contributions by exhibition users.

10 Keep looking for new ways to create a buzz around old content.

All of this must *lead to a change in the balance between capital and revenue spend during exhibition development to keep the exhibition alive after opening.* Argue the case strongly with funders that exhibitions must be built much more cheaply by cutting back on the design media, and the money saved transferred to your revenue streams.

Do not give up on existing permanent galleries where there is no money to replace them. Why not:

- Experiment with simple trails and activities, and replace them regularly – this has worked brilliantly at Mansfield, Otago and Denver, three of the case studies in this book.
- Find out which object your users find most interesting/peculiar, give it a life of its own and get it tweeting.
- Create a comfortable corner with seats in a circle.
- Have competitions and voting – encourage people to get engaged.
- Hold gallery picnics!

If you do not create a buzz, no one will do it for you.

Museums and designers

What does this mean for the museum's relationship with design companies? There is a whole commercial industry out there now, specialising in museum exhibit design. I readily admit that I would like to see a return to cheaper, simpler exhibitions, building on what many museums already do for their temporary exhibition programmes – but this does not mean do-it-yourself is the only future. Museum design can be transformative.

Bringing together museum and design objectives for any exhibition is a collaborative process – but much more so for ones whose focus is on user collaboration and engagement. When the relationship between museum and designer works well it is a delight and a creative inspiration, but all too often it can end in tears. Once designers are in place and particularly once they have control of the timetable and budget, the whole process of design and installation can become like an unstoppable juggernaut. It does not have to be like this. It is essential that there is a shared ethos around the objectives of creating a living exhibition and one that supports prolonged, meaningful engagement, and how these can best be achieved. The museum retaining full control of the process is central – something that can be difficult to do if the contract gives the design company responsibility for the budget. The general principles outlined in Box 9.3 can help towards a positive working arrangement and successful end product. Retrospectively, I wish these principles had been applied in all of the projects I have worked on.

Box 9.3 General principles for working positively with external design companies

1   Make plenty of time to imbue the designers with the *ethos of the project* – otherwise, as happens too often, the end product will be imbued with the ethos of the design company. The starting points are a great outline design brief (including key messages and core objectives) and good communication – make your expectations clear and work hard to understand your designers' expectations. This gives the underpinning for a solid working relationship.

2   The outline design brief must emphasise the 'live' nature of the exhibition – it will be a living, breathing entity that will continue to develop over time. *Flexibility* is the key. This should not mean more expensive. Lower production values may actually be a good thing if they make ongoing change easier to achieve.

3   Ensure that both sides agree on what they mean by public *collaboration* and meaningful *engagement*. Check that the designers respond positively to the concept of placing *user contributions* at the heart of the project, and do not just propose a comments board stuck in a dark corner.

4   Make sure that the outline design brief highlights the need for plenty of *spaces* and *seating* for users – *and* that your proposed content would not fill the gallery three times over.

5   Ensure that you, your staff team and the designers agree on what is meant by a *realistic timetable*. This will be longer than your director wants.

6   Focus on *cheap and cheerful* for testing ideas before developing a detailed design brief. *Always* pilot and prototype approaches with museum users before finalising and approving the brief or the design. Include a realistic budget and timetable for this from the off. The longer you can spend piloting the better – and your public will enjoy and appreciate the involvement.

7   Have a *realistic budget* and make sure, in their project tender and at interview, that the designers have agreed that the project can be achieved to the standard you expect within the budget. Make the design tender transparent so you can see, for example, how much time has been allowed for prototyping and working with users.

8   The detailed design brief must have *clear priorities* – your ambitions will invariably be greater than your budget. If you do not prioritise, the design company will have to make those decisions.

9   Ensure you have an *in-house team leader* to drive the project forward, that all core staff on the team are taken off the 'day job' so they can focus on the exhibition, and that all have 'bought in' to the concept of user collaboration and engagement. Build the skills and confidence of the staff team – remember they will have to keep the exhibition developing after opening.

10 *Never* give the design company responsibility for developing exhibition *content* on the dubious grounds that their specific expertise and understanding of how people use exhibitions means they will be able to make content more accessible to your target audiences.

11 *Never* allow the designers to chair the meetings that merge content, approach and design proposals – your issues should be the dominant ones, not the issues of the design company.

Good design will make your ideas sing. I have had both wonderful and truly awful experiences with designers. I believe strongly that what matters most is the museum's clarity of vision, expressed through the design brief, and the selection of a design team in the first place that buys into that vision. If you are not confident in your brief, the design process will be difficult, time consuming and expensive, and the end product will satisfy no one. If you are confident, you can work with your designers to develop the brief creatively in a way that results in exhibition content that delights and inspires all who engage with it.

Bibliography

AAM (1972) *Museums: Their New Audience. A Report to the Department of Housing and Urban Development by a Special Committee of the American Association of Museums*, Washington DC: American Association of Museums.

AAM (1984) *Museums for a New Century: A Report of the Commission on Museums for a New Century*, Washington DC: American Association of Museums.

AAM (2002) *Mastering Civic Engagement: A Challenge to Museums*, Washington DC: American Association of Museums.

AAM (2007) *Annual Report*, Washington DC: American Association of Museums.

AAM (2011) *2011 Mobile Technology Survey*, accessed on 31/05/2011 at www.aam-us.org/upload/AAM_Mobile_Technology_Survey.pdf

Abraham, M., Griffin, D. and Crawford, J. (1999) Organisation change and management decision in museums, *Management Decision* 37 (10), pp. 736–51.

Abram, R.J. (2005) History is as history does: the evolution of a mission-driven museum, in Janes, R.R. and Conaty, G.T. (eds) *Looking Reality in the Eye: Museums and Social Responsibility*, Calgary, Alberta: University of Calgary Press, pp. 19–42.

Abu-Shumays, M. and Leinhardt, G. (2002) Two docents in three museums: central and peripheral participation, in Leinhardt, G., Crowley, K. and Knutson, K. (eds) *Learning Conversations in Museums*, Mahwah NJ: Lawrence Erlbaum Associates, pp. 45–80.

Adams, M. (2005) *Final Report on Visitor Research for Phase 1 of the IMLS Education Interpretive Project for the Speed Art Museum, Louisville, KY*, 21 September, Edgewater MD: Institute for Learning Innovation.

Adams, M., Falk, J. and Dierking, L. (2003) Things change: museums, learning and research, in Xanthoudaki, M., Tickle, L. and Sekules, V. (eds) *Researching Visual Arts Education in Museums and Galleries*, London: Kluwer Academic Publishers.

Adams, R. (2001) *Museum Visitor Services Manual*, Washington DC: American Association of Museums.

AEA Consulting (2005) *Tyne & Wear Museum, Bristol's Museums, Galleries and Archives: Social Impact Programme Assessment*, accessed on 31/05/2011 at www.twmuseums.org.uk/about/corporatedocuments/documents/Social_Impact.pdf

Alexander, E.P. (1979) *Museums in Motion*, Nashville TN: AASLH.

Allen, S. (2002) Looking for learning in visitor talk: a methodological exploration, in Leinhardt, G., Crowley, K. and Knutson, K. (eds) *Learning Conversations in Museums*, Mahwah NJ: Lawrence Erlbaum Associates, pp. 259–303.

AMARC (2003) Website of the Australian Museum Audience Research Centre, accessed on 31/05/2011 at http://australianmuseum.net.au/Audience-Research

Ames, M. (1985) De-schooling the museum: a proposal to increase public access to museums and their resources, *Museum* 37 (1), pp. 25–31.

Anderson, D. (1997) *A Common Wealth: Museums in the Learning Age*, London: DCMS.

Anderson, D., Storksdieck, M. and Spock, M. (2007) Understanding the long-term impacts of museum experiences, in Falk, J.H., Dierking, L.D. and Foutz, S. (eds) *In Principle, In Practice: Museums as Learning Institutions*, Lanham MD: AltaMira Press, pp. 197–215.

Antrobus, A. (2010) *From Audiences to Users: Changing Art Galleries and Museums Together*, accessed on 31/05/2011 at www.claireantrobus.com/wp/wp-content/uploads/2009/11/audiencestrousers.pdf

Archibald, R. (1999) *A Place to Remember: Using History to Build Community*, Walnut Creek CA: AltaMira Press.

Archibald, R. R. (2004) *The New Town Square: Museums and Communities in Transition*, Walnut Creek CA: AltaMira Press.

Arigho, B. (2008) Ch. 14, Getting a handle on the past: the use of objects in reminiscence work, in Chatterjee, H.J. (ed.) *Touch in Museums: Policy and Practice in Object Handling*, Oxford: Berg, pp. 205–12.

Arts Council England (2006) *The Power of Art, Visual Arts: Evidence of Impact*, London: ACE.

Arts Council England (2008) *Arts Audiences Insight*, London: Arts Council England, accessed on 31/05/2011 at www.artscouncil.org.uk/media/uploads/segmentation_research/Arts_audiences_insight.pdf

Ash, D. (2002) Negotiation of thematic conversations about biology, in Leinhardt, G., Crowley, K. and Knutson, K. (eds) *Learning Conversations in Museums*, Mahwah NJ: Lawrence Erlbaum Associates, pp. 357–400.

Astor-Jack, T., Kiehl Whaley, K.L., Dierking, L.D., Perry, D.L. and Garibay, C. (2007) Investigating socially mediated learning, in Falk, J.H., Dierking, L.D. and Foutz, S. (eds) *In Principle, In Practice: Museums as Learning Institutions*, Lanham MD: AltaMira Press, pp. 217–28.

Aust, R. and Vine, L. (eds) (2007) *Taking Part: The National Survey of Culture, Leisure and Sport, Annual Report 2005/6*, London: Department for Culture, Media and Sport.

Australian Bureau of Statistics (2009) *4901.0 Children's Participation in Cultural and Leisure Activities, Australia, April 2009*, accessed on 31/05/2011 at www.abs.gov.au/ausstats/abs@.nsf/Latestproducts/4901.0

Bachman, J. and Dierking, L.D. (2010) Learning from empowered home-educating families, *Museums and Social Issues* 5 (1) Spring, pp. 51–66.

Bandelli, A. (2007) Talking together: supporting citizen debates, in McLean, K. and Pollock, W. (eds) *Visitor Voices in Museum Exhibitions*, Washington DC: Association of Science-Technology Centers, pp. 45–8.

BDRC (2009) *Visitor Attractions Trends in England 2008*, London: BDRC for VisitEngland.

Beeho, A. and Prentice, R. (1995) Evaluating the experiences and benefits gained by tourists visiting a socio-industrial heritage museum: an application of ASEB grid analysis to Blists Hill open-air museum, *Museum Management and Curatorship* 14 (3), pp. 229–51.

Been, I., Visscher, C.M. and Goudriaan, R. (2002) 'Fee or free?', paper presented at the 12th biennial conference of the Association for Cultural Economics International (ACEI), Rotterdam, The Netherlands, 13–15 June.

Bell, F.W. (2011) Guest column: museums have a major role in educational development, *Florida Times Union*, 4 March 2011, accessed on 31/05/2011 at http://jacksonville.com/opinion/letters-leaders/2011-03-04/story/guest-column-museums-have-major-role-educational

Bercow, J. (2008) *The Bercow Report: A Review of Services for Children and Young People (0–19) with Speech, Language and Communication Needs*, London: Department for Children, Schools and Families, accessed on 31/05/2011 at www.education.gov.uk/publications/eOrderingDownload/Bercow-Report.pdf

Bernstein, S. (2008) Where do we go from here? Continuing with Web 2.0 at the Brooklyn Museum, *Museums and the Web 2008*, accessed on 31/05/2011 at http://www.archimuse.com/mw2008/papers/bernstein/bernstein.html

Bernstein, S. (2011) 'Brooklyn Museum', paper presented at the MuseumNext Conference, Edinburgh, 26–27 May.

Bernstein, S. and Gittleman, M. (2010) The value of risk, *Journal of Museum Education* 35 (1) Spring, pp. 43–58.

Berry, S. and Shephard, G. (2001) Cultural heritage sites and their visitors: too many for too few, in Richards, G. (ed.) *Cultural Attractions and European Tourism*, Wallingford: CABI Publishing, pp. 159–71.

Birkett, D. (2011) quoted in *Play the Generation Game at a Museum – Everyone's a Winner*, accessed on 31/05/2011 at www.familyrapp.com/Results/archive_results_details.asp?ArticleID=4295

Birkett, D. (undated) *Dea Birkett's Eating with Kids: Museums*, accessed on 31/05/2011 at www.takethefamily.com/features/dea_birkett/eating_with_kids/museums/

Bitgood, S. (2000) The role of attention in designing effective interpretive labels, *Journal of Interpretive Research* 5 (2) Winter, pp. 31–45.

Bitgood, S. (2010) *An Attention-Value Model of Museum Visitors*, Washington DC: Center for Advancement of Informal Science Education (CAISE) and Association of Science-Technology Centers (ASTC), accessed on 31/05/2011 at

http://caise.insci.org/uploads/docs/VSA_
Bitgood.pdf

Black, G. (2005) *The Engaging Museum*, London:
Routledge.

Black, G. (2010) Embedding civil engagement in
museums, *Museum Management and Curatorship*
25 (2) June, pp. 129–46.

Black, G. (2011) Museums, memory and history,
Cultural and Social History 8 (3), pp. 415–27.

Blackwell, I. (2009) *Communication Friendly
Museums*, Stoke: Stoke Museums, accessed on
31/05/2011 at www.learning-unlimited.co.uk/
index.html

Blake, K. (2005) Teaching museum behaviours in
an interactive gallery, presented at the J. Paul
Getty Museum Symposium, 'From Content
to Play: Family-Oriented Interactive Spaces in
Art and History Museums', 4–5 June, accessed
on 31/05/2011 at www.getty.edu/education/
symposium/Blake.pdf

Block, P. (2002) *The Answer to How is Yes*, San
Francisco CA: Berrett-Koehler.

Bodo, S. (2009) Guidelines for MAP for ID Pilot
projects, in Bodo, S., Gibbs, K. and Sani, M.
(eds) *Museums as Places for Intercultural
Dialogue: Selected Practices from Europe*,
European Commission: MAP for ID, accessed
on 31/05/2011 at www.ne-mo.org/fileadmin/
Dateien/public/service/handbook_MAPforID_
EN.pdf, pp. 22–5.

Bodo, S. (2010) Intercultural spaces: a European
perspective, in *From the Margins to the Core?
Conference Notes*, Victoria & Albert Museum,
London, 24–26 March, pp. 77–84, accessed
on 31/05/2011 at www.vam.ac.uk/media/
documents/Papers_Conference_Notes.pdf

Boomerang! Integrated Marketing and Advertising
Pty Ltd (1998) *Powerhouse Museum Brand Audit
and Positioning Options*, Sydney: internal report
for the Powerhouse Museum.

Borun, M. (2008) Why family learning in museums?
The Exhibitionist 27 (1) Spring, pp. 6–9.

Borun, M. and Dritsas, J. (1997) Developing family-
friendly exhibits, *Curator: The Museum Journal*
40 (3), pp. 178–96.

Borun, M., Chambers, M., Dritsas, J. and Johnson, J.
(1997) Enhancing family learning through
exhibits, *Curator: The Museum Journal* 40 (4),
pp. 279–95.

Borun, M., Dritsas, J., Johnson, J.I., Peter, N.E.,
Wagner, K.F., Fadigan, K., Jangaard, A., Stroup, E.

and Wenger, A. (1998) *Family Learning in
Museums: The PISEC Perspective*, Philadelphia PA:
Franklin Institute.

Boston Children's Museum (2010) *Adult–Child
Interaction Inventory and Resource DVD Guide*,
Boston MA: Boston Children's Museum, accessed
on 31/05/2011 at www.informalscience.org/
documents/0000/0106/ACII.Guide_low_res.pdf

Bott, V., Grant, A. and Newman, J. (2005) *Revisiting
Collections: Discovering New Meanings for a Diverse
Audience*, London: London Museums Agency.

Bradburne, J.M. (2004) The museum time bomb:
overbuilt, overtraded, overdrawn, *The Informal
Learning Review* 65, March/April, accessed on
31/05/2011 at www.informallearning.com/
archive/Bradburne-65.htm

Braund, M.R. (2004) Learning science at museums
and hands-on centres, in Braund, M. and
Reiss, M. (eds) *Learning Science Outside the
Classroom*, London: Routledge, pp. 113–28.

Brooklyn Museum (undated) *Brooklyn Museum
Collection, Posse, and Tag! You're It!* accessed on
31/05/11 at museumsandtheweb.com http://
conference.archimuse.com/nominee/brooklyn_
museum_collection_posse_and_tag_youre_
it#ixzz0xQfkWt2P

Brown, T. (2009) *The Times*, 19 January, p. 24.

Bunting, C., Gottleib, J., Jobson, M., Keaney, E.,
Oskala, A. and Skelton, A. (2007) *Informing
Change: Taking Part in the Arts: Survey Findings
from the First Twelve Months*, London: Arts
Council of England, accessed on 31/05/2011 at
http://arts-research-digest.com/wp-content/
uploads/Informing-Change.pdf

Burnett, J. (2007) quoted in *Race* 5, February, p. 1,
accessed on 31/05/2011 at www.smm.org/race/
race_feb07.pdf

Burnham, S. (2000) Schubert and the sound
of memory, *The Musical Quarterly* 84 (4),
pp. 655–63.

Cabinet Office (2001) *Preventing Social Exclusion:
Report by the Social Exclusion Unit*, London:
Cabinet Office.

Cameron, F. (2003) Transcending fear – engaging
emotions and opinion – a case for museums in the
21st century, *Open Museum Journal* 6, pp. 1–46.

Cameron, F. (2005) Contentiousness and shifting
knowledge paradigms: the roles of history and
science museums in contemporary society,
Museum Management and Curatorship 20 (2),
pp. 213–33.

Cameron, F. (2010) Introduction, in Cameron, F. and Kelly, L. (eds) *Hot Topics, Public Culture, Museums*, Newcastle upon Tyne: Cambridge Scholars Publishing, pp. 1–16.

Cameron, F. and Kelly, L. (eds) (2010) *Hot Topics, Public Culture, Museums*, Newcastle upon Tyne: Cambridge Scholars Publishing.

Canadian Museums Association (2003) *Canadians and Their Museums: A Survey of Canadians and Their Views about Their Country's Museums*, conducted by TeleResearch Inc. for the Canadian Museums Association.

Candlin, F. (2008) Museums, modernity and the class politics of touching objects, in Chatterjee, H.J. (ed.) *Touch in Museums: Policy and Practice in Object Handling*, Oxford: Berg, pp. 9–20.

Carbonne, S. (2003) The dialogic museum, *Muse* 21, pp. 36–9.

Carlzon, J. (1987) *Moments of Truth*, New York: Harper and Row.

Carron, C.G. (2010) *The Grand Race*, Washington DC: American Association of Museums Brooking Paper on Creativity in Museums, accessed on 31/05/2011 at www.aam-us.org/getinvolved/nominate/upload/Brooking-Grand-Race.pdf

CASE (2010) *Understanding the Drivers, Impact and Value of Engagement in Culture and Sport*, London: Department for Culture, Media and Sport, Arts Council England, English Heritage, Museums Libraries and Archives Council, Sport England, accessed on 31/05/2011 at www.culture.gov//images.research/CASE-supersummaryFINAL-19-July2010.pdf

Cave, V. (2010) Planning for children and families, in MuseumsEtc (ed.) *The New Museum Community: Audiences, Challenges, Benefits*, Edinburgh: MuseumsEtc, pp. 98–125.

Center for the Future of Museums (2008) *Museums and Society 2034: Trends and Potential Futures*, Washington DC: American Association of Museums, accessed on 31/05/2011 at http://futureofmuseums.org/reading/publications/2008.cfm

Chatterjee, H.J. (ed.) (2008) *Touch in Museums: Policy and Practice in Object Handling*, Oxford: Berg.

Ciolfi, L., Bannon, L.J. and Fernström, M. (2008) Including visitor contributions in cultural heritage installations: designing for participation, *Museum Management and Curatorship* 23 (4), pp. 53–65.

Coles, A. (2009) Museum learning: not instrumental enough? in Bellamy, K. and Oppenheim, C. (eds) *Learning to Live: Museums, Young People and Education*, London: Institute for Public Policy Research and National Museums Directors' Conference, pp. 91–102, accessed on 31/05/2011 at www.nationalmuseums.org.uk/media/documents/publications/learning_to_live.pdf

Collections Management Network (2010) *Stories of the World: Collections and Communities: Revisiting Collections Implementation Research Report*, London: Collections Trust, accessed on 31/05/2011 at www.collectionslink.org.uk

Collins, S. and Lee, A. (2006) *How Can Natural History Museums Support Science Teaching and Learning? A Consultative Study*, London: DCMS, accessed on 31/05/2011 at www.nhm.ac.uk/resources-rx/files/secondary-schools-20524.pdf

Conaty, G.T. (2008) The effects of repatriation on the relationship between the Glenbow Museum and the Blackfoot People, *Museum Management and Curatorship* 23 (3), September, pp. 245–59.

Conaty, G.T. and Carter, B. (2005) Our story in our words: diversity and equality in the Glenbow Museum, in Janes, R.R. and Conaty, G.T. (eds) *Looking Reality in the Eye: Museums and Social Responsibility*, Calgary, Alberta: University of Calgary Press, pp. 43–58.

Connell, B.R., Jones, M., Mace, R., Mueller, J., Mullick, A., Ostroff, E., Sanford, J., Steinfeld, E., Story, M. and Vanderheiden, G. (1997) *Principles of Universal Design*, Version 2.0, Raleigh NC: The Center for Universal Design at North Carolina State University, accessed on 31/05/2011 at http://www.design.ncsu.edu/cud/about_ud/udprinciplestext.htm

Connerton, P. (1989) *How Societies Remember*, Cambridge: Cambridge University Press.

Connor, M. (2009) *A Manual for the 21st Century Gatekeeper*, Manchester: Cornerhouse, accessed on 31/05/2011 at http://www.cornerhouse.org/art/art-media/a-manual-for-the-21st-century-gatekeeper

Cooks, R. (1999) Is there a way to make controversial exhibits that work? *Journal of Museum Education* 23 (3), pp. 18–20.

Crane, S.A. (1997) Writing the individual back into collective memory, *American Historical Review, AHR Forum: History and Memory*, December, pp. 1372–85.

Crook, C., Cummings, J., Fisher, T., Graber, R.,

Harrison, C., Lewin, C., Logan, K., Luckin, R., Oliver, M. and Sharples, M. (2008) *Web 2.0 Technologies for Learning: The Current Landscape – Opportunities, Challenges and Tensions*, Coventry: Becta, accessed on 31/05/2011 at http://dera.ioe.ac.uk/1474/1/becta_2008_web2_currentlandscapeadditional_litrev.pdf

Crooke, E. (2007) *Museums and Community: Ideas, Issues and Challenges*, London: Routledge.

Crooke, E. (2008) An exploration of the connections among museums, community and heritage, in Graham, B. and Howard, P. (eds) *The Ashgate Research Companion to Heritage and Identity*, Aldershot: Ashgate, pp. 415–24.

Crowley, K. and Galco, J. (2001) Everyday activity and the development of scientific thinking, in Crowley, K., Schunn, C.D. and Okada, T. (eds) *Designing for Science: Implications from Everyday Classrooms and Professional Settings*, Mahwah NJ: Lawrence Erlbaum Associates, pp. 393–413.

Crowley, K. and Jacobs, M. (2002) Building islands of expertise in everyday family activity, in Leinhardt, G., Crowley, K. and Knutson, K. (eds), *Learning Conversations in Museums*, Mahwah NJ: Lawrence Erlbaum Associates, pp. 333–56.

Csikszentmihali, M. and Hermanson, K. (1995) Intrinsic motivation in museums: what makes visitors want to learn? *Museum News* May/June, pp. 34–7 and 59–61.

Cultural Heritage without Borders (2010) *The Western Balkan Regional Museum Network*, Stockholm: Cultural Heritage without Borders, accessed on 31/05/2011 at www.chwb.org/dokument/pdf/RMN.pdf

Culture and Learning Consortium (2009) *Get It: The Power of Cultural Learning*, London: Culture and Learning Consortium, accessed on 31/05/2011 at http://research.mla.gov.uk/evidence/view-publication.php?dm=nrm&pubid=1113

Cunningham, M.K. (2004) *The Interpreters' Training Manual for Museums*, Washington DC: American Association of Museums.

Curriculum Corporation (2009) *Museum and Education Digital Content Exchange: Final Report*, Canberra: Curriculum Corporation, accessed on 31/05/2011 at www.thelearningfederation.edu.au/verve/_resources/TLF_MEDCE_Report.pdf

Cuthill, M. and Fein, J. (2005) Capacity building: facilitating citizen participation in local governance, *Australian Journal of Public Administration* 64 (4), pp. 63–80.

Danilov, V.J. (2009) *Ethnic Museums and Heritage Sites in the United States*, Jefferson NC: McFarland and Company.

Danko-McGhee, K. and Shaffer, S. (undated) *Looking at Art with Toddlers*, Washington DC: Smithsonian Early Enrichment Center, accessed on 31/05/2011 at www.seec.si.edu/media/article-artwithtoddlers.pdf

Davies, S. (1994) *By Popular Demand: A Strategic Analysis of the Market Potential for Museums and Art Galleries in the UK*, London: Museums and Galleries Commission.

Davies, S. (2007a) Commentary 2, One small part: taking part and museums, *Cultural Trends* 16 (4) December, pp. 361–371.

Davies, S. (2007b) *Connecting Histories: Stage 2 Full Evaluation Report*, Birmingham: Stuart Davies Associates for Birmingham City Council, accessed on 31/05/2011 at www.connectinghistories.org.uk/Downloads%20(pdfs%20etc)/Connecting%20Histories%20Full%Evaluation%20Stage/202%20Report.pdf

Dávila, A. and Mora, M.T. (2007) *Civic Engagement and High School Academic Progress: An Analysis Using NELS Data*, University of Maryland: The Center for Information and Research on Civic Learning and Engagement, accessed on 31/05/2011 at www.eric.ed.gov/PDFS/ED495238.pdf

Davis, P. (1999) *Ecomuseums: A Sense of Place*, Leicester: Leicester University Press.

Davis, P. (2008) New museologies and the ecomuseum, in Graham, B. and Howard, P. (eds) *The Ashgate Research Companion to Heritage and Identity*, Aldershot: Ashgate, pp. 397–414.

Davison, P. (2005) Museums and the re-shaping of memory, in Corsane, G. (ed.) *Heritage, Museums and Galleries: An Introductory Reader*, London: Routledge, pp. 184–94.

DCMS (2000) *Centres for Social Change: Museums, Galleries and Archives for All*, London: Department of Culture, Media and Sport.

DCMS (Jan. 2001) *Libraries, Museums, Galleries and Archives for All: Co-operating across the Sectors to Tackle Social Exclusion*, London: Department of Culture, Media and Sport.

DCMS (2007 and ongoing) *Taking Part: England's Survey of Leisure, Culture and Sport*, accessed on 31/05/2011 at http://www.culture.gov.uk/reference_library/research_and_statistics/4828.aspx/

DCMS and DfEE (2000) *The Learning Power of Museums – A Vision for Museum Education*, London: Department of Culture, Media and Sport.

Delin, A. (2002) Buried in the footnotes: the absence of disabled people in the collective imagery of our past, in Sandell, R. (ed.) *Museums, Society, Inequality*, London: Routledge, pp. 84–97.

Delin, A. (2003) *Disability in Context*, London: Museums, Libraries and Archives Council (available on the MLA website www.mla.gov.uk as part of the Resource *Disability Portfolio*).

Denniston, H. (2003) *Holding up the Mirror: Addressing Cultural Diversity in London's Museums*, London: Helen Denniston Associates for London Museums Agency.

Denver Art Museum (2002a) *Families and Art Museums Part 1*, accessed on 31/05/2011 at www.denverartmuseum.org/files?File/family_ programs1.pdf

Denver Art Museum (2002b) *Families and Art Museums Part 2*, accessed on 31/05/2011 at www.denverartmuseum.org/files?File/family_ programs2.pdf

Destination Analysts (2009) *State of the American Traveller Survey, July 2008*, accessed on 17/06/2010 at www.destinationanalysts.com/ SATSJuly2009.pdf

Deuel, J., Ramberg, J.S., Fraser, J. and Hanchett, T. (2007) Inspiring visitor action in museums: examining the social diffusion of ideas, COURAGE and time's running out – act now, *The Exhibitionist* Fall, pp. 20–31, accessed on 31/05/2011 at http:// name-aam.org/exhibitionist

DfES (2007) *Diversity and Citizenship Curriculum Review*, accessed on 31/05/2011 at www. teachingcitizenship.org.uk/dnloads/ diversityandcitizenship.pdf

Dierking, L.D. (2010a) Laughing and learning together: what is family learning? *Family Learning Forum*, accessed on 31/05/2011 at www. familylearningforum.org

Dierking, L.D. (2010b) Why is family learning important? *Family Learning Forum*, accessed on 31/05/2011 at www.familylearningforum.org

Dierking, L.D. (2011) *Museums and Families: Being of Value*, Walnut Creek CA: Left Coast Press.

Dodd, J. and Sandell, R. (1998), *Building Bridges*, London: Museums and Galleries Commission.

Dodd, J., O'Riain, H., Hooper-Greenhill, E. and Sandell, R. (2002) *A Catalyst for Change: The Social Impact of the Open Museum*, Leicester: Research Centre for Museums and Galleries, accessed on 31/05/2011 at www.le.ac.uk/ museumstudies/research/Reports/catalyst.pdf

Dodd, J., Sandell, R., Delin, A. and Gay, J. (2004) *Buried in the Footnotes: The Representation of Disabled People in Museum and Gallery Collections*, Leicester: Research Centre for Museums and Galleries, accessed on 31/05/2011 at www.le.ac. uk/museumstudies/research/Reports/BITF2.pdf

Doering, Z. (1999) Strangers, guests or clients? Visitor experiences in museums, *Curator* 42 (2) April, pp. 74–87.

DW-World.de (2010) *Study Finds Bankruptcy Threatens Many German Cultural Institutions*, Bonn: Deutsche Welle, accessed on 08/10/2010 at http://www.dw-world.de/dw/ article/0,,5924950,00.html

East Midlands Museums Service (1996) *Knowing Our Visitors: A Market Study of East Midlands Museums*, Nottingham: East Midlands Museums Service.

Economou, M. (2004) Evaluation strategies in the cultural sector: the case of Kelvingrove Museum and Art Gallery, *Museum and Society* 2 (1), pp. 30–46.

Edwards, N. (2010) Perspectives: behind the open museum, in Glasgow Museums (ed.) *Out There: The Open Museum: Pushing the Boundaries of Museums' Potential*, Glasgow: Culture and Sport Glasgow, pp. 122–3.

Ellenbogen, K.M., Luke, J.J. and Dierking, L.D. (2007) Family learning in museums: perspectives on a decade of research, in Falk, J.H., Dierking, L.D. and Foutz, S. (eds) *In Principle, In Practice: Museums as Learning Institutions*, Lanham MD: AltaMira Press, pp. 17–30.

English Tourism Council et al. (1999) *Making the Connections: A Practical Guide to Tourism Management in Historic Towns*, London: English Historic Towns Forum, English Tourism Council and English Heritage.

Falk, J.H. (2006) An identity-centred approach to understanding museum learning, *Curator* 49 (2), pp. 151–66.

Falk, J.H. (2007) Toward an improved understanding of learning from museums: filmmaking as metaphor, in Falk, J.H., Dierking, L.D. and Foutz, S. (eds) *In Principle, In Practice: Museums as Learning Institutions*, Lanham MD: AltaMira Press, pp. 3–16.

Falk, J.H. (2009) *Identity and the Museum Visitor Experience*, Walnut Creek CA: Left Coast Press.

Falk, J.H. (2010) *Leadership Award Acceptance Speech*,

American Association of Museums EdCOM reception, May, quoted in Nolan (2010: 117)

Falk, J.H. and Dierking, L.D. (1992) *The Museum Experience*, Washington DC: Whalesback Books.

Falk, J.H. and Dierking, L.D. (2000) *Learning from Museums: Visitor Experiences and the Making of Meaning*, Washington DC: Whalesback Books.

Falk, J.H. and Dierking, L.D. (2002) *Learning without Limit: How Free-choice Learning Is Transforming Education*, Walnut Creek CA: AltaMira Press.

Falk, J.H. and Shepphard, B.K. (2006) *Thriving in the Knowledge Age: New Business Models for Museums and Other Cultural Institutions*, Lanham MD: AltaMira Press.

Falk, J.H., Dierking, L.D. and Foutz, S. (eds) (2007) *In Principle, In Practice, Museums as Learning Institutions*, Lanham MD: AltaMira Press.

Falk, J.H., Moussouri, T. and Coulson, D. (1998) The effect of visitors' agendas on museum learning, *Curator* 41 (2), June, pp. 107–20.

Faux, F., Mcfarlane, A., Roche, N. and Facer, K. (2006) *Handhelds: Learning with Handheld Technology*, Bristol: Futurelab.

Ferguson, L. (2010) Strategy and tactic: a post-modern response to the modernist museum, in Cameron, F. and Kelly, L. (eds) *Hot Topics, Public Culture, Museums*, Newcastle upon Tyne: Cambridge Scholars Publishing, pp. 35–52.

Fienberg, J. and Leinhardt, G. (2002) Looking through the glass: reflections of identity in conversations at a history museum, in Leinhardt, G., Crowley, K. and Knutson, K. (eds) *Learning Conversations in Museums*, Mahwah NJ: Lawrence Erlbaum Associates, pp. 167–211.

Figel, J. (2008) European Commissioner responsible for Education and Culture. Address at the launch of European Year of Intercultural Dialogue, quoted in Bodo, S., Gibbs, K. and Sani, M. (eds) (2009) *Museums as Places for Intercultural Dialogue: Selected Practices from Europe*, European Commission: MAP for ID, accessed on 31/05/2011 at www.ne-mo.org/fileadmin/Dateien/public/service/handbook_MAPforID_EN.pdf, p. 4.

Fillipini-Fantoni, S. (2003) 'Personalisation through IT in museums: does it really work? The case of the Marble Museum website', paper presented to Cultural Institutions and Digital Technology Conference, École de Louvre, Paris, 8–12 September, accessed on 31/05/2011 at www.archimuse.com/publishing/ichim03/070C.pdf

Finnegan, R. (2002) *Communicating: The Multiple Modes of Human Interconnection*, London: Routledge.

Finnis, J. (2009) Ch. 9, Online technology: unlocking opportunity, unlocking collections, in Bellamy, K. and Oppenheim, C. (eds) *Learning to Live: Museums, Young People and Education*, London: Institute for Public Policy Research and National Museums Directors' Conference, pp. 81–90, accessed on 31/05/2011 at www.nationalmuseums.org.uk/media/documents/publications/learning_to_live.pdf

Fleming, D. (1998) Ch. 8, Brave new world: the future for city history museums, in Kavanagh, G. and Frostick, E. (eds) *Making City Histories in Museums*, Leicester: Leicester University Press, pp. 133–50.

Fleming, D. (2005) 'Managing change in museums', paper presented to Museums and Change International Conference, Prague, 8–10 November.

Fleming, T. (2009) *Embracing the Desire Lines: Opening up Cultural Infrastructure*, accessed on 31/05/2011 at www.cornerhouse.org/Media/Learn/ReportsandStudies/Embracing_the_Desire_Lines.pdf

Fletcher, A. (2010) *Results for the Social Media Museum Research Survey*, accessed on 31/05/2011 at www.aam-USA.org

Forbes. I. (2004) quoted in *Award Winners 2004 – Killhope Mining Museum*, accessed on 31/5/2011 at www.kidsinmuseums.org.uk/awards/award-winners-2004-killhope-mining-museum/

Ford, R. (2011) One in eight British residents born abroad, *The Times*, 26 August, p. 7.

Fortney, K. and Sheppard, B. (2010) *An Alliance of Spirit: Museum and School Partnerships*, Washington DC: American Association of Museums Press.

Frankly, Green + Webb (2010) *Smartphones and Their Potential to Support Family Learning in the Cultural Sector*, accessed on 31/05/2011 at www.franklygreenwebb.com/our-reports/?aid=231&pid=223&sa=1

Gallace, A. and Spence, C. (2008) A memory for touch: the cognitive psychology of tactile memory, in Chatterjee, H.J. (ed.) *Touch in Museums: Policy and Practice in Object Handling*, Oxford: Berg, pp. 163–86.

Gardella, J. (2002) Promises to keep: making branding work for science centres, *ASTC*

Dimensions May/June, accessed on 31/05/2011 at www.astc.org/pubs/dimensions/2002/may-jun/branding.htm

Gaskins (2008) Designing exhibitions to support families' cultural understandings, *The Exhibitionist* 27 (1) Spring, pp. 11–19.

Gilman, B.I. (1918) *Museum Ideals*, Boston MA: Museum of Fine Arts.

Glasgow Museums (2007) *Towards an Engaged Gallery*, Glasgow: Glasgow Museums.

Glasgow Museums (ed.) (2010) *Out There: The Open Museum: Pushing the Boundaries of Museums' Potential*, Glasgow: Culture and Sport Glasgow.

GLLAM (2000) *Museums and Social Inclusion*, Leicester: Group for Large Local Authority Museums.

Graham, J. (2008) *First Steps: Providing for the Early Years in Museums*, London: London Museums Hub, accessed on 31/05/2011 at www.learning-unlimited.co.uk/page4/files/First_Steps.pdf

Graham, J. (2009) *'Which way shall we go? OK, I'll follow you . . .' Providing Resources that Help Parents and Carers to Engage with Museum Collections and Buildings*, Bristol: Renaissance South-West.

Greater Philadelphia Cultural Alliance (2009) *Research into Action: Pathways to New Opportunities*, Philadelphia PA: Greater Philadelphia Cultural Alliance, accessed on 31/05/2011 at www.philaculture.org/sites/default/files/Research%20into%20Action%20(full%20report).pdf

Griffin, D. and Abraham, M.(2001) The effective management of museums: cohesive leadership and visitor-focused public programming, *International Journal of Museum Management and Curatorship* 18 (4), pp. 335–68.

Griffin, J. (2002) 'Museum visitor experiences and learning', notes on a paper presented at Why Learning? seminar, Australian Museum/University of Technology, Sydney, 22 November, accessed on 31/05/2011 at http://australianmuseum.et.au/Uploads/Documents/9322/janetteg.pdf

Griffin, S.S. (2010) *Funding Note: Using Institute of Museum and Library Services Grants to Support Out-of-School-Time Programmes*, Washington DC: Institute of Museum and Library Services, accessed on 31/05/2011 at www.financeproject.org/publications/UsingInstituteofMuseum-FN.pdf

Groundwater-Smith, S. and Kelly, L. (2003) 'As we see it: improving learning in the museum', paper presented to the British Educational Research Annual Conference, Edinburgh, September.

Gurian, E.H. (2006) Threshold fear, in Gurian, E.H., *Civilizing the Museum*, London: Routledge, pp. 115–26.

Guzmán, J. and Tortolero, C. (2010) The National Museum of Mexican Art: a new model for museums, *Journal of Museum Education* 35 (1) Spring, pp. 83–92.

Gyllenhaal, E.D. (2006) *A Generalised Developmental Framework for Planning Cultural Exhibitions and Programs*, Selinda Research Associates, accessed on 31/05/2011 at www.selindaresearch.com/Cultural_Developmental_Framework_01.doc

Hague, C. (2010) *'It's not chalk and talk anymore': School Approaches to Developing Students' Digital Literacy*, Bristol: Futurelab.

Ham, S.H. (1992) *Environmental Interpretation: A Practical Guide*, Golden CO: Fulcrum Books.

Harvard Family Research Project (2005) Complementary learning, special edition of *The Evaluation Exchange*, 11 (1) Spring, Cambridge MA: Harvard School of Education, accessed on 31/05/2011 at www.hfrp.org/var/hfrp/storage/original/application/9aa95169b0118cf821e26167fa55769d.pdf

Hawkey, R. (2004) Learning with digital technologies in museums, science centres and galleries, *FutureLab Series, Report 9*, Bristol: FutureLab.

Hein, G.E. (1998) *Learning in the Museum*, London: Routledge.

Hein, G.E. (2011) Museum education, in Macdonald, S. (ed.) *A Companion to Museum Studies*, Chichester: Wiley-Blackwell, pp. 340–52.

Hellman, B. (2010) *Can Augmented Reality 'Cross the Chasm' for Use in Museums and Galleries?*, a report submitted in partial fulfilment of the requirements for the MBA degree and the Diploma of Imperial College London, December.

Henning, M. (2006) *Museums, Media and Cultural Theory*, Maidenhead: Open University Press.

Heritage Lottery Fund (2010) *Investing in Success: Heritage and the UK Tourism Economy*, London: Heritage Lottery Fund, accessed on 15/06/2010 at www.hlf.org.uk/aboutus/howwework/Documents/HLF_Tourism_Impact_single.pdf

Heywood, F. (2010) Renaissance cuts would be ruinous, *Museums Journal* September, p. 15.

Hilke, D.D. (1988) Strategies for family learning in museums, in Bitgood, S., Roper, J.T., Jr. and

Benefield, A. (eds) *Visitor Studies: Theory, Research and Practice*, Jacksonville FL: Center for Social Design, pp. 120–5.

Hill, K. (2001) Because it just makes sense: serving the museum visitor, in Adams, R. (ed.) *Museum Visitor Services Manual*, Washington DC: American Association of Museums, pp. 11–12.

Hill, R.W. (2007) Regenerating identity: repatriation and the Indian frame of mind, in Watson, W. (ed.) *Museums and Their Communities*, London: Routledge, pp. 313–23.

Hill Strategies Research Inc. (2007) A profile of the cultural and heritage activities of Canadians in 2005, *Statistical Insights on the Arts* 5 (4), accessed on 31/05/2011 at www.arts.on.ca/AssetFactory. aspx?did=1481

Hollows, V. (2010) Contemporary art and human rights, in *From the Margins to the Core? Conference Notes*, Victoria & Albert Museum, 24–26 March, pp. 91–102, accessed on 31/05/2011 at http://media.vam.ac.uk/ media/documents/conferences/2010/margins- to-the-core/v&a-fromthemarginstothecore- compiledpapers&notes.pdf

Holo, S. (2009) Ethnic-specific museums: why they matter and how they make a difference, in Holo, S. and Alvarez, M. (eds) *Beyond the Turnstile: Making the Case for Museums and Sustainable Values*, Lanham MD: AltaMira Press, pp. 40–4.

Hood, M.G. (1983) Staying away: why people choose not to visit museums, *Museum News*, April, pp. 50–7.

Hood, M.G. (1993) After 70 years of audience research, what have we learned? Who comes to museums, who does not, and why? *Visitor Studies* 5 (1), pp. 16–27.

Hood, M.G. (1996) Audience research tells us why visitors come to museums – and why they don't, in *Towards 2000: Evaluation and Visitor Research in Museums*, Sydney: Powerhouse Museum.

Hooper-Greenhill, E. (1994) *Museums and Their Visitors*, London: Routledge.

Hooper-Greenhill, E. (2000) *Museums and the Interpretation of Visual Culture*, London: Routledge.

Hooper-Greenhill, E. (2003) 'Museums and social value: measuring the impact of learning in museums', paper presented at the ICOM-CECA Annual Conference, Oaxaca.

Hooper-Greenhill, E. (2004) Measuring learning outcomes in museums, archives and libraries: the Learning Impact Research Project (LIRP), *International Journal of Heritage Studies* 10 (2), pp. 151–74.

Hooper-Greenhill, E. (2007) *Museums and Education: Purpose, Pedagogy and Performance*, Abingdon: Routledge.

Humphrey, T. and Gutwill, J.P. (2005) *Fostering Active Prolonged Engagement*, Walnut Creek CA: Left Coast Press.

IMLS (2001) *Perspectives on Outcome-Based Evaluation for Libraries and Museums*, Washington DC: Institute of Museum and Library Services, accessed on 31/05/2011 at www.imls.gov/pdf/ pubobe.pdf

IMLS (2007) *Outcome Based Evaluation Overview*, Washington DC: Institute for Museum and Library Services, accessed on 31/05/2011 at www.imls.gov/applicants/basics.shtm

IMLS (2009a) *Museums, Libraries and 21st Century Skills*, Washington DC: Institute of Museum and Library Services, accessed on 31/05/2011 at www.imls.gov/pdf/21stcenturyskills.pdf

IMLS (2009b) *The Future of Museums and Libraries: A Discussion Guide*, Washington DC: Institute of Museum and Library Services, accessed on 18/03/2011 at www.imls.gov/pdf/ discussionguide.pdf

International Association for Public Participation (2009) *A Model for Engagement*, accessed on 31/05/2011 at www.dse.vic.gov.au/effective- engagement/developing-an-engagement-plan/a- model-for-engagement#h3

Internet World Statistics (2010) *Internet Usage Statistics 2010*, accessed on 31/05/2011 at http://www.internetworldstats.com/stats.htm

IOM (2010) *World Migration Report*, Geneva: International Organisation for Migration, accessed on 10/12/2010 at http://publications. iom.int/bookstore/free/WMR_2010_ ENGLISH.pdf

Jackson, A. and Kidd, J. (2008a) *Performance, Learning and Heritage Research Project: Executive Summary*, University of Manchester: Centre for Applied Theatre Research, accessed on 31/05/2011 at www.plh.manchester.ac.uk

Jackson, A. and Kidd, J. (2008b) *Performance, Learning and Heritage Research Project: Full Report*, University of Manchester: Centre for Applied Theatre Research, accessed on 31/05/2011 at www.plh.manchester.ac.uk

Janes, R.R. (ed.) (1997) *Museums and the Paradox of*

Change, Calgary, Alberta: University of Calgary Press.

Janes, R.R. (2009) *Museums in a Troubled World*, London: Routledge.

Janes, R.R. and Conaty, G.T. (2005) Introduction, in Janes, R.R. and Conaty, G.T. (eds) *Looking Reality in the Eye: Museums and Social Responsibility*, Calgary, Alberta: University of Calgary Press, pp. 1–17.

Jelinek, M. (undated) *The Unknown*, accessed on 31/05/2011 at www.jewishmuseum.cz/en/aidentifikace.htm

Jeong, J.-H. and Lee, K.-H. (2006) The physical environment in museums and its effects on visitors' satisfaction, *Building & Environment* 41 (7) July, pp. 963–9.

Johns, N. (1999) Ch. 9, Quality, in Leask, A. and Yeoman, I. (eds) *Heritage Visitor Attractions: An Operation Management Perspective*, London: Cassell, pp. 127–43.

Johns Hopkins University (2010) Recession pressures on non-profit jobs, *The Listening Post Project Communiqué No. 19*, Baltimore MD: Johns Hopkins Center for Civil Society Studies, accessed on 31/05/2011 at http://ccss.jhu.edu

Johnson, J.I. and Rassweiler, J.L. (2010) Connecting museum, school and community: collaborations for learning, in Fortney, K. and Sheppard, B. (eds) *An Alliance of Spirit: Museum and School Partnerships*, Washington DC: American Association of Museums Press, pp. 65–72.

Johnson, S. (2007) *Evaluation of the Use of Mobile Phone Technology (OOKL) as a Recording Tool and Indicating Children's Reaction to Working Both Indoors and out of Doors at Kew Gardens*, London: Institute of Education, accessed on 31/05/2011 at http://ookl.files.wordpress.com/2008/10/kew-institute-of-education-evaluation-at-kew-sept-07.pdf

Johnsson, E. (2004) *Pupils' Ideas about Museum Experiences*, London: London Museums Hub.

Jolly, E.J. (2009) Testimony of Dr. Eric J. Jolly, president, Science Museum of Minnesota on 'Examining the role of museums and libraries in strengthening communities' before the House Committee of Education and Labor at the Subcommittee on Healthy Families and Communities, 11 September 2008, in Alivar, T.V. (ed.) *Role of Museums and Libraries in Strengthening Communities*, New York: Nova Science Publishers, Inc., pp. 87–97.

Jones-Rizzi, J. (2008) Contextualising culture, *The Exhibitionist* 27 (1) Spring, pp. 20–8.

Kanics, I.M. and Scrivner-Mediates, H. (2008) Creating universally accessible play environments for all, *The Exhibitionist* 27 (1) Spring, pp. 37–43.

Katz. P.M. (2010) *Service Despite Stress: Museum Attendance and Funding in a Year of Recession*, Washington DC: American Association of Museums.

Kavanagh, G. (ed.) (1990) *History Curatorship*, Leicester: Leicester University Press.

Kavanagh, G. (2000) *Dream Spaces: Memory and the Museum*, London: Leicester University Press.

Kelly, L. (2001) 'Developing a model of museum visiting', paper presented at the Museums Australia annual conference National Cultures, National Identity, Canberra.

Kelly, L. (2002) 'Play, wonder and learning: museums and the preschool audience', paper presented at the Australian Research in Early Childhood Education 10th Annual Conference, University of Canberra, January.

Kelly, L. (start date 2002) *Exhibitions as Contested Sites: The Role of Museums in Contemporary Society International Research Project*, accessed on 31/05/2011 at http://australianmuseum.net.au/research/Exhibitions-as-Contested-Sites

Kelly, L. (2003) 'Museums as sources of information and learning: the decision making process', paper presented at the symposium Exhibitions as Contested Sites: The Contemporary Role of the Museum, Australian Museum, Sydney, 28 November.

Kelly, L. (2007) *The Inter-relationships between Adult Museum Visitors' Learning Identities and Their Museum Experiences*, a thesis submitted for the degree of Doctor of Philosophy, University of Technology, Sydney, accessed on 31/05/2011 via http://australianmuseum.net.au/staff/lynda-kelly

Kelly, L. (2008) 'Museum 3.0: informal learning and social media', paper presented at the Social Media and Cultural Communication conference, Sydney: Museum of Sydney and Australian Museum, 28–29 February, accessed on 31/05/2011 at http://audience-research/wikispaces.com/file/view/Kelly+Museum+3.0+paper.pdf

Kelly, L. (2011) 'Audience research in the museum without walls', paper presented at the MuseumNext conference, Edinburgh, 26–27 May.

Kelly, L. and Gordon, P. (2002) Developing a community of practice: museums and reconciliation in Australia, in Sandell, R. (ed.) *Museums, Society, Inequality*, London: Routledge, pp. 153–74.

Kelly, L. and Russo, A. (2010) From communities of practice to value networks: engaging museums in Web 2.0, in Cameron, F. and Kelly, L. (eds) *Hot Topics, Public Culture, Museums*, Newcastle upon Tyne: Cambridge Scholars Publishing, pp. 281–98.

Kelly, L., Bartlett, A. and Gordon, P. (2002) *Indigenous Youth and Museums*, Sydney: Australian Museums Trust, accessed on 31/05/2011 at http://australianmuseum.net.au/uploads/Documents/2588/iym_full_report.pdf

Kelly, L., Main, S., Dockett, S., Perry, B. and Heinrich, S. (2006) *Listening to Young Children's Voices in Museum Spaces*, Australian Association for Research in Education, accessed on 31/05/2011 at www.aare.edu.au/06pap/kel06341.pdf

Kiihne, R. (2008) Following families: from tracking to transformations, *The Exhibitionist* 27 (1) Spring, pp. 54–60.

Kirshenblatt-Gimblett, B. (1998) *Destination Culture: Tourism, Museums and Heritage*, Berkeley: University of California Press.

Korza, P., Bacon, B.S. and Assaf, A. (2005) *Civic Dialogue, Arts and Culture: Findings from Animating Democracy*, Washington DC: Americans for the Arts.

Koster, E.H. and Baumann, S.H. (2005) Liberty Science Center in the United States: a mission focused on external relevance, in Janes, R.R. and Conaty, G.T. (eds) *Looking Reality in the Eye: Museums and Social Responsibility*, Calgary, Alberta: University of Calgary Press, pp. 85–111.

Kotler, N., Kotler, P. and Kotler, W. (2nd edn 2008) *Museum Marketing and Strategy: Designing Missions, Building Audiences, Generating Revenue and Resources*, San Francisco CA: Jossey-Bass.

Kotler, P. and Andreasen, A. (5th edn 1996) *Strategic Marketing for Non-Profit Organizations*, New York: Simon and Schuster.

Kotler, P., Kartajaya, H. and Setiawan, I. (2010) *Marketing 3.0: From Products to Customers to the Human Spirit*, Hoboken NJ: John Wiley and Sons.

Kreamer, C.M. (2002) Defining communities through exhibiting and collecting, in Karp, I., Kreamer, C.M. and Lavine, S.D. (eds) *Museums and Communities: The Politics of Public Culture*, Washington DC: Smithsonian Institution Press, pp. 367–81.

Kreps, C. (2009) Foreword, in Bodo, S., Gibbs, K. and Sani, M. (eds) *Museums as Places for Intercultural Dialogue: Selected Practices from Europe*, European Commission, accessed on 31/05/2011 at www.ne-mo.org/fileadmin/Dateien/public/service/handbook_MAPforID_EN.pdf

Lavanga, M. (2006) *Artistic Explorations in Cultural Memory: Research Workshop*, University of Leiden: Faculty of Creative and Performing Arts, 3–4 November, accessed on 31/05/2011 at www.eurocult.org/uploads/docs/488.pdf

Leadbeater, C. (2009) *The Art of With*, Manchester: Cornerhouse, accessed on 31/05/2011 at www.cornerhouse.org/media/Learn/The%20Art%20of%20With.pdf

Lehman, A.L. (2010) Response from the Director of Brooklyn Museum, letter in *The New York Times*, 7 August, accessed on 31/05/2011 at www.nytimes.com/2010/08/08/arts/design/08alsmail-BROOKLYNMUSEUM-LETTERS.html

Lehmann, S. and Murray, M.M. (2005) The role of multisensory memories in unisensory object discrimination, *Cognitive Brain Research* 24, pp. 326–34.

Leinhardt, G. and Knutson, K. (2004) *Listening in on Museum Conversations*, Walnut Creek CA: AltaMira Press.

Leinhardt, G., Crowley, K. and Knutson, K. (eds) (2002) *Learning Conversations in Museums*, Mahwah NJ: Lawrence Erlbaum Associates.

Leinhardt, G., Tittle, C. and Knutson, K. (2002) Talking to oneself: diaries of museum visits, in Leinhardt, G., Crowley, K. and Knutson, K. (eds) *Learning Conversations in Museums*, Mahwah NJ: Lawrence Erlbaum Associates, pp. 103–33.

Leonard, A. (2001) Visitor services defined, in Adams, R. (ed.) *Museum Visitor Services Manual*, Washington DC: American Association of Museums, pp. 1–3.

Lewis, W.J. (1994) *Interpreting for Park Visitors*, Philadelphia PA: Eastern Acorn Press.

Light, D. and Prentice, R.C. (1994) Who consumes the heritage product? Implications for European heritage tourism, in Ashworth, G.J. and Larkham, P.J. (eds) *Building a New Heritage: Tourism, Culture and Identity in the New Europe*, London: Routledge, pp. 90–116.

Lila Wallace-Reader's Digest Fund (2000) *Service to People: Challenges and Rewards. How Museums Can Become Much More Visitor-Centred*, New York: Wallace Foundation, accessed on 31/05/2011 at www.wallacefoundation.org/ SiteCollectionDocuments/WF/Knowledge%20 Center/Attachments/PDF/Services%20to%20 People-Challenges%20and%20Rewards.pdf

Lohman, J. (2010) quoted in *Making It Happen* DVD on leadership and diversity in the heritage and culture sector, London: Victoria & Albert Museum.

Loomis, R.J. (1996) How do we know what the visitor knows? Learning from interpretation, *Journal of Interpretation Research* 1 (1), accessed on 31/05/2011 at www. journalofinterpretationresearch.org

Lord, B. (ed.) *The Manual of Museum Learning*, Lanham CA: AltaMira Press.

Low, T.L. (1942) *The Museum as a Social Instrument*, New York: Metropolitan Museum of Art for the American Association of Museums.

Lubar, S. (1997) Exhibiting memories, in Henderson, A. and Kaeppler, A.L. (eds) *Exhibiting Dilemmas: Issues of Representation at the Smithsonian*, Washington DC: Smithsonian Institution, pp. 15–27.

Luke, J.L. and McCreedy, D. (2010) Introduction: making parent involvement a community issue, *Museums & Social Issues* 5 (1) Spring, pp. 5–14.

Lynch, B. (2001) If the museum is a gateway, who is the gatekeeper?, *engage* 11 Winter, pp. 1–12, accessed on 31/05/2011 at www.engage.org/ downloads/152E22BED_11.%20Bernadette%20 Lynch.pdf

Lynch, B. (2011) *Whose Cake Is it Anyway?* London: Paul Hamlyn Foundation, accessed on 31/07/2011 at www.phf.org.uk/page. asp?id=1417

Lynch, B. and Alberti, S. (2010) Legacies of prejudice: racism, co-production and radical trust in the museum, *Museum Management and Curatorship* 25 (1) March, pp. 13–35.

MacArthur, M. (2010) Do we need a social media policy? *Museum* November/December, pp. 29 and 58–9.

MacDonald, G.F. and Alsford, S. (2007) Canadian museums and the representation of culture in a multicultural nation, in Watson, S. (ed.) *Museums and Their Communities*, London: Routledge, pp. 276–91.

Mackay, L. (2010) *Visitors Are Doing it for Themselves: How Can User-generated Content Create New Narratives for Collections and Increase Audience Engagement?* Unpublished dissertation for M. Litt Museum and Gallery Studies, University of St Andrews.

Marable-Bunch, M. (2010) Meeting teachers' needs, in Fortney, K. and Sheppard, B. (eds) *An Alliance of Spirit: Museum and School Partnerships*, Washington DC: American Association of Museums Press, pp. 9–14.

Maslow, A.H. (2nd edn 1970) *Motivations and Personality*, New York: Harper and Row.

Maximea, H. (2002) Projecting display space requirements, in Lord, B. and Lord, G. (eds) *The Manual of Museum Exhibitions*, Walnut Creek CA: AltaMira Press, pp. 76–90.

Maxted, P. (1999) *Understanding Barriers to Learning*, London: Campaign for Learning.

McCarthy, K.F. and Jinnett, K. (2001) *A New Framework for Building Participation in the Arts*, RAND, accessed on 31/05/2011 at www.rand. org/pubs/monograph_reports2005/MR1323. pdf

McCormick Foundation (undated) *McCormick Foundation Civics Program*, accessed on 31/05/2011 at www.mccormickfoundation.org/ Civics/programs/

McLarty, L. (2010) *Evaluation of Campaign! Make an Impact: Interim Report*, Leeds: Dubit Limited on behalf of Museums, Libraries and Archives Council.

McLean, F. and Cooke, S. (2003) Constructing the identity of a nation: the tourist gaze at the Museum of Scotland, in *Tourism, Culture and Communication*, 4 (3), pp. 153–62.

McLean, K. (1993) *Planning for People in Museum Exhibitions*, Washington DC: Association of Science-Technology Centers.

McLean, K. (2007a) Surviving in two-way traffic, in McLean, K. and Pollock, W. (eds) *Visitor Voices in Museum Exhibitions*, Washington DC: Association of Science-Technology Centers, pp. 8–13.

McLean, K. (2007b) Do museum exhibitions have a future?, *Curator* 50 (1), pp. 109–21.

McLean, K. and Pollock, W. (2007a) Crafting the call, in McLean, K. and Pollock, W. (eds) *Visitor Voices in Museum Exhibitions*, Washington DC: Association of Science-Technology Centers, pp. 14–20.

McLean, K. and Pollock, W. (eds) (2007b) *Visitor Voices in Museum Exhibitions*, Washington DC: Association of Science-Technology Centers.

McManus, P. (1994) Families in museums, in Miks, L. and Zavala, A. (eds) *Towards the Museum of the Future*, London: Routledge, pp. 81–118.

McManus, P.M. (1996) Visitors: their expectations and social behaviour, in Durbin, G. (ed.) *Developing Museum Exhibitions for Lifelong Learning*, London: The Stationery Office, pp. 59–62.

McNealy, S. (2005) *Oracle Open World Keynote Speech*, 21 September, reported in press release at www.highbeam.com/doc/1G1-136472784.html

McRainey, D.L. (2008) New directions in adult education, *Journal of Museum Education* 33 (1), pp. 33–42.

McRainey, D.L. (2010) Ch. 7, A sense of the past, in McRainey, D.L. and Russick, J. (eds) *Connecting Kids to History with Museum Exhibitions*, Walnut Creek CA: Left Coast Press, pp. 155–72.

Merriman, N (1991) *Beyond the Glass Case*, Leicester: Leicester University Press.

Merritt, E.E. and Katz, P.M. (eds) (2009) *2009 Museum Financial Information*, Washington DC: American Association of Museums.

Mezaros, C. (2008) Un/Familiar, *Journal of Museum Education* 33 (3) Fall, pp. 239–46.

Mintz, R. (2011) 'Driving participation and giving', paper given at the Museum Next conference, Edinburgh, 26–27 May.

Misztal, B. (2003) *Theories of Social Remembering*, Maidenhead: Open University Press.

MLA (2001) *Renaissance in the Regions: A New Vision for England's Museums*, London: MLA.

MLA (2004) *Visitors to Museums and Galleries 2004*, London: MORI/Museums, Libraries and Archives Council.

MLA (undated) *Inspiring Learning: An Improvement Framework for Museums, Libraries and Archives*, London: Museums, Libraries and Archives Council, accessed on 31/05/2011 at www.inspiringlearningforall.org.uk

MLA Renaissance West Midlands (2010) *Transforming Museum Education in the West Midlands: The Impact of Renaissance in the Regions 2004–2010*, Birmingham: Renaissance West Midlands, accessed on 31/05/2011 at www.mla.gov.uk/what/programmes/renaissance/regions/west_mids/about_us/~/media/West_Mids/files/2010/PDF/Renaissance%20-%20 Transforming%20Museum%20Education%20 2010.ashx

Morgan, J., Williamson, B., Lee, T. and Facer, K. (2007) *Enquiring Minds*, Bristol: Futurelab, accessed on 31/05/2011 at www.enquiringminds.org.uk/pdfs/Enquiring_Minds_guide.pdf

MORI (May 1999) *Visitors to Museums and Art Galleries in the UK*, London: Museums and Galleries Commission.

MORI (2001) *Visitors to Museums and Galleries in the UK*, London: Resource.

MORI (2003) *The Impact of Free Entry to Museums*, London: MORI, accessed on 31/05/2011 at http://www.ipsos-mori.com/researchpublications/publications/publication.aspx?oItemId=541

Morris, G. and McIntyre, A. (undated) *Insight Required*, Manchester: Morris, Hargreaves, McIntyre, accessed on 31/05/2011 at www.creativenz.gov.nz/assets/ckeditor/attachments/69/seven_pillars_of_audience_focus.pdf

Munley, M.E., Roberts, R.C., Soren, B. and Hayward, J. (2007) Envisioning the customized museum: an agenda to guide reflective practice and research, in Falk, J.H., Dierking, L.D. and Foutz, S. (eds) *In Principle, In Practice: Museums as Learning Institutions*, Lanham MD: AltaMira Press, pp. 77–90.

Museum of the University of St Andrews (undated) *MUSA Collections Centre: Creating an Open Access Store for Recognised Collections*, accessed on 31/05/2011 at http://www.museumsgalleriesscotland.org.uk/what-we-do/case-studies/case-study/32/musa-collections-centre-creating-an-open-access-store-for-recognised-collections

NACCCE (1999) *All Our Futures: Creativity, Culture and Education*, London: National Advisory Committee on Creative and Cultural Education, accessed on 31/05/2011 at www.cypni.org.uk/downloads/alloutfutures.pdf

Nakou, I. (2005) 'Oral history, museums and history education', paper presented at Can Oral History Make Objects Speak? conference, ICOM: ICME, Greece, October, accessed on 31/05/2011 at www.museumsnett.no/alias/HJEMMESIDE/icme/icme2005/nakou.pdf

National Literacy Trust (2006) *Reading for Pleasure: A Research Overview*, London: National Literacy Trust, accessed on 31/05/2011 at

www.literacytrust.org.uk/assets/0000/0562/
Reading_pleasure-2006.pdf

National Museum of American History (undated) *Sweatshops in America*, accessed on 31/05/2011 at http://americanhistory.si.edu/sweatshops/intro/intro.htm

National Trust (2004) *Informed Welcome*, unpublished.

NEA (2nd edn 2004) *Imagine: Introducing Your Child to the Arts*, Washington DC: National Endowment for the Arts, accessed on 31/05/2011 at www.nea.gov/pub/imagine.pdf

NEA (2009) *2008 Survey of Public Participation in the Arts*, Washington DC: National Endowment for the Arts.

Newman, A. (2001) Social exclusion zone, *Museums Journal* September, pp. 34–6.

Nolan, T.R. (2010) History repeats itself: American museums in a time of recession: will we ever learn?, *Journal of Museum Education* 35 (1) Spring, pp. 117–20.

Nowlen, P. (2009) Video interview for Center for the Future of Museums' *Voices of the Future*, accessed on 31/05/2011 at http://www.youtube.com/watch?v=VzG1Iua_j7k

O'Neill, M. (2002) Preface, in Dodd, J., O'Riain, H., Hooper-Greenhill, E. and Sandell, R., *A Catalyst for Change: The Social Impact of the Open Museum*, Leicester: Research Centre for Museums and Galleries, accessed on 31/05/2011 at www.le.ac.uk/museumstudies/research/Reports/catalyst.pdf, pp. 2–5.

Ocello, C.B. (2010) Getting out of the subject box, in Fortney, K. and Sheppard, B. (eds) *An Alliance of Spirit: Museum and School Partnerships*, Washington DC: American Association of Museums Press, pp. 45–50.

Office of the First Minister and Deputy First Minister (2005) *A Shared Future: Policy and Strategic Framework for Good Relations in Northern Ireland*, Belfast: Government for Northern Ireland, accessed on 31/05/2011 at www.ofmdfmni.gov.uk/asharedfuturepolicy2005.pdf

Oltman, M. (2000) Creating exhibits for the very young, in National Association for Interpretation, *Legacy* 11 (6), November/December, pp. 14–19.

OP&A (2002) *Exhibition Concept Models*, Washington DC: Smithsonian Institution, Office of Policy and Analysis, accessed on 31/05/2011 at www.si.edu/opanda/Reports/BackgroundPapers/Exhibitions/WPExConcepts.pdf

OP&A (2004) *Increasing and Diversifying Smithsonian Audiences*, Washington DC: Smithsonian Institution Office of Policy and Analysis, accessed on 31/05/2011 at www.si.edu/opanda/Reports/Oct04SICmtg.pdf

OP&A (2007a) *2030 Vision: Anticipating the Needs and Expectations of Museum Visitors of the Future*, Washington DC: Smithsonian Institution, Office of Policy and Analysis, accessed on 31/05/2011 at www.si.edu/opanda/docs/Rpts2007/2030vision.final.pdf

OP&A (2007b) *Museum Visitation as a Leisure Time Choice*, Washington DC: Smithsonian Institution, Office of Policy and Analysis, accessed on 31/05/2011 at www.si.edu/opanda/docs/Rpts2007/RegentsAudiences.final.pdf

OP&A (2010) *Smartphone Services for Smithsonian Visitors*, Washington DC: Smithsonian Institution, Office of Policy and Analysis, accessed on 31/05/2011 at http://smithsonian-webstrategy.wikispaces.com/file/view/OP%26A+SIAAppReport.1407.Final.pdf

Open Museum, Glasgow (2010) *Out There: Contemporary Contexts for Museums*, accessed on 31/05/2011 at http://openmuseumoutthere.wordpress.com/about

Orend, R.J. (1989) *Socialization and Participation in the Arts*, Princeton NJ: Princeton University Press, accessed on 31/05/2011 at http://arts.endow.gov/research/reports/NEA-Research-Report-21.pdf

Osterman, M.D. and Sheppard, B. (2010) Museums and schools working together, in Fortney, K. and Sheppard, B. (eds) *An Alliance of Spirit: Museum and School Partnerships*, Washington DC: American Association of Museums Press, pp. 1–8.

Ostrower, F. (2005) *The Diversity of Cultural Participation: Findings from a National Survey*, Washington DC: The Urban Institute/Wallace Foundation, accessed on 31/05/2011 at http://armuz.typepad.com/armuz/files/TheDiversityofCulturalParticipation.pdf

Paris, S.G. (2000) Situated motivation and informal learning, in Hirsch, J.S. and Silverman, L.H. (eds) *Transforming Practice: Selections from the Journal of Museum Education 1992–1999*, Washington DC: Museum Education Roundtable, pp. 200–11.

Paris, S.G. (ed.) (2002) *Perspectives on Object-Centred Learning in Museums*, Mahwah NJ: Lawrence Erlbaum Associates.

Paris, S.G. and Mercer, M.J. (2002) Finding self in

objects: identity exploration in museums, in Leinhardt, G., Crowley, K. and Knutson, K. (eds) *Learning Conversations in Museums*, Mahwah NJ: Lawrence Erlbaum Associates, pp. 401–23.

Paterson, T. (2008) A harsh lesson for Germany, courtesy of its socialist past, *The Independent* 22 October, accessed on 31/05/2011 at www.independent.co.uk/news/world/europe/a-harsh-lesson-for-germany-courtesy-of-its-socialist-past-968642.html

Perkin, C. (2010) Beyond the rhetoric: negotiating the politics and realising the potential of community-driven heritage engagement, *International Journal of Heritage Studies* 16 (1 and 2), pp. 107–22.

Pew Internet (2009) *Twitter and Status Updating, Fall 2009*, Susannah Fox, Kathryn Zickuhr and Aaron Smith for Pew Internet, accessed on 15/06/2010 at http://www.pewinternet.org/Reports/2009/17-Twitter-and-Status-Updating-Fall-2009.aspx

Phillips, L. (2008) Reminiscence: recent work at the British Museum, in Chatterjee, H.J. (ed.) *Touch in Museums: Policy and Practice in Object Handling*, Oxford: Berg, pp. 199–204.

Pine, B.J. and Gilmore, J.H. (1999) *The Experience Economy*, Boston MA: Harvard Business School.

Pingdom (2010) *The Incredible Growth of the Internet since 2000*, posted by Pingdom on 22 October, accessed on 31/05/2011 at http://royal.pingdom.com/2010/10/22/incredible-growth-of-the-internet-since-2000

Pitman, B. and Hirzy, E. (2011) *Ignite the Power of Art: Advancing Visitor Engagement in Museums*, New Haven CT: Yale University Press and Dallas Museum of Art.

PLB Consulting (2001) *Developing New Audiences for the Heritage*, London: Heritage Lottery Fund.

Pollock, W. (2007) Voice of the people, in McLean, K. and Pollock, W. (eds) *Visitor Voices in Museum Exhibitions*, Washington DC: Association of Science-Technology Centers, pp. 3–7.

Prentice, R.C. (1989) Ch. 7, Pricing policy at heritage sites: how much should visitors pay? in Herbert, D.T., Prentice, R.C. and Thomas, C.J. (eds) *Heritage Sites: Strategies for Marketing and Development*, Aldershot: Avebury, pp. 231–71.

Prentice, R. (1998) Recollections of museum visits: a case study of remembered cultural attraction visiting on the Isle of Man, *Museum Management and Curatorship* 17 (1), pp. 41–64.

Prentice, R., Davies, A. and Beeho, A. (1997) Seeking generic motivations for visiting and not visiting museums and like cultural attractions, *Museum Management and Curatorship*, 16 (1), pp. 45–70.

Pringle, E. (2006) *Learning in the Gallery: Context, Process, Outcomes*, London: engage, accessed on 31/05/2011 at www.en-quire.org/downloads/LEARNINGINTHES_finaltext.doc

Prochaska, J.O., Norcross, J.C. and DiClimente, C.C. (1994) *Changing for Good: A Revolutionary Six Stage Programme for Overcoming Bad Habits and Moving Your Life Positively Forward*, New York: William Morrow and Co.

Prown, J.D. (1993) The truth of material culture: history or fiction? in Lubar, S. and Kingery, W.D. (eds) *History from Things: Essays on Material Culture*, Washington DC: Smithsonian, pp. 1–19.

Rabinovitch, V. (2003) Museums facing Trudeau's challenge: the informal teaching of history, *Canadian Issues* October, accessed on 31/05/2011 at www.civilization.ca/cmc/explore/resources-for-scholars/essays/museology/victor-rabinovich/museums-facing-trudeaus-challenge-teaching-of-history

Rainie, L. (2006) 'Life online: teens and technology and the world to come', speech to the Public Library Association annual conference, Boston, 23 March.

Rand, J. (2001) Visitors' bill of rights, in Adams, R. (ed.) *Museum Visitor Services Manual*, Washington DC: American Association of Museums, pp. 13–14.

Rand, J. (2010a) Write and design with the family in mind, in McRainey, D.L. and Russick, J. (eds) *Connecting Kids to History with Museum Exhibitions*, Walnut Creek CA: Left Coast Press, pp. 257–84.

Rand, J. (2010b) *Adventures in Label Land*, Powerpoint presentation, accessed on 31/05/2011 at http://familylearningforum.org/images/presentation-rand-11-15-10.pdf

Rawson, E.R. (2010) It's about them: using developmental frameworks to create exhibitions for children (and their grown-ups), in McRainey, D.L. and Russick, J. (eds) *Connecting Kids to History with Museum Exhibitions*, Walnut Creek CA: Left Coast Press, pp. 49–73.

RCMG (2002) *Learning through Culture: The DfES Museums and Galleries Education Programme*, Leicester: Research Centre for Museums and Galleries, accessed on 31/05/2011 at www2.

le.ac.uk/departments/museumstudies/rcmg/
publications

RCMG (2004a) *Inspiration, Identity, Learning: The Value of Museums – The Evaluation of DCMS/ DfES Strategic Commissioning 2003–2004: National/Regional Museum Partnerships*, University of Leicester: Research Centre for Museums and Galleries, accessed on 31/05/2011 at www2.le.ac.uk/departments/museumstudies/ rcmg/publications

RCMG (2004b) *What Did You Learn at the Museum Today? The Evaluation of the Renaissance in the Regions Education Programme in the Three Phase 1 Hubs*, Leicester: Research Centre for Museums and Galleries, accessed on 31/05/2011 at www2. le.ac.uk/departments/museumstudies/rcmg/ publications

RCMG (2006) *What Did You Learn at the Museum Today? Second Study – Evaluation of the Outcome and Impact of Learning through the Implementation of the Renaissance in the Regions Education Programme Delivery Plans across Nine Regional Hubs (2005)*, University of Leicester: Research Centre for Museums and Galleries, accessed on 31/05/2011 at www2.le.ac.uk/departments/ museumstudies/rcmg/publications

RCMG (2007a) *Inspiration, Identity, Learning: The Value of Museums, Second Study – An Evaluation of the DCMS/DCSF National/Regional Museum Partnership Programme 2006–2007*, University of Leicester: Research Centre for Museums and Galleries, accessed on 31/05/2011 at www2. le.ac.uk/departments/museumstudies/rcmg/ publications

RCMG (2007b) *Engage, Learn, Achieve: The Impact of Museum Visits on the Attainment of Secondary Pupils in the East of England 2006–2007*, University of Leicester: Research Centre for Museums and Galleries, accessed on 31/05/2011 at www2.le.ac.uk/departments/museumstudies/ rcmg/publications

Reach Advisors (May 2010) *Museum Audience Insight: History Visitors*, accessed on 31/05/2011 at http://reachadvisors.typepad.com/ museum_audience_insight/history_visitors/

Reach Advisors (February–April 2011) *Museum Audience Insight: National Museum Visitor Survey*, accessed on 31/05/2011 at http://reachadvisors. typepad.com/museum_audience_insight

Regnier, V. (1997) Children's museums: exhibit issues, in Maher, M. (ed.) *Collective Vision:*

Starting and Sustaining a Children's Museum, Washington DC: Association of Youth Museums.

Renaissance North-East (2010) *Exploring Literacy through Museums*, London: MLA, accessed on 31/05/2011 at www.mla.gov.uk/what/ programmes/renaissance/regions/north_east/ info_for_sector/~/media/North_East/ files/2010/Exploring_Literacy_Through_ Museums_publication.pdf

Renaissance North-West (2005) *Towards Best Practice in Developing New Audiences for Museums: Results of a Workshop on Developing Audiences and Collections, Manchester Museum 21 June*, Manchester: Renaissance North-West.

Renaissance North-West (2008) *Write On: How to Use Museums and Galleries to Improve Children's Literacy*, Manchester: Renaissance North-West, accessed on 31/05/2011 at http://i.dmtrk.com/ CmpDoc/2008/479/238_write-on-literacy-booklet.pdf

Renaissance South-West (2008) *Close Encounters with Culture: Museums and Galleries as part of the Early Years Foundation Stage*, Bristol: Renaissance South-West, accessed on 31/05/2011 at www. learning-unlimited.co.uk/index.html

Rennie, L.J. and McClafferty, T.P. (1996) Science centres and science learning, *International Journal of Science Education* 27, pp. 53–98.

Richards, G. (ed.) (2001a) *Cultural Attractions and European Tourism*, Wallingford: CABI.

Richards, G. (2001b) The market for cultural attractions, in Richards, G. (ed.) *Cultural Attractions and European Tourism*, Wallingford: CABI Publishing, pp. 31–53.

Ringel, G. (2005) 'Designing exhibits for kids: what are we thinking?', paper presented at the J. Paul Getty Museum symposium, From Content to Play: Family-Oriented Interactive Spaces in Art and History Museums, 4–5 June, accessed on 31/05/2011 at www.getty.edu/education/ symposium/Ringel.pdf

Rosenthal, E. and Blankman-Hetrick, J. (2002) Conversations across time: family learning in a living history museum, in Leinhardt, G., Crowley, K. and Knutson, K. (eds) *Learning Conversations in Museums*, Mahwah NJ: Lawrence Erlbaum Associates, pp. 305–29.

Rowlands, M. (2008) Aesthetics of touch among the elderly, in Chatterjee, H.J. (ed.) *Touch in Museums: Policy and Practice in Object Handling*, Oxford: Berg, pp. 187–98.

Royal Ontario Museum (1976) *Communicating with the Museum Visitor: Guidelines for Planning*, Toronto: Royal Ontario Museum.

Rubenstein, R. and Loten, J. (1996) *Cultural Heritage Audience Studies: Sources and Resources*, Rubenstein and Associates for Heritage Policy and Research Division, Department of Canadian Heritage.

Runyard, S. and French, Y. (1999) *Marketing and Public Relations Handbook for Museums, Galleries and Heritage Attractions*, London: The Stationery Office.

Russell, C.A., Mielke, M.B. and Reisner, E.R. (2009) *Evidence of Programme Quality and Youth Outcomes in the DYCD Out-of-School-Time Initiative: Report on the Initiative's First Three Years*, New York: Policy Studies Associates Inc, accessed on 31/05/2011 at www.wallacefoundation.org

Russell, R.L. (2005) Designing for thinking in museums, *Informal Learning Review* 71, March/April, accessed on31/05/2011 at www.informallearning.com/ilr-archive.htm.

Russell, R.L. (2006) Informal learning in context, *Informal Learning Review* 77, March/April, accessed on 31/05/2011 at www.informallearning.com/ilr-archive.htm

Sachatello-Sawyer, B., Fellenz, R.A., Burton, H., Gittings-Carlson, L, Mahony, J.L. and Woolbaugh, W. (2002) *Adult Museum Programs: Designing Meaningful Experiences*, Walnut Creek CA: AltaMira Press.

Samis, P. (2007) New technologies as part of a comprehensive interpretive plan, in Din, H. and Hecht, P. (eds) *The Digital Museum: A Think Guide*, Washington DC: American Association of Museums, pp. 19–34.

Sandell, R., Dodd, J. and Garland-Thomson, R. (2010) *Re-Presenting Disability: Activism and Agency in the Museum*, London: Routledge.

Sanford, C.W. (2009) *Let's Give 'Em Something To Talk About: How Participation in a Shared Museum Experience Can Seed Family Learning Conversations at Home*, unpublished PhD thesis, accessed on 31/05/2011 at http://etd.library.pitt.edu/ETD/available/etd-12072009-152924/unrestricted/SanfordCamelliaW2009Dissertation.pdf

Schlageck, K. (2010) Schools in the 21st century, in Fortney, K. and Sheppard, B. (eds) *An Alliance of Spirit: Museum and School Partnerships*, Washington DC: American Association of Museums Press, pp. 15–22.

Science Museum of Minnesota (2007) *RACE* exhibition press release, accessed on 31/05/2011 at www.smm.org/race/race_talkingcircle.pdf

Scott, C. (2000a) Branding: positioning museums in the 21st century, *International Journal of Arts Management* 2 (3), pp. 35–9.

Scott, C. (2000b) Positioning museums in the 21st century, in Lynch, R., Burton, C., Scott, C., Wilson, P. and Smith, P., *Leisure and Change: Implications for Museums in the 21st Century*, Sydney: Powerhouse Museum and University of Technology, pp. 37–48.

Scott, C. (2007) 'What difference do museums make: using values in sector marketing and branding', paper given to MPR-ICOM conference, Vienna, 20 August, accessed on 31/05/2011 at http://mpr.icom.museum/html-files/papers/2007-scotttxt.pdf

SEEC (2009) *Smithsonian Early Enrichment Center 2008 Annual Report of the Board of Directors*, Washington DC: Smithsonian Early Enrichment Center, accessed on 31/05/2011 via www.seec.si.edu

Serrell, B. (1996) *Exhibit Labels: An Interpretive Approach*, Walnut Creek CA: AltaMira Press.

Serrell, B. (1998) *Paying Attention: Visitors and Museum Exhibits*, Washington DC: American Association of Museums.

Sharples, M., Lonsdale, P., Meek, J., Rudman, P. and Vavoula, G.N. (2007) Evaluation of MyArtSpace, a mobile learning service for school museum trips, in Norman, A. and Pearce, J. (eds) *Proceedings of 6th Annual Conference on Mobile Learning*, mLearn, Melbourne, pp. 238–44, accessed on 31/05/2011 at https://lra.le.ac.uk/handle/2381/8257

Silverman, L. (2010) *The Social Work of Museums*, London: Routledge.

Silverstein, L.B. and Layne, S. (2010) *Teaching for Creativity through the Arts: Why, What, and How*, Washington DC: The John. F. Kennedy Center for the Performing Arts, accessed on 31/05/2011 at http://bit.ly/teachingcreativity

Simon, N. (2007) Beyond hands-on: Web 2.0 and new models for engagement, *Hand to Hand* 21 (4), Winter, accessed on 28/01/2011 at www.museumtwo.com/publications/beyond_hands_on.pdf

Simon, N. (2008) *Museum 2.0 blogspot 20/11/2008: Free2Choose and the Social Dimension of Polling Interactives*, accessed on 22/02/2011 at http://museumtwo.blogspot.com/2008/11/free2choose-and-social-dimension-of.html

Simon, N. (2010) *The Participatory Museum*, Santa Cruz CA: Museum 2.0, also accessible at www.participatorymuseum.org

Smithsonian Institution (2009) *Web and New Media Strategy*, Washington DC: Smithsonian Institution, accessed on 31/05/2011 at http://smithsonian-webstrategy.wikispaces.com/Strategy+--+Table+of+Contents

Spalding, J. (2010) Perspectives: behind the Open Museum, in Glasgow Museums (ed.) *Out There: The Open Museum: Pushing the Boundaries of Museums' Potential*, Glasgow: Culture and Sport Glasgow.

Spock, D. (2010) Imagination – a child's gateway to engagement with the past, in McRainey, D.L. and Russick, J. (eds) *Connecting Kids to History with Museum Exhibitions*, Walnut Creek CA: Left Coast Press, pp. 117–35.

Stainton, C. (2002) Voices and images: making connections between identity and art, in Leinhardt, G., Crowley, K. and Knutson, K. (eds) *Learning Conversations in Museums*, Mahwah NJ: Lawrence Erlbaum Associates, pp. 213–57.

Stevens, M. (2009) *Stories Old and New: Migration and Identity in the UK Heritage Sector*, London: Institute for Public Policy Research, accessed on 31/05/2011 at www.baringfoundation.org.uk/Stories.pdf

Stoke Speaks Out (undated) *About Us*, accessed on 31/05/2011 at www.stokespeaksout.org/home/About%20Us

Surowiecki, J. (2004) *The Wisdom of Crowds*, New York: Doubleday.

Taylor, M.J. and Twiss Houting, B.A. (2010) Is it real? Kids and collections, in McRainey, D.L. and Russick, J. (eds) *Connecting Kids to History with Museum Exhibitions*, Walnut Creek CA: Left Coast Press, pp. 241–56.

Thomas, C.J. (1989) The role of historic sites and reasons for visiting, in Herbert, D.T., Prentice, R.C. and Thomas, C.J. (eds) *Heritage Sites: Strategies for Marketing and Development*, Aldershot: Avebury, pp. 62–93.

Tilden, F. (3rd edn 1977) *Interpreting Our Heritage*, Chapel Hill: University of North Carolina Press.

The Times (2011) The protest network (leading article), *The Times*, 2 February, p. 2.

Tinsley, P. (2009) *Guest Post: Top 40 Countdown at the Worcester City Museum*, 30 November 2009, accessed on 31/05/2011 at http://museumtwo.blogspot.com/2009/11/guest-post-top-40-countdown-at.html

Tissier, D. and Nahoo, S.S. (2004) *Black and Minority Ethnic Engagement with London's Museums: Telling It Like It Is – Non-User Research*, London: StUF, accessed on 31/05/2011 at http://research.mla.gov.uk/evidence/documents/Telling_it_like_it_is_rpt.pdf

Tonkin, E., Corrado, E.M., Moulaison, H. Lea, Kipp, M.E.I., Resmini, A., Pfeiffer, H.D. and Zhang, Q. (2008) Collaborative and social tagging networks, *Ariadne* 54, January, accessed on 31/05/2011 at www.ariadne.ac.uk/issue54/tonkin-et-al

Tourism Research Australia (2008) *Snapshot: Cultural and Heritage Tourism in Australia 2008*, accessed on 31/05/2011 at http://www.australiacouncil.gov.au/research/arts_sector/reports_and_publications/cultural_tourism

Trant, J. (2009) Tagging, folksonomy and art museums, accessed on 31/05/2011 at http://conference.archimuse.com/jtrants/stevemuseum_research_report_available

Trevelyan, V. (ed.) (1991) *'Dingy places with different kinds of bits': An Attitudes Survey of London Museums amongst Non-visitors*, London: London Museums Service.

Tyne & Wear Archives and Museums (undated) *Tyne & Wear Museums Mission Statement*, Newcastle: Tyne & Wear Archives and Museums, accessed on 31/05/2011 at www.twmuseums.org.uk/about/ourmission

Underhill, P. (1999) *Why We Buy: The Science of Shopping*, London: Orion Publishing.

US Department of Commerce and the President's Committee on the Arts and the Humanities (2005) *A Position Paper on Cultural and Heritage Tourism in the United States*, Washington DC: Department of Commerce, accessed on 31/05/2011 at http://www.pcah.gov/pdf/05WhitePaperCultHeritTourism.pdf

USS Constitution Museum (2010a) *Developing Content to Engage Families*, accessed on 31/05/2011 at http://familylearningforum.org/engaging_text/family-content/developing-content.htm

USS Constitution Museum (2010b) *Writing for a Family Audience*, accessed on 31/05/2011 at http://familylearningforum.org/engaging_text/writing-for-families/writing-for-families.htm

V & A (undated) *Designing Museum Activity*

Backpacks for Families, London: Victoria & Albert Museum, accessed on 31/05/2011 at http://www.vam.ac.uk/school_stdnts/museum_educators/design_backpacks/index.html

Vargas, J.A. (2007) Students make connections at a time of total disconnect, *The Washington Post*, 17 April, quoted in OP&A, *2030 Vision: Anticipating the Needs and Expectations of Museum Visitors of the Future*, Washington DC: Smithsonian Institution, p. 2.

Varine, H. de (1993) 'Tomorrow's community museums', lecture given in the Senate Hall, University of Utrecht, 15 October, accessed on 31/05/2011 at http://assembly.coe.int/Museum/ForumEuroMusee/Conferences/tomorrow.htm

Veverka, J. (1994) *Interpretive Master Planning*, Helena MT: Falcon Press.

Vygotsky, L.S. (1978) *Mind in Society: Development of Higher Psychological Processes*, Cambridge MA: Harvard University Press.

Walker, K. (2007) Visitor-constructed personalised learning trails, in Trant, J. and Bearman, D. (eds) *Museums and the Web 2007: Proceedings*, Toronto: Archives and Museum Informatics, 31 March, accessed on 31/05/2011 at www.archimuse.com/mw2007/papers/walker/walker.html

Wallace Foundation (2008) *A Place to Grow and Learn: A Citywide Approach to Building and Sustaining Out-of-school Time Learning Opportunities*, New York: Wallace Foundation, accessed on 31/05/2011 at www.wallacefoundation.org

Wallace Foundation (2009) *Engaging Audiences: Report on the Wallace Foundation Arts Grantee Conference, Philadelphia PA 1–3 April 2009*, New York: Wallace Foundation, accessed on 31/05/2011 at www.wallacefoundation.org/KnowledgeCenter/KnowledgeTopics/CurrentAreasofFocus/ArtsParticipation/Documents/Engaging-Audiences-Wallaconference.pdf

Watson, S. (2010) Myth, memory and the senses in the Churchill Museum, in Dudley, S.H. (ed.) *Museum Materialities: Objects, Engagements, Interpretation*, Oxford: Routledge, pp. 204–23.

Webb, R.C. (2000) The nature, role and measurement of affect, *Journal of Interpretation Research* 5 (2) Winter, pp. 15–30.

Weil, S. (1999) From being about something to being for somebody: the ongoing transformation of the American museum, *Daedalus* 128 (3) Summer, pp. 229–58.

West, R. and Chesebrough, D.E. (2007) New ways of doing business, in Falk, J.H., Dierking, L.D. and Foutz, S. (eds) *In Principle, In Practice: Museums as Learning Institutions*, Lanham MD: AltaMira Press, pp. 139–52.

White, R. (2010) *The Future of Out-of-Home Entertainment*, accessed on 31/05/2011 at www.whitehutchinson.com/leisure/articles/OutOfHomeEntertainmentFuture.shtml

Wilkening, S. and Chung, J. (2009) *Life Stages of the Museum Visitor: Building Engagement over a Lifetime*, Washington DC: American Association of Museums.

Williams, C. (2010) The transformation of the museum into a zone of hot topicality and taboo representation: the endorsement/interrogation response syndrome, in Cameron, F. and Kelly, L. (eds) *Hot Topics, Public Culture, Museums*, Newcastle upon Tyne: Cambridge Scholars Publishing, pp. 18–34.

Wilton, J. (2006) Museums and memories: remembering the past in local and community museums, *Public History Review* 12, pp. 58–79, accessed on 31/05/2011 at www.australianhumanitiesreview.org/archive.html

Wolins, I.S., Jensen, N. and Ulzheimer, R. (1992) Children's memories of museum field trips: a qualitative study, *Journal of Museum Education* 17 (2), pp. 17–27.

Wong, J.L. (2002) Who we are, *Interpretation Journal* 7 (2) Summer, pp. 4–7.

Woroncow, B. (2001) 'Heritage for all: ethnic minority attitudes to museums and heritage sites', paper presented to the ICOM Triennial Conference, Barcelona.

Worts, D. (2006) Measuring museum meaning: a critical assessment framework, *Journal of Museum Education* 31 (1), pp. 41–9, accessed on 31/05/2011 at http://douglasworts.org/wp-content/uploads/2009/06/worts_jme_final.pdf

Yerkovich, S. (2007) 'Museums engaging controversy', paper presented to ICOM Triennial Conference, Vienna, August.

Zimmer, R., Jefferies, J. and Srinivasan, M. (2008) Touch technologies and museum access, in Chatterjee, H.J. (ed.) *Touch in Museums: Policy and Practice in Object Handling*, Oxford: Berg, pp. 150–9.

Zohar, D. and Marshall, I. (2004) *Spiritual Capital: Wealth We Can Live By*, London: Bloomsbury.

Index